Albert Camus as Political Thinker

Albert Camus as Political Thinker

Nihilisms and the Politics of Contempt

Samantha Novello
University of Torino, Italy

First published 2010 by
PALGRAVE MACMILLAN

Palgrave Macmillan in the UK is an imprint of Macmillan Publishers Limited, registered in England, company number 785998, of Houndmills, Basingstoke, Hampshire RG21 6XS.

Palgrave Macmillan in the US is a division of St Martin's Press LLC, 175 Fifth Avenue, New York, NY 10010.

Palgrave Macmillan is the global academic imprint of the above companies and has companies and representatives throughout the world.

Palgrave® and Macmillan® are registered trademarks in the United States, the United Kingdom, Europe and other countries.

ISBN 978–0–230–24098–8   hardback

This book is printed on paper suitable for recycling and made from fully managed and sustained forest sources. Logging, pulping and manufacturing processes are expected to conform to the environmental regulations of the country of origin.

A catalogue record for this book is available from the British Library.

Library of Congress Cataloging-in-Publication Data

Novello, Samantha, 1974–
    Albert Camus as political thinker : nihilisms and the politics of
        contempt / Samantha Novello.
            p. cm.
        ISBN 978–0–230–24098–8 (hardback)
1. Camus, Albert, 1913–1960—Political and social views.   2. Camus,
    Albert, 1913–1960—Criticism and interpretation.   3. Nihilism (Philosophy)
    4. Political science—Philosophy.   I. Title.
B2430.C354A6N69 2010
320.092—dc22   2010023961

10   9   8   7   6   5   4   3   2   1
19 18 17 16 15 14 13 12 11 10

Printed and bound in Great Britain by
CPI Antony Rowe, Chippenham and Eastbourne

In memory of Jacqueline Lévi-Valensi

Contents

Acknowledgements

After working on Camus's writings for some years, I have acquired many debts of gratitude. I am very grateful to Simona Forti for the invaluable support she offered during the writing of this book; she read several drafts of the manuscript and I have benefited from her intelligent comments, her competence and encouragement. This book draws on material I wrote for my two PhD theses at the European University Institute of Florence (2005) and at the University of Turin, which benefited from comments and suggestions made by Peter Wagner, Maurice Weyemberg and Pier Paolo Portinaro. I would like to thank Quentin Skinner for encouraging me to pursue my doctoral studies. I am very grateful to the European University Institute for offering me a research grant and, as an alumna, for putting the collections of the EUI library at my disposal. I am especially grateful to the *POLIS* Department of the Università del Piemonte Orientale and to the Political Studies Department of the Università degli Studi di Torino, Italy, which freed me from teaching for four years and supported this research project, allowing me to complete this book.

Special thanks go to my mother, Sue, and to Margot Wylie, for their knowledge and patience in correcting the book, and to Sarah and Pierre Fredj for their hospitality and support during my innumerable trips to Paris. I would like to thank Mita Jonca, Emmanuel Vintiadis, Roberto Salerno and Fabio Macciò for their illuminating inspiration, true friendship and support.

Participating in the new Pléiade edition of Camus's complete works has also been of great value for the writing of this book. My heartfelt thanks go to Catherine Camus and Raymond Gay-Crosier for their support, patient assistance and advice, which have proved invaluable. All my gratitude goes to my mentor, Jacqueline Lévi-Valensi, whose intellectual generosity, support and encouragement have been inestimable in my passionate undertaking of this research. To my greatest sorrow, she died before this work was achieved. The book is dedicated to her and to the 'Camusian friendship' with which she honoured me.

Note on the Texts and Abbreviations

References to quotes are given immediately in the text. I have translated the French quotes personally wherever the English translation did not exist and, without explicit indication, I have slightly modified existing translations for the sake of accuracy. All extracts from the four volumes of Albert Camus, *Œuvres complètes* © **Éditions Gallimard**. Given the various editions available, references to Nietzsche's works are to sections, not to page numbers, unless a specific translation is quoted. Works frequently cited throughout the text and in notes are identified by the following abbreviations. Full references can be found in the Bibliography.

I, II, III, IV	Albert Camus, *Œuvres Complètes*, I. 1931–44; II. 1944–48; III. 1949–56; IV. 1957–59.
CAC4	Albert Camus, *Cahiers Albert Camus, 4. Caligula. Version de 1941.*
CAC8	*Camus à Combat, Cahiers Albert Camus. 8*, ed. J. Lévi-Valensi.
EE	Albert Camus, *L'Envers et l'Endroit* in I, pp. 29–72.
E	Albert Camus, *L'Étranger* in I, pp. 139–213.
MS	Albert Camus, *Le Mythe de Sisyphe*, in I, pp. 217– 315.
DES	Albert Camus, *Métaphysique chrétienne et néoplatonisme* in I, pp. 999–1081.
LAA	Albert Camus, *Lettres à un ami allemand*, in II, pp. 1–29.
N	Albert Camus, *Noces*, in I, pp. 99–137.
RR	Albert Camus, *Remarque sur la révolte*, in III, pp. 325–33.
HR	Albert Camus, *L'Homme révolté*, in III, pp. 61–324.
EO	Jean Grenier, *Essai sur l'esprit d'orthodoxie.*
A	Friedrich Nietzsche, *Aurore.*
GM	Friedrich Nietzsche, *On the Genealogy of Morality.*
NP	Friedrich Nietzsche, *La Naissance de la philosophie a l'époque de la tragédie grecque.*

NT	Friedrich Nietzsche, *La Naissance de la tragédie*.
EH	Friedrich Nietzsche, *Ecce homo*.
CI	Friedrich Nietzsche, *Le Crépuscule des Idoles*.
HTH	Friedrich Nietzsche, *Humain, trop humain*.
VPI, II	Friedrich Nietzsche, *La Volonté de Puissance*, vols I, II.

Introduction: An 'Untimely' Political Thought for Serious Times

In the late 1960s, a French philosopher provocatively maintained that a book of philosophy must be, on one hand, a very special kind of detective story and in a way, on the other, a sort of science fiction.[1] By detective story, he meant that when writing or investigating a book of philosophy, concepts must be conceived to be made and unmade on a mobile horizon and always in relation to a specific 'drama' or theme. Concepts intervene to solve particular problems, exert their sphere of influence on a 'local situation', and change and evolve along with the questions from which they stem. Furthermore, insofar as the author dislocates his concepts, which he inherits from his own time and tradition, and re*creates* them, his work is necessarily 'untimely'; irreducible to both the philosophy of history and the philosophy of the eternal, his personal philosophy delves into the questions regarding the unknown or that which is still not well known and, in this sense, it has something to do with science fiction.

As Albert Camus himself observed in his *Mythe de Sisyphe*, a profound thought is in a constant state of becoming; it adopts the experience of a life and assumes its shape. In 1952, he wrote: 'Je ne suis pas un philosophe, en effet, et je ne sais parler que de ce que j'ai vécu. J'ai vécu le nihilisme, la contradiction, la violence et le vertige de la destruction. Mais dans le même temps, j'ai salué le pouvoir de créer et l'honneur de vivre. [...] Je ne m'intéresse qu'à la renaissance. (No, I am not a philosopher and I am only able to speak of that which I have lived. I have lived and experienced nihilism, contradiction, violence and the fever of destruction. But at the same time, I have hailed the power to create and the honour to live. [...] I am only interested in *renaissance*.)' (III, p. 411).

Camus lived in 'serious times' when poets and artists could be imprisoned, tortured and executed, like Garcia Lorca, because their words and

1

very existence contradicted those in power ('Preface to *L'Espagne libre'* (1945), II, p. 667); as he observed in 1951, to create in 'serious times' is to create *dangerously*. This is the 'horizon' or experience that shapes Camus's thoughts and positions; in the contemporary 'age of fear', which he considered to be dominated by a passion for servitude, especially, widespread among right as well as left-wing intellectuals, Camus conceived the artists, silenced by means of denigration and violence in the name of the imperative of utility and efficacy, to be testimonies to and of freedom.

'Pourquoi suis-je un artiste et non un philosophe? C'est que je pense selon les mots et non selon les idées. (Why am I an artist and not a philosopher? Because I think in words and not in ideas.)' (II, p. 1029). Camus understood the works of an artist to be the successive and multiple faces that strengthen his or her sole creation. His works are not isolated testimonies, but rather aspects of an evolving whole that complement, correct, overtake, or even contradict, one another (*MS*, p. 297). He observed that the greatest homage readers can pay to a writer does not consist in 'venerating' the written works, thus, turning them into fixed forms, but rather to comprehend and *continue* the writer's thought processes and creative effort (III, p. 410).

Scholars have warned against the temptation of transforming Camus into an '*écrivain à message*' by extracting from his work a selection of philosophical concepts (e.g. 'absurd', 'revolt', 'nihilism', 'love'), which are then exploited as catchwords for the most different and varied purposes. Camus is an '*écrivain du texte*' and concepts interweave with his creative process functioning as poles of complex metaphoric constellations from which they receive their fragile consistency and constantly moving meaning. The meaning of Camus's sole creation can only be fully understood in light of the specific 'drama' or question his concepts are called to shed light upon. The importance that Camus himself assigned, throughout his works, to consistency and exact use of words, accurate imagination, clear language and 'classicism', attests to the necessity that we take what he thinks and writes seriously, *to the letter*, particularly when he makes a strong distinction between the artist and the philosopher, both of whom he conceives to exemplify two alternative modes of thinking.

Critics have observed that Camus is not a political *theorist* (Braun 1974; Abbou 1986); others assert that he is a political theorist of a very special kind, namely, one 'who defies conventional theoretical labels and methods' and displays a coherent view of politics, as well as an ethical sensitivity, both of which are uncommon traits among political writers (Isaac 1992, p. 15). Camus was trained in and extensively studied philosophy, but was educated in Algiers; a child of the empire, born on the eve of the First World War in the milieu of the *petits colons*, he was an outsider to the Kantian tradition of the Collège de France, where the French intelligentsia was formed (Hughes 2007; Amiot and Mattéi 1997). Tuberculosis made it impossible for him to begin a teaching career, which may have led him to become an academic political philosopher. Although Camus was not a philosopher, that is, he did not practise philosophy as a profession, he was seen, nonetheless, to be endowed with a 'philosophical *nature*' (Amiot and Mattéi 1997, p. 2), which refused to blindly accept the established forms of twentieth-century philosophy and expressed itself in a variety of genres (lyrical essays, political articles, literary and musical critiques, short stories, novels, tragedies), including philosophical essays, that were reminiscent of the Cartesian tradition and of the literature of the French *moralistes*.

Political scientists and philosophers have invoked Camus's refusal of abstraction and of a coherent intellectual system to prove that he was 'unsuited' for political thinking and, therefore, could not be considered to be on the levels of the great authors of the philosophical political canon (Braun 1974; Isaac 1992); his philosophical arguments were ultimately judged to be not especially good and his novels were pronounced, probably on the grounds of their editorial success, to be his finest works (Sherman 2009).

Dismissed as a political thinker, Camus was recognised, nonetheless, to have been a 'political creature' (Isaac 1992), constantly concerned with political events throughout his life. An adolescent during the world economic crisis, he was 20 when Hitler came into power in Germany; the war in Spain, the Second World War, and four years of occupation completed the education of his generation, which was confronted with the unprecedented experience of mass destruction caused by the bombing of urban centres and civilians, the extermination camps and the nuclear bomb. Rather than providing a coherent political thought, Camus has been seen to contribute to political thinking with his fine insights on the human condition (Braun 1974) and on those practical problems of politics connected to the idea resistance to oppression, the limits of politics itself, and democratic alternatives to mass politics (Isaac 1992, p. 18).

The impression one gets from these critical assessments of Camus's writings is that they seem more to be asking, 'what is their *use*?' than, 'What is Camus saying?'. His thoughts and written works are judged to be 'fit' or 'unfit' according to a generally accepted idea of what philosophy, political theory, politics are and ought to be; those who have analysed his work, however, neglect to investigate, *to the letter*, what Camus himself understood philosophy, politics and thinking to be, what he wrote about them, how and why he did so.

For Camus, thinking is, above all else, the desire to create a world. As he noted in 1939, present events ('l'actualité') constitute matter for the creator only insofar as they provoke 'untimely' issues (*'inactuels'*) that give them a meaning; in other words, they constitute matter only insofar as the artist is able to transcend them and create his own universe (*MS*, p. 288). Camus admitted his own inability to think outside of lived experience and he described his creative process to be the obstinate repetition of particular aspects of that experience in which his thought passed repeatedly along ancient paths, nevertheless, without ceasing to be beyond and *over* them (*'surplomber'*) (Camus 1972, p. 1615). In concurrence with Nietzsche's 'untimely' method of thought,[2] to which he explicitly alludes, Camus writes exclusively of what he has *overcome* or moved *beyond*; his written works attest to the creator's 'wonderful and puerile universe' (*MS*, p. 284), namely, to the rigorous self-discipline (*ascesis*) and the mode of thinking of the artist, who indefatigably recreates concepts in relation to the 'untimely' issue(s) that the present events call to his attention.

Even in 1943, Maurice Blanchot emphasised the 'untimeliness' of Camus's reflections that were developed in *Le Mythe de Sisyphe* by affirming that there was more to his essay on the absurd than a mere history of contemporary sentiments and ideas. Blanchot may be considered to be among those rare subtle critics and philosophers who understood that, by *recreating* such concepts as absurd, freedom, nihilism, revolt, Camus called the philosophical political tradition from Plato to contemporary ideologies into question and moved *beyond* it. Thus, simply affirming Camus's distance from political theory or philosophy, as well as from practical or 'realistic' politics, is not enough.

The scope of this book is to interpret the various 'facets' of Camus's thought and creative processes, or at least some of them, from his own perspective, with his own defined categories and following Camus's own line of reasoning rather than *in spite* of all these elements. The ambition of this book is to be a book of philosophy (in the aforementioned sense) on an artist. With an act of modesty before the author's work and with an act of confidence in his thinking and writing, the book proceeds as though it were a kind of detective story; it goes in search of the clues that may shed light on Camus's creative process by individuating the horizon in which his concepts are to intervene and the problem(s) they were intended to resolve and in relation to which they themselves change. This is essential in order for the meaning and implications of what I consider to be Camus's 'untimely' political thought to be made clear, a political thought which demands from his readers more than a simple 'contextualisation' or historical account of the themes and positions of their author, but a change in the way one thinks, a 'transfiguration' of life, morality, politics, political action and creation.

Chapter 1 begins by individuating the 'drama', which Camus delineates in his texts of the late 1950s, in particular, 'Le Pari de notre génération' ('The Wager of Our Generation') and 'L'Artiste et son Temps'. The author denounces a generalised attitude of hatred, on which a widespread practice of humiliation, abasement, denigration of men and women is based, on all levels of daily intercourse, as well as a systematic perversion of language, which makes communication impossible. 'Lies' are not just intentional falsifications or mystifications of reality, for instance, for ideological or 'realistic' purposes; Camus also uses this term to designate a form of inconsistent reasoning or 'intellectual vice', which uses the instruments of reason, its categories and logic connections to *prove* an opinion, affirm its absolute right beyond all doubt and objection, and to silence the antagonist by disparaging his opinions and his very existence. The opponent is transformed into an 'enemy', who is banned from the circle of peers and characterised through the use of negative moral terms; this linguistic treatment is a prelude to his intellectual and, eventually, physical annihilation. Hatred and lie are seen to be constitutive of the twentieth century, they are the techniques of fear and politics of contempt that form the abysmal legacy that has willingly been inherited by our twenty-first century.

From his first article in the early 1930s to his last book, Camus struggled with the devious practices of degradation (III, p. 454), which are ingrained in the very fabric of economic, social, and political relationships and in the way thought and action in these sectors are structured. The 'untimely' issue, that the artist draws from contemporary events and that constitutes the ambit of Camus's thinking is that of nihilism or, more precisely, of nihilism*s*. As mentioned, Camus articulates his creative process basing it on a perspective that changes along with the concepts that are introduced and constantly recreated by the artist. Referring to nihilism with its plural form, 'nihilisms', reminds the reader that Camus shapes his investigation on a particular historical situation and through the use of concepts that he has drawn from a variety of sources.

With whom and on what political and philosophical issues did Camus have regular exchanges and discussions? What did he read and when? The first three chapters of the book attempt to answer these questions with the intention of shedding light on Camus's 'untimely' problem and on the genealogy of the concepts he employs and develops. The book delves into the ancient paths of Camus's thought processes that may be traced back to the early 1930s, when, as a poor schoolboy admitted with a bursary to the Lycée of Algiers, he attended Jean Grenier's Philosophy classes. Philosopher, friend of Jean Paulhan and collaborator of the prestigious Parisian review, *La Nouvelle Revue Française*, Grenier's influence in bringing the question of nihilism to the attention of young Camus is indubitable.

Under the direction of his teacher, Camus identified nihilism to be an essentially political question, which called into question the understanding of action in the Western tradition of political philosophy, as well as the relationship between rationalism and contemporary power politics and, in particular, in the German and Russian revolutionary movements of the early decades of the twentieth century. In that nihilism is associated with an appetite for total destruction – of authority, moral values, tradition, life – and an instinct of death, Camus, through his readings of Nietzsche and Max Scheler, identifies nihilism with a 'philosophy' or mode of thinking, the origins of which may be found in an attitude of contempt (*ressentiment*). Culminating in moral and political fanaticism, nihilism coincides with a specific *use* rather than a *loss* of 'reason'.

As it openly appears in his early articles and 'reveries' between 1932 and 1934, Camus's criticism of rationalism and his understanding of nihilism are deeply associated with and correlated to Nietzsche's perspective on the matter. The influence that the German philosopher's work had on Camus's creative process, as the inventories of the French writer's private library would suggest, is commonly assumed as much as it is unexplored in critical assessments of his philosophical political reflections. Investigating the French editions of Nietzsche's books that were in Camus's possession, in the chronological order in which he plausibly read them, has disclosed the young author's early methodological concerns and has shed light on his search for an alternative mode of thinking, which attempts to go beyond the limits posed by philosophers' 'reason'.

In Chapter 3, I demonstrate how reading Nietzsche, Bergson, Plotinus, and the mystics provides Camus with the concepts through and with which he creates and develops his personal language and mode of thinking. It is through the use of these sources that Camus brings the role that art plays, in evading the servile teleology of Western reason and in 'liberating' intelligence from the modern fetishistic belief in the objectiveness and immutable character of economic, social and political constructs, into full focus. The artist's writings of the 1930s express a perspective or mode of thinking that dislocates teleological reason and defines a different understanding of political action that goes beyond the modern rationalist theories, as well as the contemporary varieties of 'political romanticism' and the mystic Fascist appeals to 'Unity'. Camus rejects the concepts of 'nature' and 'creation' of the philosophical political tradition on which the Nazi aestheticisation of politics is based, and brings the question of liberation from Western logic to the foreground.

Camus makes Nietzsche's criticism of the link between the logic, ontology, and language of the Western tradition his own and, in concurrence with Georges Bataille, he identifies freedom with the liberation from the 'servile' logic of utility and efficacy of the philosophers' *moral* reason, which he detects at the core of such diverse acts as war, suicide and terrorism. He considers this type of logic to be responsible for 'enslaving' modern man to a fetishistic system of economic and political relationships of domination that reduce living beings to mere cogs or functions of a machine, which they themselves have created. This reduction of man to (no)thing is characteristic of what Camus calls '*romantic* nihilism' (III, p. 452), which he sees to be inherent in Western civilisation and which he links to an attitude of hatred or contempt of the world and men.

The obvious influence that Max Scheler's phenomenological analysis of *ressentiment* had on Camus's thoughts and ideas, perceptible in his writings of the mid-1930s – in the lyrical essays and the 1936 dissertation in Philosophy on Christian Metaphysics and Neoplatonism – to *Le Mythe de Sisyphe* and his essays on revolt of the 1940s, later reworked in his 1951 *L'Homme revolté,* casts essential light on Camus's 'nihilisms'.

'Romantic' or 'absolute' or 'radical' nihilism constitutes the fundamental question, which is brought to the foreground by contemporary political events and with which the French writer was confronted throughout his entire life and work. Camus conceives that his art goes *beyond* the nihilistic logic of modernity that governs economic, social, moral, and political life and combats the 'enslavement' of men and women and their consequent humiliation and exploitation by increasing their freedom and responsibility (IV, pp. 583–4). In Chapters 4 and 5, I explore the *logic* of nihilism, which Camus detects at the core of the contemporary totalitarian understanding of political action as the transformation of the world and men. The idea of a demiurgic creation of the ideal political community, on which the right- and left-wing revolutionary movements are based, is perceived by Camus to be the expression of a resentful attitude of hatred of the world that is manifestly indebted to the metaphysical constructs of free will and finality (*telos*) of the Platonic–Aristotelian tradition of political philosophy.

I propose to interpret Camus's definition of '*good* nihilism' in his *Le Mythe de Sisyphe*, taking into account the artist's effort to 'liberate' thinking and action from the abasing and murderous logic of Western theory and revolutionary practice by providing an alternative, 'illogical' or *a*-teleological, perspective from which to *recreate* or re-evaluate existence outside the limits imposed by the systems of fear and contempt. A close textual examination of Camus's sources, in particular, Nietzsche's written fragments on the pre-Platonic philosophers in the age of tragedy, provides some illuminating clues that allow us to interpret the Absurd reasoning as an 'aesthetic' or non-fabricative mode of thinking that breaks the finalistic straitjacket of reason by placing itself outside and beyond the mode of *ressentiment* and 'transfigures' existence from the artist's perspective of 'love' (of the world).

Inseparable from the famous words of Nietzsche, 'God is dead', Camus's *good* nihilism is fully captured in Dostoyevsky's formula 'Everything is permitted', which indicates a 'divine' way of thinking that evades the structures of domination that are intrinsic to the linguistic, logical, social, moral, and political constructs of the Western tradition, which culminate in the phrase 'Everything is possible' of *radical* nihilism.

In Chapters 6 and 7, I demonstrate that Camus, especially in the articles of *Combat* but also in his essays and tragedies of the 1940s, delineates a political experience that is shaped by and acquires its full meaning and consistency from the 'aesthetic' thought of the Absurd. In *Le Mythe de Sisyphe*, the experience of absurdity, to which death, suffering, and humiliation confront men, strips existence of the 'servile' constructs by means of which reason had, to that point, traditionally *made sense* of it, and imparts a different 'economy' of life – an 'economy' of honour, greatness, generosity – which is irreducible to that of *ressentiment*.

Absurd thinking then goes beyond the initial negative movement of absurdity and 'says yes', in other words, it testifies that human life exceeds the nihilistic attempt to reduce man to a simple function according to the logic of power, as may be illustrated by Camus's tragedy *Caligula*. Camus's notion of revolt is not opposed to the Absurd, but rather is ingrained into the absurd or *tragic* thinking of *Le Mythe*, which is essential to be able to understand his criticism of the totalitarian declaration and attempt to succeed in totally (re)creating man and the world.

The three 'cycles' that, in Camus's own words, constituted his sole creation (Camus 1972, p. 1610) should not be understood as a dialectical progression – from the absurd (thesis) to revolt (antithesis) and to love (synthesis/origin) – but as different 'facets' of his way of thinking that, by repeating ancient routes, dwells on different aspects – suicide and *logical* murder or terror(ism) – which he has drawn in his own time.

Camus places the creation or re-evaluation of politics, economy, and existence outside and beyond the desire for power and the structures of domination, which inform the modern modes of apprehending and behaving in the world and which culminate in the 'right to dishonour' that is characteristic of moral and political fanaticism (IV, p. 241). In that it lies beyond *radical* nihilism, Camus's absurd thinking 'transfigures' political action, removing it from the modern enslavement to final objectives, utility and success; it is on this that an 'untimely' political constellation is founded and presents an alternative to the twentieth-century politics of contempt, the categories (power, freedom, revolution) and the logic (modern realism) of which it rejects.

In his lecture at the University of Uppsala, after he was awarded the Nobel Prize for Literature in 1957, Camus declared that 'we live in an interesting era' (IV, p. 247) or, in any case, in one that no longer allows men and women to be *disinterested* in it (Camus 1961, p. 176). The artist refuses the alternative engagement *vs.* disengagement of traditional, especially, Existentialist–Marxist political discourse, which Camus identifies in the two sides of the same nihilistic or teleological model of action. By refusing art in both 'the ivory tower' and in the service of party politics, Camus's absurd thinking transforms the creator from being a modern conqueror into a 'testimony to and of freedom' (II, p. 488), namely, to a political action that is a stranger to the 'passion for enslavement' that subjects the contemporary age to the logic of use, power and efficacy. The artist rejects the alternative 'victim'/ 'executioner' that is characteristic of the *moral* or finalistic justification of existence, which is human reason's most ominous side, as well as the system of the death penalty or *logical* murder that on such interpretation is based. By refusing the humiliation and murder of the opponent, the artist cannot be defined a conqueror or a political man; he replaces reason's 'radicalism' or fanaticism with a profound vocation to defend the rights of those who do not share his opinions. The 'untimeliness' of Camus's political thinking lies in the following words, which he wrote in the late 1940s:

[U]n des sens de l'histoire d'aujourd'hui et plus encore de demain, c'est la lutte entre les artistes et les conquérants, et si dérisoire que cela puisse paraître, entre les mots et les balles. ([O]ne of the meanings of today's and, even more so, of tomorrow's history, is the struggle between the artists and the conquerors and, so derisory as it may seem, between words and bullets.) (III, p. 364)

1
The Twentieth-Century Politics of Contempt

> La passion la plus forte du XXe siècle : la servitude.
> (Camus, *Carnets* 1950)

'Virtue' *vs.* 'crime', 'progress' *vs.* 'reaction', 'rational' *vs.* 'irrational', are only some of the linguistic indicators of the contemporary radicalism that prevails in political discourse. Radicalism, also referred to as Jacobinic hyperbolism, consists in a specific mode of thought and language that neutralises political conflict by disqualifying the opponent's conduct and opinions, 'blackening' (in Latin *denigrare*, 'to denigrate') the antagonist to the point where he or she is no longer recognised as a peer. In what may also be described as a hyper-moralisation of political discourse and action political confrontation dissolves into a Manichean struggle of Good *versus* Evil.

Criticism, denigration and spitefulness (IV, p. 583), which are used as a means to invalidate political conflict *inter pares* by disparaging and throwing discredit upon the opponent, are found at the core of what Camus defines as the contemporary 'age of fear' (*CAC8*, p. 608). When interviewed in October 1957,[1] Camus resorts to the term 'nihilism' to speak of this radical mode of thought, which he identifies in the contemporary understanding of political action and, especially, in the Existentialist-Marxist understanding of 'engagement' within party politics. In the same interview, he explicitly distinguishes this 'nihilistic' form of commitment from his own understanding of political militancy, thus suggesting that the comprehension of the problem of nihilism is essential to grasp the singularity of his own political position that hovers in the margins of political philosophies and the post-war horizon of terrorisms.

Over the last 20 years, 'nihilism' has been the object of sociological and philosophical criticisms.[2] The term has been used to designate a condition in which there is a disjunction between our experience of the world and the conceptual apparatus we have at our disposal, which we have inherited, to interpret it (Ansell-Pearson 1994, pp. 35–6); in other words, nihilism has been seen as a short circuit between our experience and the symbolic paradigms we use to think and contemplate our actions. Thus, nihilism has been understood primarily as a cultural problem – the failure to impart a sense of meaning and the loss of self-understanding – which eventually affects the political sphere, in some cases with murderous effects. As post-totalitarian attempts to rethink the notions of democracy and community clearly attest (Lacoue-Labarthe and Nancy 1983), nihilism, by dislocating the individual's ability to act as an agent (Warren 1985, p. 190), is seen to call the metaphysical concept of agency of liberal and conservative political thought dramatically into question.

The term 'Nihilism' in that it is used as a synonym for radical destruction – of values, laws, and life (Crépon 2005, p. 85) – is traced back to the phrase 'Nothing is true, everything is permitted', which announces the death of God in Turgenev, Dostoevsky and Nietzsche, and is used in philosophical political analyses to account for a heterogeneous series of phenomena in the twentieth and twenty-first centuries, from totalitarianism to genocidal wars and terrorist attacks. This has contributed to a diffused marginalisation and 'devolution' of the term, which in sociological analyses and in the established political discourse has been replaced by the terms 'anti-democratic', 'terroristic', and 'fundamentalist' (Clemens and Feik 2000, p. 18).

Recent attempts to challenge nihilism's status as a politically forceful philosophical discourse (Clemens and Feik 2000, p. 19), however, have focused on the historical roots of this contemporary political phenomenon, which was associated with 'demonology', namely, with a monstrous synthesis of modern State bureaucracies and early nineteenth-century Russian terrorist movements (Clemens and Feik 2000, pp. 31–3) and, therefore, Dostoevsky was seen to have established 'the legacy of nihilism for the twentieth century' (Clemens and Feik 2000, p. 31). As Hannah Arendt noted, Dostoevsky's formula 'Everything is permitted' powerfully condensed what was commonly understood as 'nihilism' in sociological and political studies of the post-war years, namely, the dismantling of metaphysics and the attack against the supra-sensuous and transcendent ideas, which, since Plato's time, were intended to measure, judge, and give meaning to existence (Arendt 1961, p. 30). By linking nihilism and bureaucratic activity together, recent research draws attention to the strictly *political* problem of nihilism, but it seems to neglect what Arendt considered to be even more relevant for the investigation of our time than nineteenth-century demonology and rebellions against traditions, that is to say, the unprecedented phenomenon of *radical nihilism* (Arendt 1961, p. 34). The phenomenon that she refers to as 'radical nihilism' was experimented for the first time in totalitarian ideologies and terror, which overthrew the assertion that 'everything is permitted' by proclaiming instead that 'everything is possible' (Arendt 1994, p. 431).

Arendt seems to be particularly concerned with the psychological attitude of contempt towards existence, which is characteristic of radical nihilism. In *The Origins of Totalitarianism*, she calls attention to how, from the time of the Greeks, political life has been seen to breed a deep resentment towards the disturbing miracle of existence, wherein each of us is made as he or she is (Arendt 1951b, p. 301). Arendt, in her 1953 American lectures, then outlines this contempt that resides at the core of the Western tradition of political philosophy and links it to the Marxian understanding of political action.[3] By reviving and applying the Nietzschean category of *ressentiment* ('resentment') to the political phenomena of the twentieth century, Arendt suggests that, in order to shed light on contemporary politics, we ought to investigate the particular *creativeness* of nihilism rather than its sheer destructiveness.

Camus identifies nihilism in the systematic use of criticism, denigration and spitefulness that are employed as a form of political action (IV, p. 583) and, like Arendt, refers to a *radical* mode of thought, which is rooted in a psychological-political attitude of resentment toward existence, bringing the relationship between creation and political action to the foreground in contemporary 'politics of fear'. As I will argue in Chapter 4, Camus's definition of nihilism cannot be understood without referring, in particular, to Max Scheler's *L'Homme du ressentiment*, which emphasises the creativeness of an attitude that was already explored by Nietzsche under the French appellation of *ressentiment* in his *Genealogy of Morals*. Some of the symptoms of this widespread attitude include maliciousness (*méchanceté*), a tendency to denigrate (*malignité*), as well as a sterile form of criticism, which, in the intent to defend one's opinions, refuses to confront these last with reality (Scheler 1958, p. 47).

Etymologically, spitefulness is derived from the verb spite, 'insult' or 'outrage', 'treat maliciously' (from the Latin verb *despectare*, 'to regard with contempt'). Emphasis is placed on the particular top-down perspective that accompanies resentment; to contemn, or to treat or regard with contempt, signifies to despise (from Lat. *despicere*). In turn, despise carries the connotation of 'looking *down* on' someone or something. In his translation of 'The Wager of our Generation', Justin O'Brien chooses the word 'disparage' to render the signification of the French term *dénigration* (from Lat. *denigrare* 'to blacken') (Camus 1961, p. 170); this word choice not only reinforces the sense of a difference of rank (from *par* 'equal', 'peer'), it also clearly conveys the act of stripping someone of the status of peer.

The way in which language is used reveals the devaluation that *ressentiment* entails. The echo of Nietzsche's forceful etymological analyses in the first dissertation of the *Genealogy of Morals* is apparent in Camus's definition of nihilism, yet he nonetheless, takes his distances from Scheler's study in one crucial respect. According to the latter, resentment postulates the equality between the offender and the offended; the 'feeling of equality' that kindled the violent reaction against the aristocracy during the French revolution provides the historical example of the disruptive and levelling force of *ressentiment* with respect to social hierarchies and traditional values (Scheler 1958, pp. 20–1 n.1). In Camus's view, resentment denotes a 'radical' way of thinking, speaking, and acting, which disparages the opponent, linguistically and physically expelling him from the rank of peer, and terminates in the nihilist affirmation of a 'droit au *déshonneur* (right to dishonour)' (IV, p. 241).

Camus develops his political reflection around the word couple 'honour'/'dishonour' (see Chapter 6). These two terms refer to two distinct and irreducible political constellations. Honour, or respect of the opponent, recurs in Nietzsche's *Genealogy of Morals* to designate a way of relating to the enemy by recognising him as a peer. The free man does not look *down* on his antagonists nor does he disparage them as 'evil', but honours them as enemies *inter pares* (*GM*, I, 10) – Nietzsche observes in the 'Twofold prehistory of good and evil' in *Human, All too Human* (I, 2, 45), the Trojan and the Greek in Homer are both 'good'. Insofar as the particular evaluation of *ressentiment* regards the opponent as an '*evil*doer', it incorporates a God-like perspective, introducing a top-down relation, which literally 'abstracts' and removes the enemy from the living context of the relationships with his peers and paves the way to the nihilistic 'right to dishonour'. Resentment excludes horizontality (*inter pares*) and introduces a vertical master-slave relationship of dominion, which influences the notion of freedom of action; when this disposition exists in the individual a community can hardly arise (Nietzsche 1986, p. 37). It is no surprise that in the opening pages of the 1951 essay *L'homme révolté*, Camus refers to Tertullian's famous passage of *De spectaculis*, also cited by Nietzsche in his *Genealogy of Morals* (I, 15), as a masterly illustration of resentment (*HR*, p. 75). The creativeness of this attitude consists in re-directing suffering through a re-evaluation of man and the world, in which contempt is regarded as a peculiar form of appraisal or appreciation (from lat. *ad*, 'to' *pretium*, 'price'), which belittles man by setting a low value or 'price' upon him (*GM*, III, 25). Camus appropriates the Nietzschean idea that the categories through which the world and man have traditionally been apprehended and appraised, similarly to those in Tertullian's representation of the 'eternal blessedness' in Christian paradise, are *created* by hate (*GM*, I, 15). In other words, they replace the horizontal relationship of respect and honour (*inter pares*) with the vertical relationship of dominion, which is the sign of a dynamic of *ressentiment*.

The relation that exists between hatred, fear and power in the contemporary understanding of political action is a pivotal question in Camus's reflection during the years of the Résistance and in the immediate aftermath of the Liberation (see Chapter 6); in his articles for *Combat*, the resistance newspaper for which he was the editor between 1944 and 1947, the idea of a 'freedom in honour' (*CAC8*, p. 26) challenges the traditional notion of freedom of action of Liberal and Conservative, as well as of revolutionary theories, and denounces the 'right to dishonour', namely, the right to humiliate (from Lat. *humilis* 'low', 'that lies under'), insult, disrespect, and hold contempt for in the political arena of the twentieth 'century of fear' (*CAC8*, p. 608). The parallel between Tertullian's heavenly 'spectacle' of cruelty on Judgment Day and the public gatherings on the occasion of capital executions (*HR*, p. 75) attests to the political relevance that Camus accords to the question of nihilism.

Camus had been introduced to this issue by his teacher Jean Grenier in the early 1930s and became so absorbed with it as to make it his own in time. Professor of philosophy at the Lycée Bugeaud of Algiers, friend of Jean Paulhan and collaborator of *La Nouvelle Revue Française* (hereinafter *NRF*), Grenier is a key figure in the young writer's philosophical political 'apprenticeship'. His classes were structured to be as a philosophical *work-in-progress*,[4] thus, it is more than likely that some arguments of his reflection were brought to the attention of his students. The question of nihilism in particular appears to be crucial to Grenier's philosophical considerations, as is confirmed by the essay 'Le Nihilisme Européen et les Appels de l'Orient', which he published in *Philosophies* in 1924 using a pseudonym.[5]

This essay is an important source in that it sheds light on the beginnings of Camus's political thought. First, it provides an interpretation of nihilism that is explicitly modelled on the Nietzschean notion of *ressentiment*; Grenier understands nihilism in the sense of the German word *Schadenfreude*, also referred to as 'self-vivisection', 'intoxication', 'romanticism', or 'will to nothingness' in the posthumous fragments of Nietzsche's *La Volonté de puissance* (Caves 1924a, p. 56). This self-contempt, that Camus's teacher had detected in early twentieth-century European thought, is illustrated in Germany by Oswald Spengler's best-selling *The Decline of the West* on one hand, and, on the other, by the editorial project of the *Nietzsche Archiv* committee, and is traced back to the 'creative' power of *ressentment* in stirring and redirecting frenzied affections for the purpose of anaesthetics (*GM*, III, 15). In his essays and letters of the late 1930s, Grenier especially dwells on the adverse effects that enthusiasm combined with political action has had in the contemporary right- and left-wing ideologies; the content of these considerations is evoked in Camus's political reflection of the 1940s and 1950s.

Secondly, in his 1924 essay, Grenier suggests that a relation between nihilism and the Western concept of political action exists; this was bound to leave a profound mark on Camus's early opinions and con-templations. In the first part of 'Le Nihilisme Européen et les Appels de l'Orient', Grenier focuses on Oswald Spengler's theses in *The Decline of the West* and on Hermann Keyserling's appeals to Oriental wisdom. He views them as the historical illustrations of those philosophical catego-ries which, in his opinion, culminate in the early twentieth-century Europeans' 'universel désarroi' (universal helplessness) and appetite for destruction. More than a decade later, in his 'L'âge des orthodoxies' (1936), Grenier draws attention to a widespread feeling of helplessness ('désarroi') engendered by academic rationalism (Grenier 1967, p. 39). Camus uses the same terminology in his 1942 draft of a foreword to *Le Mythe de Sisyphe*: 'L'intelligence moderne est en plein désarroi. La connaissance s'est distendue à ce point que le monde et l'esprit ont perdu tout point d'appui. C'est un fait que nous souffrons de nihilisme. (Modern intelligence is in a complete state of helplessness. Knowledge has stretched to the point that the world and the mind have lost all sup-port. It is a fact that we are suffering from nihilism.) (II, p. 948).

In the second part of his 1924 essay, Grenier goes yet further: defin-ing the political phenomenon of the so-called 'Russian Nihilism' as the extreme peak of European Nihilism, he assumes political nihilism to be the most logical outcome and daring actualisation of the fun-damental ideas of the eighteenth century (Caves 1924b, p. 186), as well as the magnifying glass through which the inner logic of Western philosophical thought ought to be investigated. Almost 30 years before

Hannah Arendt's *The Human Condition* and her lectures on *Karl Marx and the Tradition of Western Political Thought*, Grenier links the issue of nihilism to the Western concept of political action. He believes that the apparent destructiveness of nihilism is the other side of the philosophical understanding of action as a process of *realising* a superior ideal through violence ('just idea'/ 'just cause'). This teleological concept of action (from Gr. *telos*, 'end') justifies the destruction of existing institutions, laws, communities as a preliminary condition (*pars destruens*) to the future (re)construction (*pars construens*) of a model society capable of achieving ultimate 'happiness'.

Grenier draws attention to the Platonic–Aristotelian idea of 'perfection' that is implied in the notion of end or final cause and which he detects in the traditional understanding of political action as the realisation or actualisation of the 'ideal'. On one hand, he identifies two key concepts of the Western political tradition, violence and progress, in the notion of realisation; these are concepts on which the nihilist discourse in nineteenth-century Russia was built, culminating in the twentieth-century revolutionary theories that combined the Russian 'seductiveness of destruction' and the Jacobinic radical principle of 'just anger' (Caves 1924b, p. 187). Thus, Russian nihilism exposes the teleocratic logic of the Western 'fabricative' model of action and power. On the other hand, the notion of realisation calls into question the matter, discussed by Grenier in the concluding pages of the essay, regarding the traditional distinction made between thinking (the philosophical *vita contemplativa*) and acting (the political *vita activa*) and between action as synonym of power and inaction as synonym of powerlessness.

According to Camus's teacher, the so-called 'Russian mind' that was immortalised in Dostoevsky's novels is the historical illustration of *ressentiment*: crime and punishment – the former as pleasure of persecution and destruction (*GM*, II, 16), the latter as a specific way of directing that pleasure of destruction against oneself – are two facets of the same principle. Dostoevsky's nihilist characters take pleasure in the act of recounting their crimes and displaying their shame and guilt in public confessions; thus they incorporate the God-like perspective of the spectator that was detected by Nietzsche in the moral understanding of 'punishment as festival' (*GM*, II, 13). According to the German philosopher, if one considers the deed in and of itself, crime and punishment coincide: the criminal, the police and the judges resort to the same type of actions (rape, torture, manslaughter, imprisonment) (*GM*, II, 14), the only difference being that the punisher commits the deed systematically and *without passion* – fear, cunning and 'coldness' are the 'symptoms' of the perspective of punishment, which is an indication of the presence of *ressentiment* (*GM*, II, 15).

In a perspective of punishment, two elements that are crucial for the analysis of nihilism are introduced. First, power is identified with 'cold-heartedness', where effective action is rooted in the capacity of the calculating subject to master or negate his/her desires. Second, every deed is interpreted within the temporal frame of *telos*, that is to say, as a 'means-to-an-end' (utilitarian principle); in nineteenth-century Russian nihilism, as well as in twentieth-century revolutionary ideologies, action is etched into a 'History' (millenarianism) which puts the deed between brackets. The Subject/agent of this teleological action that reaches toward achievement is the *Gewaltmensch* or '*homme de puissance*' (Caves 1924a, p. 61). According to Grenier, the notion of achievement accounts for both Western and Oriental philosophies, which are both founded on the idea of outward and inward struggle and domination. These traditions, respectively represented by Faust and Krishna as two variants of the figure of the warrior, negate the limit, finitude or incompletion of the world and of the human condition in favour of boundlessness (*ivresse*) and the quest for perfection. The way in which the Western world conceives of power in terms of effective action and the Oriental ideal of contemplation, understood to mean a withdrawal from the world and the internalisation of the Western outward struggle for domination, are two sides of the same nihilistic coin.

Thus, in Grenier's view, philosophy is confronted with a deceitful alternative that brings the political implications of European nihilism into full light: on one hand, the reduction of political action to the cult of efficacy leads to the unbridled rule over the masses (Bolshevism); on the other, the separation of philosophical contemplation from political action through abstention (refusal to vote, refusal to command/obey) leads to the creation of 'islands' of retreat from the public space, as was the case in the Epicurean and Stoic schools of the late Roman Empire, in which the exercise of thought is identified with passiveness and inaction (Caves 1924b, p. 196). In his 1924 essay, as well as in his 1938 collection of political writings, *Essai sur l'esprit d'orthodoxie*, Grenier openly challenges the political statute of philosophical thinking: 'engaged' philosophy committed to party policy and the so-called philosophy in the 'ivory tower' are two declinations of the same Platonic–Aristotelian teleocratic concept of action as realisation, which logically and historically leads to the twentieth-century impasse of nihilism.

One should not forget that in the early 1930s, under the guide of his teacher, Camus studied to become a philosopher and his first attempts at literary creation are imbued with philosophical references (see Chapter 2). The role Grenier played in drawing Camus's attention to nihilism as an eminently political question, by touching upon the relation between theory and action and, therefore, between philosophical reason and the nihilistic logic of achievement in the Western tradition of political thought, is indubitable. In order to understand the genesis of Camus's reflection in the 1930s, Grenier's considerations on nihilism are crucial, and shed light on the young student's concern for the criticism of modern rationalism and his quest for an alternative method of thought.

I propose that we read Camus's 1932 philosophical writings as an attempt to bring the connection between the Western concept of reason and the nihilistic impasse of action/effectiveness *versus* inaction/powerlessness into focus; along with evaluating the possibility of defining a different way of considering action so that it is no longer perceived and contemplated within the bounds of the logic of nihilism but rather outside and beyond.

2
'Undisguised influences'

Albert Camus, in his interview with Jean-Claude Brisville in 1959, recalls having wanted to be a writer already at the age of 17 (I, p. ix; Brisville 1959, p. 256). Rather than a 'vocation' or a profession, in the Weberian sense, he conceived his artistic creation to be an endless interrogation that evades the categories of analytical reason ('clarity') and goes back to a poverty or 'denudement', which he experienced in the sensory and sensual plenitude of the Algerian ecstatic nature (*EE*, pp. 32–3). A stranger to the romantic emphasis on demiurgic will (I, p. x), Camus's artistic process is said to elude *ressentiment* and escape the humiliation of misery and ugliness.

In 1930, at the age of 17, the author begins his intense literary and philosophical 'apprenticeship' with Jean Grenier. While the reading of André Richaud's *La Douleur* is said to have unveiled the world of creation to the young student, born of a poor family from a working-class area of Algiers,[1] there is little doubt that it was through the reading of Jean Paulhan's *NRF*, 'the first literary journal in France', of which Grenier was a regular collaborator, that the international philosophical political debate of the 1930s was disclosed to Camus.[2]

In 1932, the young philosophy student respectively devotes a review and a short dissertation to Bergson's *Les Deux Sources de la Morale et de la Religion*,[3] and to the aesthetic theories of Schopenhauer and Nietzsche,[4] which were published in *Sud*, the Algerian review of literature and art directed by Grenier's students. According to the young commentator, the twentieth century 'en mal d'action (desperate for action)' is imbued with Bergson's anti-rationalistic thinking that cautions against the dangers of analysis ('intelligence and reason'). Reason is seen to dissolve society and drive the individual to despair (I, p. 544); Camus's reference to the contemporary mind (*genie*), grievously wandering in want of a new instinctive philosophy beyond rationalism (I, p. 545) calls to mind Jean Grenier's sombre reflections on European Nihilism, as well as the philosophical analyses in the *NRF* of those years.[5]

By replacing immediate knowledge or intuition for science and rational argumentation (I, p. 543), '(la) philosophie (de Bergson) me paraissait la plus belle de toutes, car elle était une des rares avec celle de Nietzsche qui refusa tout à la Raison. (Bergson's philosophy seemed to be to me the most beautiful of all philosophies, for it was one of the rare ones, along with Nietzsche's, that denied everything to Reason.)' (I, p. 544.) *Les Deux Sources de la Morale et de la Religion*, however, proves to be a disappointment to Camus, who had expected it to be the application of this method and, thus, found the new 'intuitive' religion of the century.

The criticism of rationalism is also a pivotal element of Camus's longer article, 'Sur la musique'. According to the bibliography of the manuscript version of the text (I, p. 1363), Camus reads *Le Cas Wagner*, *Nietzsche contre Wagner* and consults *La Naissance de la tragédie*. In particular, he focuses his attention on Nietzsche's 'An Attempt at Self-Criticism', the late preface to the third edition of the 1872 book on tragedy (Arnold 1979, p. 97); the fact that Camus approaches the philosopher's theory on aesthetics and moulds his commentary of *La Naissance de la tragédie*, not only matching the perspective but also adopting the terminology used in the 1886 preface, sheds important light on the author's early writings, which relate the question of art to Nietzsche's methodological investigation. The idea that is introduced in Nietzsche's 'Attempt at Self-Criticism' posits that the world's existence can only be justified as an aesthetic phenomenon, and therefore remains *outside* the moral interpretation of reason. In art, the possibility for the creative will to be 'liberated' from the practical and theoretical utilitarianism of modern rationalism is presented; art reaches beyond the logic upon which moral and political fanaticism are founded (*NT*, 'Essai d'une critique de soi-même', 2, 5).

Dismissed as a scholastic exercise (Le Ridier 1999, p. 143), it is in the 1932 'Sur la musique' that the still largely unexplored question of Camus's Nietzscheanism is raised. Contrary to what has been generally assumed, I argue that from the very beginning of the young author's questioning of an anti-rationalistic method of thought, Nietzsche's writings of the 1880s were determinant in preventing Camus from falling prey to that idealistic, 'self-satisfied neo-romanticism', which critics have often imputed to his early writings (Arnold 1984, p. 126),[6] and in introducing him to the criticism of the modern philosophical political ideas.

Camus makes the radical challenge of the Platonic concept of Beauty (I, p. 530) that pervades Nietzsche's 1886 prefaces his own and propounds that the Greek perception of beauty is rooted in a deep sense of pain – creatively evaded through artistic illusion ('Dream') – rather than in a teleological aspiration to reach perfection. In his commentary of the Nietzschean relationship between beauty, or aesthetic Apollonian creation, and 'rapture' (*ivresse*), the Dionysian ecstatic negation of identity, that is brought about by music (I, p. 531), Camus particularly hones in on the philosopher's struggle against discouragement and his 'heroic optimism', which does not 'romantically' or 'idealistically' negate pain, but rather is rooted in it (I, p. 529). The young student places the Nietzschean 'artist's nature' in opposition to the anguished lament of the rationalist Subject (I, p. 532); thus, he demonstrates his understanding of tragic 'ecstasy' to be the negation of philosophical reason and considers it to be disruptive of the modern utilitarian way of thinking existence, rather than as the dissolution of life *tout court*. The echoes of Grenier's Nietzschean analyses of the relation between the European will for destruction, Western rationalism and the teleological concept of action as realisation and perfection are apparent in Camus's analysis of the 'radical aesthetics' of *La Naissance de la tragédie*.[7]

The five short texts along with the prologue, which Camus writes between May and October 1932 and groups together under the programmatic headings of *Intuitions*, may be read as a 'dramatisation' of Nietzsche's aesthetic anti-rationalism. This work, to which he assigns benchmark importance, is said to contain 'some really bad things, some undisguised influences, but also something of myself' (Camus and Grenier 1981, p. 11). The apparent Bergsonian influence reflected in the title should not mislead us: in the introductory lines of his work, Camus attributes his first literary attempt to the desire of his 'too mystical soul' (I, p. 941); thus, openly declaring the influence that Nietzsche's methodological remarks in the 'Attempt at Self-Criticism' had on his work. The emphasis Nietzsche places on the mystical 'new' soul that strives to find its own language to sing what cannot be said, namely, to express a thought that goes beyond the boundaries of grammar and logic of philosophical reason, is reflected in Camus's own understanding of aesthetic creation.

Camus perceives aesthetic creation to be a 'new birth', in other words, it is the act of giving order to an obscure desire to speak which is brought about in reading or conversation through the encounter with a 'perfect language' that brings the artist's personal awkward and timid *singing* to light (IV, p. 623). The constant confrontation with and imitation 'in the spiritual sense of the word' (IV, p. 623) of the ideas and work of his teacher, Jean Grenier,[8] define the artist's relation to this last and also describe his connection to the work of Nietzsche that is first evident in *Intuitions* and continues to manifest itself throughout his entire life.

In the early 1930s, Camus reads Henri Albert's French translations of the German philosopher (Arnold 1979; Favre 2004).[9] But *what* Nietzsche did he actually read? In October 1932, along with each text of his *Intuitions*, Camus signs and dates a copy of Nietzsche's *Ecce homo*, indicating the importance this work has for him at the beginning of his intellectual production (Arnold 1979, p. 96). Through the 1886 preface to *La Naissance de la tragédie* and *Ecce homo*, the young writer is confronted with the questions and terminology of the mature Nietzsche and is introduced to *Aurore* (*Daybreak*), the 1881 book that establishes the philosopher's attack on moral 'prejudices' and the immoralist research of a transvaluation of all values.

The reading of the preface to *Aurore* is likely to have brought the relation between modern rationalism and contemporary moral and political fanaticism to Camus's attention.[10] In his violent attack of the eighteenth century political theories of 'enthusiasm', Nietzsche uses the term 'fanaticism' to address the virulent influence that the philosophy of the 'moral tarantula' Rousseau had on both Kant's criticism of pure reason and on Robespierre's revolutionary programme for the realisation of the empire of 'wisdom', 'justice' and 'virtue' on earth (*A*, 'Avant-Propos', 3). Addressed as the 'Circe of philosophers' and considered to be an art of intellectual seduction and persuasion that excites action by stirring frenzied passions, morality denotes a specific way of thinking or interpreting existence which incorporates a perspective of contempt or hatred of the 'world' and fear of beauty.

The political issue of moral fanaticism, raised by modern revolutionary theories, radically calls into question the Western belief in the fundamental 'objective' character of reason and its logical judgements; according to Nietzsche, traditional logic and modern rationalism are *moral* phenomena, they are primarily a means to comprehend and (de)valuate the world and human life and incorporate the abasing and despising perspective characteristic of *ressentiment*. Notions such as 'God', 'soul', 'free will', 'virtue', 'sin', and 'truth', which are forever 'drawing us upward' and precisely thereby for ever 'bringing us down' (*A*, 'Avant-Propos', 4), are the deceitful creations ('lies') of human imagination and are rooted in the instincts of revenge re-directed against the fundamental conditions of life.

In his 1932 *Intuitions*, Camus openly follows in the steps of 'the first *immoralist*' thinker (*EH*, 'Pourquoi je suis un destin', 2), and links his own interrogation to the Nietzschean effort of artistic (re)evaluation to evade contemporary rationalism. The analysis of Nietzsche's intellectual biography by Lou Andréas-Salomé confirms that the young author identified his own methodological research with that of the tragic philosopher.[11] Andréas-Salomé portrays Nietzsche to be a thinker 'rongé par mille *incertitudes* (consumed by a thousand *uncertainties*)' (Andréas-Salomé 2002 [1932], p. 285), who is struggling with his overwhelming desires, but who senses in them a 'new ideal of knowledge' (Andréas-Salomé 2002, p. 155).

'Incertitudes' ('Uncertainties') is the heading of the first text in Camus's *Intuitions*.[12] The thematic continuity with the argument of 'Sur la musique' is apparent in its opening lines – 'La musique s'était tue et les deux hommes se taisaient (The music had stopped and the two men were silent)' (I, p. 941). When the music stops, reason begins to speak once again: Camus imagines himself as the silent spectator of a dialogue between two figures, two opposed projections of the author's own Self, which he tries to conciliate in vain (I, p. 943). Thus, he associates reason with *dédoublement*, the internal division of one's self, and perceives this to engender *lassitude* and indifference (I, p. 943). The two characters speak the language of power and dominion: on one hand, there is an active figure who bases his ability to command on the capacity to negate his desires (I, p. 942); on the other, there is a passive character who longs for the infinite. This last apparently rejects the vertical power relation of command and obedience but takes pleasure in lamentation without actually interrupting or stepping out of the relation. In 'Incertitudes', the influence of Grenier's political analysis of modern nihilism and, especially, of the relation between rationalism and the Western opposition action/inaction, efficacy/powerlessness is manifest; Camus represents these two sides of the nihilistic phenomenon as two 'voices' of his own divided self, dismissing all forms of indifference towards the (false) alternative force/lassitude as 'lie' (*mensonge*). In his opinion, reason does not offer a viable way out of the self-destructive impasse of traditional power politics.

By radically calling 'science' and rationalism into question, Nietzsche's work is an example of interrogation that challenges the relation between domination, power and *ressentiment* supported and perpetuated by philosophical reason. In her biography, Andréas-Salomé insists that Nietzsche displaces the primacy of intellect and logical clarity in favour of a philosophy that is resolutely hostile to the values of reason

(Andréas-Salomé 2002, p. 152). She portrays him as a thinker who, exactly like young Camus, is searching for a different method of thought that reaches beyond the nihilistic methods of rationalism (Andréas-Salomé 2002, p. 157).[13]

The texts compiled in *Intuitions* develop two themes that are pivotal to the philosophical experience of Nietzsche: *dédoublement* and madness. Andréas-Salomé relates the separation of the author's self into two distinct parts (*dédoublement*) to the philosopher's effort to bestow order upon his disharmonious and labyrinthic nature[14] by disciplining the multiplicity of his instincts and bringing them to the highest degree of lucidity (Andréas-Salomé 2002, p. 40). The result is not the (con)fusion of passions in an unchanging and harmonious unitary being, but rather that the individual suffers from an internal tragic split; Andréas-Salomé goes on to describe the philosopher as one who is contemplating his own self through a reflecting lens and is caught in an insoluble dualism, Spectator–Actor. This paralyses the flow of his instincts, while the violence of his passions tends to *dislocate the sovereignty of intelligence* (Andréas-Salomé 2002, pp. 43–4).[15]

According to Salomé, Nietzsche distinguishes the harmonious and homogeneous nature of the man of action – the unbroken *'âme de maître* (soul of a master)'* (Andréas-Salomé 2002) – from the thinker's heterogeneous nature, which demands the most rigorous self-discipline.[16] The Nietzschean thinker turns his own life into an instrument of knowledge – in a touching autobiographic fragment, probably dated around 1934, Camus, who had contracted tuberculosis and was faced with a precocious death, writes: 'Je sais maintenant que la vraie vie est la santé et que le corps est un moyen de connaissance (I now know that true life is health and that the body is a means of knowledge')' (I, p. 95).[17]

Four of the five texts which constitute *Intuitions* – 'Délires' ('Deliriums'), 'La volonté de mensonge' ('The Will to Lie'), 'Souhait' ('Desire') and 'Retour sur moi-même' ('Return Back to Myself') – are developed around a dialogue between the Author and the Dyonisian figure of the Madman or Fool (*le Fou*). Also defined as the Conciliator (I, p. 945), the Fool preaches that the internal contradictions (*dédoublement*) caused by the analytical faculty of 'intelligence' must be overcome by stripping existence of the four-fold principle of reason through which man has traditionally made sense of the world (I, pp. 943–4). 'Delirium', which is associated to laughter, is the manifestation of the dissolution of ordinary knowledge (I, p. 945), namely, of the moral straitjacket of reason. The Fool is the embodiment of the Nietzschean criticism of rationalism, who in art, action, in the natural elements and in God traces those forms of *love* that suppress reason's deceitful creations of *ressentiment* and culminate in ecstatic communication ('oblivion') (I, p. 946).

The flagrant influence of Nietzsche's 1880s' writings leaves no doubt as to the philosophical political implications of Camus's reveries: the anti-romantic aesthetics propounded by the Fool reject the 'false' alternative force/weakness that Grenier has detected at the core of the European 'will for destruction' and which Camus finds residing in such 'lies' of reason as 'personality', 'Soul' or 'Subject'. From the tragic (Dyonisian) perspective of the Fool, to become God(s) holds no other meaning than that of stepping out of the vertical power relation and of the nihilistic identification of action with efficacy and force (I, p. 946), which is doubly bound to the *principium individuationis* of rationalistic utilitarian logic. Thus, echoing Nietzsche, Camus does not understand ecstatic love and 'perpetual desire' as a reduction to sheer 'stupid animality' (I, p. 947), but rather as a higher 'spiritual' process of liberation from the metaphysical straitjacket through which life has traditionally been apprehended and evaluated.

The text of 'Délires' calls to mind Andréas-Salomé's intellectual biography, which dwells on the role that madness plays in Nietzsche's philosophy, and, particularly, in *Aurore*, where the 'delirium of dream and madness' (Andréas-Salomé 2002, pp. 282) give access to the instinctual roots of humanity, the Fool being the masque worn by 'all those superior men irresistibly driven to break the yoke of any kind of morality, and to proclaim new laws' (Andréas-Salomé 2002, p. 283). The influence Andréas-Salomé's biography has had on Camus in relating the motive of madness to the methodological issue of 'immoralism' in Nietzsche's work is apparent; in 'Délires', Camus evokes the Nietzschean 'superior men' who break the yoke of morality and create new values:

> Vers des îles lointaines voguent des *hommes déchaînés*, qui goûtent avec force l'âcreté des cieux et la splendeur vigoureuse de la brise marine. Ils ne regardent pas derrière eux, dédaignant le *lâche* sillage qui fuit l'hélice et meurt. (*Men who have broken their chains* sail towards faraway islands, tasting the pungent skies and the vigorous splendour of the sea breeze. They do not look back, disdaining the *cowardly* wake that flees from the propeller and dies') (I, p. 947; Camus 1980, p. 128; my italics).

This passage strongly evokes *Ecce homo*, where the image of navigation is associated with Zarathustra's 'seekers' (*EH*, 'Pourquoi j'écris de si bons livres', 3), the conquerors and discoverers of new lands and new values, who break with all that is *behind* them and embark on terrible seas. These 'argonautes of the ideal' (*EH*, 'Pourquoi j'écris de si bons livres', 'Zarathustra', 2) bravely reject the fetters of tradition, namely, the modes of thought and language of philosophical or moral reason, which the modern 'last men', fascinated by the Ideal of Progress but incapable of looking forward (*EH*, 'Pourquoi j'écris de si bons livres', 'Zarathustra', 3), are still cowardly submissive to. In *Ecce Homo*, 'lâcheté' (cowardice) and 'faiblesse' (weakness) are associated with the nihilistic or romantic flight from reality into the 'Ideal', which Nietzsche grounds in a nay-saying disparaging judgement upon existence (*ressentiment*) and opposes to the audacious knowledge of the 'Dyonisian' yes-saying adventurers. When Camus opposes his own weakness and cowardice to the courage 'to no longer be a man' (I, p. 947), he openly echoes the Nietzschean figure of the superior man (*Übermensch* or *surhomme*), who is free from the nihilistic logic of moral reason.

In 'Souhait' ('Desire'), Camus dramatises the methodological remarks of Nietzsche's 1886 preface to *Aurore* in a dialogue between the actor and the spectator of his divided reflecting self (I, p. 951): 'Je me per-suadais aisément aussi que l'intelligence que nous considérons généra-lement comme claire et méthodique n'était qu'un obscur et tortueux labyrinthe à côté de ces presciences immédiates. (I persuaded myself easily, too, that the intelligence we generally consider as clear and methodical is nothing other than an obscure and tortuous labyrinth[18] compared to these immediate presciences.) (I, p. 950; Camus 1980, p. 133). Camus adopts Nietzsche's criticism of the Cartesian method and displaces intelligence from the key role that it has been assigned to in modern philosophical and scientific knowledge.

The young writer explicitly resorts to the Nietzschean term 'rumina-tions' to define his own process of thinking as one which enters *deeply into himself* (I, p. 950). Like Nietzsche's mole, the 'subterranean' animal that pierces and digs its way into the depths of the soul in order to find its own '*aurore*' ('daybreak') (*A*, Preface, 1), the author attentively probes his own self, replacing metaphysical objectiveness with the 'intuitions soudaines qui éclairaient la nuit de mes incertitudes (sudden intuitions which illuminated the night of my uncertainties)' like innumerable fleeting 'éclairs de lucidité presque matérielle (flashes of almost material lucidity)' (I, p. 950). Tracing 'truth*s*', rather than Truth,[19] in intuition, philosophical reason is dislocated and the corporeal and instinctual dimension that was dismissed or even condemned by the Platonic–Christian tradition as 'passion' and 'delirium' is re-evaluated.

Intuitive thinking 'lights up in a flash' (*éclair*) and illuminates that which is concealed or 'counterfeited' by dialectical thought (*EH*, 'Pourquoi j'écris de si bon livres' – 'Ainsi parlait Zarathoustra', 3); this image that is used in *Ecce homo* to convey the thinker's inspiration confirms Camus's early attempt to mould his reveries to Nietzsche's philosophical example. The metaphoric constellation of light/lightning/clarity in reference to the thinker's ruminations, as opposed to the dialectics of philosophical reason, recurs in two of Camus's sources: Andréas-Salomé's biography and Charles Andler's *Le pessimisme esthétique de Nietzsche*.[20] In particular, Andler associates Nietzsche's 'flashing' intuition, which displaces philosophy, with the creative power of human thought as source of representations, norms and values (Andler 1958b, pp.15–16). The creative or *artistic* drive of the man of knowledge is a pivotal element in Camus's 1932 writings and attests to the influence Nietzsche's thought had on his later gnoseologic, ethical and political reflections.[21]

In *Intuitions*, Camus explicitly thematises the Nietzschean 'will to lie', linking the criticism of Western rationalism to the problem of action. Aware of the deceitful character of those 'reasons' (*lies*), by means of which he justifies his conduct (I, p. 943), and confronted with the superhuman example of Zarathustra's 'conquerors', the author suffers from his all too human weakness to live up to the Fool's 'divine' word, namely, to break free from the oppressiveness of *ratio* (I, p. 943):

> Quand donc se lèvera pour moi *l'aurore audacieuse* de mes résolutions? Quand aurai-je *le courage de ne plus être un homme ?*
> Vers des îles lointaines voguent des hommes déchaînés [...]
> (When will the *audacious daybreak* of my resolutions rise up for me ? When will I have *the courage to no longer be a man?*
> Men who have broken their chains sail toward faraway islands [...]).
> (I, p. 947, my italics)

Camus openly follows in the footsteps of *Ecce homo*, where the image of the dawn evokes the liberation from the straitjacket of rationalism that supports traditional morality and which announces a whole series of new mornings, or *revaluations* of all values (*EH*, 'Pourquoi j'écris de si bons livres' – 'Aurore', 1; 'Pourquoi je suis un destin', 1).

Furthermore, the image of the 'faraway islands' also seems to confirm that Camus embraces Nietzsche's criticism of morality: in the second part of *Thus Spoke Zarathustra*, the 'blissful Islands' and faraway seas evoke a *change of perspective*, the liberation of the *Übermensch* (Overman) from the logical and moral chains of reason.[22] It is essential that we do not understand this 'liberation' as the unleashing of man's unbound irrational drives, but rather as a radical change in the way of thinking.

Zarathustra's exhortation to take the limits of what is humanly think-able, visible, and sensible upon oneself turns the 'will to truth' into a deconstructing and destabilising thought process that calls such notions as 'Being', 'Perfection', 'God'– in other words, everything that has thus far been called holy, good, untouchable, and divine – into question and conceives of the world as having been created and shaped by men in their own image in order to be able to master reality.

In *Ecce homo*, Nietzsche – the 'first honest' thinker – reveals that the concepts that have grounded the constellations of power for centu-ries ('Truth', 'justice', 'virtue') are 'lies' or symbolic constructions (*EH*, 'Pourquoi je suis un destin', 1). By re-appropriating the immanence of values and allocating them as fictitious, anthropomorphic schemes or products of the human creative will, Nietzsche rejects the 'fetishistic' relation of human thought with existing values, ideas and power struc-tures. The German philosopher uses the term 'fetishism' to denote a specific mode, which he detects in traditional metaphysics and moral reasoning, of thinking and acting according to traditional values, ideas and structures as if they were transcendent and objective ('Idealism').

Philosophical rationality is conceived by Nietzsche to be the glue of the moral interpretation of existence that is typical of 'Christians and *other* nihilists'; this last negates Dionysian aesthetic philosophy and is rooted in *ressentiment*.[23] In *Ecce homo*, the term 'nihilism' does not denote a crisis of authority (Ansell-Pearson 1994, p.102), but rather a specific practical-historical structure of authority identified with Western *ratio* (Vattimo 1999, pp. 295–6). Therefore, Nietzsche's emphasis on the creative will brings about a change in the way values and ideas are related to, as well as nature. This challenges the traditional moral, metaphysical and socio-economical structures, and paves the way for a radical rethinking of the traditional categories of political philosophy to take place.

In *Ecce homo* and *Aurore*, 'immoralism' is the key to the criticism of Western rationalism. Denoting a new way of thinking the world, the body, and action that defetishises all moral, social and political values and 'liberates' the human creative will, 'immoralism' challenges the modern *faith* in reason for its fetishistic refusal at all costs to see reality as it is (*EH*, 'Pourquoi je suis un destin', 4). For their lack of truthfulness and cowardice, modern men refuse to see the fictional character of the concepts ('Truth', 'God', 'Virtue', 'Justice'), schemes or socio-economic and political structures, as the 'objective', immutable yokes to which they have submitted.

Deeply ingrained in this radical questioning of rationalism is Nietzsche's criticism of terms associated with modern political discourse, such as 'objectivity', 'scientific', 'historical sense', 'progress'. In both *Aurore* and *Ecce homo*, the 'immoralist' re-appropriation of the *artistic* or creative drives of men has clear social and political implications and brings the logic that supports and perpetuates the traditional constellations of power to the foreground. Having read both texts in the early 1930s, Camus in his early years is already fully aware of the political dimension of 'immoralism', and, in my opinion, his early reflections attest to his precocious internalisation of Nietzsche's methodological investigation, which explored a 'liberation' or *transformation of the mind* that reached outside of and beyond the bounds of the fetishistic perspective of Western rationalism.[24]

As early as 1932, Camus becomes acquainted with Nietzsche's criticism of modernity and, especially, of the utilitarian logic of contemporary 'petty politics'; in *Ecce homo*, the modern phenomenon of party politics may be traced to a *moral* or 'fetishistic' mode of thinking and interacting, which creates a form of personal spiritual and physical enslavement. The modern 'individuals' intentionally enter into and support an economic and political system of relations based on subordination and which turn them into mere 'cogs'; Nietzsche detects a utilitarian logic in the modern agents' choice to *be* whatever their superiors *make* of them and, therefore, to accept being *used* as a spendable or replaceable element (*A*, III, 166)[25] to the point of extreme self-negation or martyrdom (*A*, III, 183).

The criticism of this modern form of slavery plays an important part in Nietzsche's analyses of the contemporary constellations of power and in his criticism of party politics. In *Aurore*, the moral 'fetishistic' structure of modern thought – also referred to as 'romanticism' or 'idealism' – is traceable in Socialist political programmes, which are seen to perpetuate rather than eliminate the fetishistic relationship intrinsic to the economic system by reversing the sign of the worker's enslavement from dishonour (shame) into honour (virtue) and by placing the transformation of the workers' condition *outside* the workers themselves. Nietzsche detects a teleological or utilitarian logic in the anticipation political actors have of future change (hope), for which they must be prepared; the belief that constant expectation (*attente*) will fatally bring about Revolution (*A*, III, 206) is founded upon such logic. In his mature political writings, Camus's criticism of Marxist revolutionary doctrine is developed around the Nietzschean analyses of the fetishistic teleolocratic way in which political action is thought of. I suggest that Camus already internalises and makes use of this analysis in the early 1930s.

It is in *Intuitions*, in particular, that the reception of Nietzsche's question of liberation from the modern economic, political and cultural
enslavement is most evident (I, p. 943). Confronted with the over-human
appeal to break the chains of tradition, Camus is caught between two
ways to understand the future (*avenir*): on one hand, the future is conceived of in traditional terms of *telos* as the 'end' and 'perfection' of the
present, which entails applying an 'idealistic' and utilitarian way of relating to what ought to be/exist as some*thing* that ought to be waited *for*
(*attente*); on the other, the future is perceived as the 'immoralist' effort to
think beyond the existing structures of authority (*EH*, 'Pourquoi j'écris de
si bons livres' – 'Ainsi parlait Zarathoustra', 6 and 8). In 'Délires', Camus
relates the expectation of the future to the question of happiness and, as
the emphasis on his 'mystic' spirit confirms,[26] he addresses the temporal
dimension of '*l'attente*' from the perspective of the Dyonisian liberation
from the *moral* or fetishistic relations that establish the traditional forms
of authority ('Où donc est la vraie vie, heureuse,/ puisqu'elle n'est pas
l'attente. (Where then is the true, happy life,/ since it is not expectation)'
(I, p. 947).

Between 1932 and 1933, the problem of 'liberation' is expressed in
Camus's writings with an explicit 'immoralist' overtone. In my view, the
experience of illness plays a crucial role in radically calling into question how existence is thought of, liberating the thinker from the utilitarian 'chains' of *ratio*. Constantly confronted with the ineluctability of
death, the 'honest' thought unveils the moral lies and fetishistic logic
on which the social political structures and discourses are grounded; in
an autobiographical fragment of the mid-1930s, Camus writes that a
man sentenced to death does not *cheat* – he is aware, for instance, that
he will not 'pay his debt to society' but that he will have his head cut off
(I, p. 95). In this nuance lies the question of fanaticism that was brought
to Camus's attention by reading Nietzsche.

In the draft of a preface to a new collection of essays ideated around
1933, the refusal 'to cheat' (*tricher*) is explicitly related to 'immoralism'
as the rejection of a specific way of thinking, that the author detects in
ordinary discourses:

> Ça ennuie les gens qu'on soit lucide et ironique. On vous dit: 'Ça
> montre que vous n'êtes pas bon' : je ne vois pas le rapport. Si j'entends
> dire à quelqu'un : 'Je suis immoraliste', je traduis : 'J'ai besoin de me
> donner une morale' ; à un autre : 'Sus à l'intelligence', je comprends :
> 'Je ne peux pas supporter mes doutes.' Parce que ça me gêne qu'on
> triche. Et le grand courage c'est de s'accepter soi-même – avec ses

contradictions. (People are annoyed when one is lucid and ironic. They say: 'It shows that you are not good'. I do not see the connection. If I hear someone saying: 'I am immoralist', I translate: 'I need to give myself a morality'; to another: 'Down with intelligence', I understand: 'I cannot bear my doubts.' Because it bothers me when someone cheats. And the great courage is to accept oneself – with one's contradictions.) (I, p. 73)[27]

The mode of thinking Camus alludes to is described by Nietzsche in *Aurore* and consists in a form of argumentation or logical connection aimed at securing one's opinions or ideals for fear of doubt. This 'intellectual vice' (*A*, V, 543) is associated to moral and political fanaticism. According to Nietzsche, fanatics cannot bear their doubts and resort to the logic and categories of reason in order to blur or falsify evidence when it testifies against their theories ('radical idealism'). Kant's second Critique exemplifies this process by means of which the constructs of reason ('lies') are 'sanctified', that is to say, they are placed beyond the reach of critical objections and examination.

Camus associates 'immoralism' with courage:

Si vous voyez un sourire sur les lèvres désespérées d'un homme, comment séparer celui-ci de celles-là? Ici l'ironie prend une valeur métaphysique sous le masque de la contradiction. (If you see a smile on a man's desperate lips, how is one to separate this one here from those ones there? Here, irony acquires a metaphysical value under the mask of contradiction.) (I, p. 73).

In *Aurore*, the hopeless smile of the Phrygian slave, Epictetus, illustrates an example of conduct that is opposed to the fetishistic intellectual vice of modern 'idealists' and slaves; it combines courage and a look that is tirelessly turned inward rather than outward; a strict and rigorous use of reason is applied and at the same time *fear* (of God/master) is absent.[28] Nietzsche's remarks are essential to shed light on Camus's early 'immoralist' questioning, which challenges the 'fetishistic' modes of Western rational thought and moral fanaticism.

Nietzsche's Epictetus anticipates the pages of *Le Mythe de Sisyphe* and *L'homme révolté* and provides the example of a man who does not hope; although he lives in a condition of slavery, he is not a slave to the expectation of a 'happiness' that comes from *outside* and from above (God's grace), therefore, he is independent and evades the vertical relation of submission of fanatic reason. Camus evokes this type of conduct as a political model of action in the immediate aftermath of the declaration of war in his article 'Considérations inactuelles', published in *Le Soir républicain*. The young journalist explicitly refers to his Nietzschean source and praises the virtue of independence as a process of spiritual liberation from 'prejudices' that actively refuses to support the politics of enslavement and 'domestication', namely, a fetishistic (bureaucratic) way of thinking and acting, which, as in the case of war, culminates in death (I, pp. 771–2).

3
Tragic Beginnings

[...] on ne se remet pas du tragique entrevu aux commencements.

(R. Schürmann, *Des hégémonies brisées*)

In the previous chapter, I sought to shed light on the beginnings of
Camus's thought processes and constellations of notions, as well as to
bring to the foreground his early concern for the problem of method
in relation to his teacher Jean Grenier's analysis of European nihilism.
Taking Camus's anti-intellectualist approach seriously by exploring in
particular detail the Nietzschean sources of his early writings, I have
individuated in the German philosopher's 'immoralist' criticism of
modern rationalism and of the Western tradition of political philosophy one of the influences that had a strong impact on the young student's contemplations in the 1930s.

One question lies at the beginning of Camus's investigation: how
to think beyond Western *ratio*? In a short note to his friend Max-Pol
Fouchet, dated 1933, the young author rejects 'la *pure intelligence* vide
et méprisable (the empty and despicable *pure intelligence*)' (I, p. 953, my
italics) and places 'Dream', or Art and Action beyond the reach of the
petty Logic of utilitarian thinking (I, p. 954).[1]

Dream (Art)	Action
Ordinary Life	
(Utilitarian Logic)	

Availing himself of the terminology used in Bergson's *L'évolution
créatrice*, Camus's 1933 notes and writings suggest that Bergsonism is

more than just an erudite reference and provides a cluster of questions and notions with which the young author formulates his personal 'immoralist' mode of thought. In particular, Grenier's pupil makes the Bergsonian research of a method of 'liberation' from the utilitarian straitjacket of 'pure' intelligence his own (I, p. 543).

At about 20 years of age, tuberculosis drags Camus 'au seuil de la vie et avant tout entreprise (to the threshold of life and before any undertaking' (I, p. 960), and provokes in him a deep disgust for the pettiness and futility of the mechanical chain of acts and events that constitute ordinary mundane existence: 'Son orgueil révolte la vie quotidienne qui se montre plus humiliante alors. (His pride revolts at everyday life, which grows even more humiliating.)' (I, p. 960; Camus 1980, p. 171).[2] Pain cracks the surface of the 'servile' logic that governs everyday life, and reveals the absurdity of an existence that the ridiculous sense of traditional ideals or 'prejudices' conceals.[3] The young author doubts

> des idées générales, des conventions sociales, de tout ce qu'il a reçu. Chose plus grave, il doute des sentiments plus profonds : Foi, Amour. Il prend conscience qu'il n'est rien. [...] Mais il sait qu'il désire, donc qu'il peut être quelque chose : il lui faut à tout prix définir ses virtualités. (general ideas, social conventions, all he has received. A graver matter, he also doubts the deepest feelings: Faith, Love. He becomes aware that he is nothing. [...] But he knows that he desires, thus that he can be something: he must at all cost define his virtualities.) (I, p. 960).

In these opening lines of the 1933 *L'Art dans la Communion* (*Art in Communion*), Camus formulates his personal discourse on method, merging his 'immoralist' perspective with the Bergsonian idea of the liberation of thought and action from the despotic Logic of habit, positivist science and metaphysical thinking, which the term 'virtuality' precisely evokes.

Beyond the utilitarian logic and abstractions of discursive reason, art is defined as a process of crystallisation of the artist's impressions in a 'screen' (*écran*), or 'happy prism' between everyday life and human conscience, which frees from the tyranny of *ratio*: 'Au-dessus de la vie, au-dessus de ses cadres rationnels, se trouve l'Art, se trouve la Communion (Beyond life, beyond its rational frameworks, Art is found, Communion is found)' (I, p. 961). Art is said to *create* life anew by fixing the objects of its contemplation in images, signs or gestures (I, p. 963).[4] Camus links Nietzsche's emphasis on the emancipatory power of art with Bergson's criticism of utilitarian reason,[5] thus placing artistic creation beyond space, time, and causality. Art is understood as a 'Pause' (*Arrêt*) (I, p. 965), a 'mystic intuition' that interrupts the logic of ordinary life (I, p. 964), and discloses an a-teleological perspective:

> On pourrait nous reprocher d'abaisser l'Art, en le considérant comme un moyen. Mais les moyens sont parfois plus beaux que les fins et la recherche plus belle que la vérité. Qui n'a rêvé d'un livre ou d'une œuvre d'art qui ne soit qu'un *commencement* et qui espère, profondément *inachevé* ? (Some might reproach us for lowering Art, by considering it a means. But the means sometimes are more beautiful than the ends and the quest more beautiful than the truth. Who has not dreamt of a book or a work of art that is nothing other than a *beginning*, and that hopes, profoundly *unfinished*?) (I, p. 964, my italics)

Art replaces achievement with beginning, where the 'divine' is understood as the final cause or end of the creative process. In the early 1930s, the rejection of *telos* (from Gk. 'the end') is a prominent concern in Grenier's essays on Oriental philosophy and in *Les Îles*, the 1933 collection of texts, that had a profound influence on Camus's internal development and work.[6] The rejection of *telos* is also salient in Bergson's work[7] and from this the young student is able to bring liberation from the servitude to utilitarian reason into focus, as well as to consider art and action as a 'means-without-end'. In *L'Art dans la Communion*, Giotto's frescoes are said to create '*perfect* action', namely, one which is not in the service of ordinary life (I, p. 961), but is 'fixed' in the twofold sense of immobilised and corrected by the creator's rigorous effort (I, p. 962).

In Camus's reflection on aesthetics, perfection does not coincide with the realisation of a work of art that slips away ('*se dérobe*') from its creator (I, p. 975), but rather, with the 'pause' (*arrêt*) that is generated by the creative process in 'l'équilibre entre deux forces puissantes, puisqu'on y voit l'immobilité torturée d'une lutte trop égale – aussi la délicieuse fusion du combat [.] (the equilibrium between two powerful forces, since one sees in it the tortured immobility of a struggle that is too equally balanced – also the delicious fusion of the combat [.])' (I, p. 965). Camus resorts to the Bergsonian image of a 'miracle ceaselessly renewed' (I, p. 964) to convey the perfection that exists beyond the achievement of an *end*less creative process. The influence Bergson had on his work is apparent in Camus's definition of artistic creation as a logical effort to immortalise the object(s) of aesthetic contemplation (I, p. 960)[8] that 'stops' the temporal flow (I, p. 965) and creates a new order beyond the servile logic of reason. Thus, Camus rejects the traditional teleological concept of creation as realisation, and shifts the focus from the end-product to the artist's beginning and also draws attention to the role of 'ce manique de l'Unité (this maniac for Unity)' (I, p. 964) in unifying dispersed phenomena into a logical form – as he notes in April 1933, art is impossible without constraints (*contraintes*) (I, p. 958).

Influenced by Grenier, Bergson and Émile Bréhier's Bergsonian commentaries,[9] Camus is likely to have resorted to Plotinus as a means to provide an alternative to the Platonic–Aristotelian teleological way of conceiving art and beauty. In *L'Art dans la Communion*, he quotes a long passage from the *Enneads* I, 6, 3, where the Hellenic philosopher defines beauty as an internal unitary principle, as the form or 'scheme' (*logos*) of a being or artwork. By identifying in particular the beauty of physical bodies in their unity rather than in the symmetry of their parts, Plotinus turns to aesthetic contemplation, rather than to artistic production, to illustrate the distinct creative process that brings a being 'back to *unity*' (*Enneads*, I, 6, 1–2). Thus, the artist's 'comparison' and 'adjustment' to the form of beauty (*logos*), which culminates in the judgement that his creation is beautiful, replaces the traditional teleological understanding of creation as the violent 'submission' of a shapeless dispersed matter to an ideal form that is *external* to it. Plotinus uses the musical metaphor of 'harmony' (*accord*) to convey this 'adjustment', and the same image recurs in Bergson's writings to define a form of creative action that evades traditional teleology. Aesthetic judgement provides a model of 'connaissance immaculée de toute relation pratique (knowledge cleansed of all practical relation)' (Bréhier 1982, p. vi);[10] it is no surprise that the metaphor of harmony/accord also recurs in Camus's lyrical texts of the 1930s.

In Camus's early writings, creation goes beyond *telos* and evades the 'despotic' reasons or final ends of a demiurgic will, which are detected in the philosophical model of action. In Nietzsche and Grenier, the criticism of creation is connected to their criticism of teleological reason and of the 'servile' concept of perfection that is understood to be the final cause and achievement of creative action and which 'enslaves' modern men to the nihilistic logic of the efficacy of contemporary power politics. In Camus, the 'immoralist' criticism of Western rationalism terminates in aesthetics: liberation from teleology does not allow for 'libertinage métaphysique (metaphysical licentiousness)' (I, p. 960), but rather is explicitly moulded on Grenier's understanding of freedom as a free choice of one's dependency (I, p. 960), which finds its clearest example in the artist's logical effort to be coherent (I, p. 964).

In his 1933 writings, Camus places the constraints of an aesthetic *logos* beyond the bounds of *ratio*. This shift has important consequences for how the relationship that subsists between thinking and action is understood. As Hannah Arendt notes in *The Life of the Mind*, 'with this shift [from *ratio* to *logos*], the criterion for truth has shifted from the agreement of knowledge with its object – the *adequatio rei et intellectus*, understood as analogous to the agreement of vision with the seen object – to the mere *form* of thinking, whose basic rule is [...] consistency with itself, that is, to what Kant still understood as the merely negative 'touchstone of truth' (Arendt 1978, p. 122). Moreover, 'the criterion of *logos*, coherent speech, is not truth or falsehood, but meaning' (Arendt 1978a, p. 98); in chapter 6, I demonstrate how the question of meaning as opposed to that of 'truth' plays an essential part in Camus's political thinking.

Commentators fail to adequately note how the artist's logical effort may be identified with his need for *coherence*, which replaces the traditional notion of truth with his 'mystic intuition' (I, p. 964). Influenced by Grenier and Bergson's views (I, p. 544),[11] Camus detects in mystical thought a way or 'method' to evade the logic of modern rationalism without, however, embracing the widespread irrationalism and voluntarism typical of the early twentieth-century philosophical and political doctrines.

In his lyrical works, from the 1933 *La Maison Mauresque* to the collections of essays of *L'Envers et l'Endroit* (1937) and *Noces* (1939), 'Communion' primarily denotes a way to obtain liberation from the hideous dominion of *ratio*, which has the characteristics of a mystic supra-rational procession of 'ecstasy' and 'love'. Camus, after reading the mystics in the first half of the 1930s, moulds his notion of creation by using a mystical language that is essential to understand in order for it to shed light on the way he personally conceives of action as going beyond the reach of the teleological model of the Western tradition.

Strongly recalling Plotinus' remarks on the concept of beauty, *La Maison Mauresque* develops a parallel between the young author's personal artistic creation and the process of contemplation that allows him to 'ascend' from the dispersed contradictoriness of *ratio* to the unity of 'Communion', which goes past the bounds of reason (I, p. 968); Camus also designates this Communion as rapture (*'ivresse'*) and love. After ascent, comes then 'descent' from ecstasy to a way of life that is renewed by the memory and recollection of this radical experience.[12]

'Communion' is attained through the contemplation of living nature that has been wrapped in a robe of sunlight, which marks the presence of a syncope/halt (*arrêt*) to the mechanical necessity of ordinary life and, thus, provokes a sensory and sensual egress from the social and cultural constructs of the Self ('sortir de moi-même' (I, p. 970)). In anticipation of the essays in *Noces*, Camus describes 'Communion' as a process of *simplification*; the author is 'resorbé dans l'unique sensation de chaleur envahissante (resorbed in the unique sensation of invading heat)', which, without realizing it, arouses 'le machinal désir de retrouver l'anéantissement premier (the automatic desire to rediscover the original annihilation)' (I, pp. 970–1).

Nevertheless, the dissolution of the servile 'dreamy insignificance' (I, p. 971) of ordinary existence does not terminate in a substantial fusion with nature, but rather in a distinct relation of *consent* (from Latin, *cum-sentire*, *cum* 'together'; *sentire*, 'to feel'). From his 1933 lyrical writings on, the sensual liberation from *ratio* in the ecstatic rapture (*ivresse*) of 'Communion' is not understood by Camus as the annihilation of human conscience in a *reductio ad unum* to 'biological' or 'mineral' life (Agamben 1995), but rather, as the beginning of a different form of conscience and a higher form of life that goes beyond the defined categories created by modern rationalist and materialistic interpretations.

Mystic 'communion' with nature

It is essential that the notion of 'Communion' is clarified in order to dispel a misunderstanding concerning Camus's reflections. According to this misunderstanding, the author of *Noces* speaks of nature in an unreflective way and comprehends the latter, in an essentialist acceptation, as the immanent foundation of human finitude and rebellious action, therefore, in flagrant contrast with the absurdist character of his general philosophy (Isaac 1992, pp. 231–2). From the analyses of the contemporary French libertarians (Vertone 1989, pp. 16, 36–7) to the more recent feminist political theorisations (Bartlett 2004, pp. 8 and 131 ff.), the emphasis on the 'strong naturalistic tendencies' in Camus's thought (Isaac 1992, p. 232) attests, in my opinion, to a persistent misinterpretation of the ecstatic 'return' to Nature (Werner 1972, p. 67) and to the opposition nature *vs.* history that may be found in his lyrical and political writings.[13]

By neglecting to effectuate a systematic exploration of his early texts and their sources, philosophical political studies of Camus's work fail to 'situate' his thought in the intellectual climate of the 1930s, where the so-called 'return to Nature' was a pivotal issue in the anti-rationalist political doctrines of the early twentieth century. It was particularly central to the German political 'romanticism' and could be noted in Ludwig Klages, as well as in Alfred Rosenberg's vitalistic and racial mysticism that concurred with the National-Socialist 'revolution against reason' and were analysed and brought to the attention of the French public by Paulhan's *NRF*.

Camus is likely to have become acquainted with the German philosophical political debate of the time through his teacher Jean Grenier, as well as from reading the articles devoted to Hitlerism, which inaugurated the 1933 political anti-Fascist turn of the *NRF*. In the draft of a foreword for *Le Mythe de Sisyphe* of September 1942, the author certainly has these ideologies in mind when rejecting the contemporary 'prêches sur les "retours". Retour au Moyen Âge, à la mentalité primitive, à la terre, à la religion, à l'arsenal des vielles solutions. (preachings on the "returns". Return to the Middle Ages, to the primitive mentality, to the earth, to religion, to the arsenal of old solutions.)' (II, p. 948.)[14] The text calls to mind Brice Parain and George Blumberg's analysis of the National-Socialist 'prêche (de) l'évangile [...] du retour à la terre (preaching of the gospel [...] of the return to the earth)' in the *NRF* (Parain-Blumberg 1933, pp. 257, 259) In the final version of the 1942 foreword that was addressed to Gallimard, Camus changes the expression 'return to the earth' into 'return to the so-called "natural" life' (I, p. 320) and takes a clear position against its ideological exploitation as an inadequate solution to the unprecedented problem of the twentieth century, the disorientation (*désarroi*) of modern intelligence (II, p. 948) – in one word, nihilism (I, p. 320).

The Nietzschean inspiration of Camus's argument is apparent in his emphasis on the aesthetic power of the mind in 'recreating chaos using its own means' (II, p. 948), and thus, on the emancipation of thought from its submission to metaphysical or *moral* reason, which may be considered the undeniable acquisition of the twentieth century. The irrationalism and naturalism of the 'romantic' political ideologies, as well as the vitalistic appeals of racial aestheticism, which culminate in the Nazi identification of European nihilism with the negation of *organic* life, link the creative will to a return to the 'blood and soil'.[15] Camus considers these to be the 'old solutions' (II, p. 948), which pretend to negate nihilism with the teleological, *moral* and 'nihilistic' instruments denounced by Nietzsche in his writings of the 1880s.

In the early 1930s, the young author cannot ignore the political implications of these returns to 'natural life' or to the 'earth'. Around 1933–34, Bergson warned against the dangers of the 'imitation' of nature, indicating the Platonic project of a demiurgic re-creation or re-foundation of the political body that was entailed in the Nazi appeals to a mystical unity or 'return to the origins' (Soulez 1989, p. 307ff.). In the mid-1930s Brecht and Benjamin's famous formula 'the aestheticisation of politics' also draws attention to the voluntaristic and organicistic interpretations of the Nietzschean notion of creation, that interpret political action in the light of the teleological model of the Western philosophical tradition and identify politics with plastic art, or the violent realisation *by any and all means* of the unitary body politic. From this perspective, the mystical return to 'nature' denotes the realisation of the political Unity or 'natural' community, understood in the Aristotelian sense as final cause and perfection (*physis*).[16]

Georges Bataille, a talented and lucid witness of the political implications of Nietzsche's aestheticism in rethinking freedom and free action beyond the confines of traditional forms of authority, defends the German philosopher against the Nazi's political appropriations of his work in the 1937 'Propositions' in *Acéphale*. Bataille's criticism of the Fascist 'monocephalic' society (Bataille 1937a, p. 18) is grounded, precisely, on the author's rejection of *telos* and of the organicistic identification of Unity, Nature, or the Earth, as the finality and the achievement of the political community. Contemporary racist, fascist and communist ideologies interpret the Nietzschean liberation of the creative will in 'servile' terms, judging political creation from the perspective of efficacy and utility (Risset 1987). Thus, they submit action to teleocratic reason and identify it with the organisation and realisation of a 'closed' homogeneous organism under one Head (*arché*).[17] Bataille's model of a free, unachieved (*'inachevée'*), *poly-* or *a*-cephalic society links freedom to the retreat or negation of achievement, which is represented by a 'headless' (*an*archic) creation, a superior synthesis of earthly '*in*organic' life (Bataille 1937b, p. 21) that extends beyond the bounds of the servile logic of *ratio*. It culminates in an experience of ecstatic rapture (*ivresse extatique*), a mystic experience without God, namely, without any fetishistic 'objective' reference outside of itself.[18]

Camus shares Bataille's Nietzschean criticism of the 'enslavement' of modern, liberal and socialist, *homo oeconomicus* and also rejects *telos*, placing art and action in 'Communion' (*'ivresse'*) beyond the limits of petty utilitarian *ratio*. His lyrical essays of the 1930s, from *La Maison Mauresque* to *Noces*, describe a mystical experience of freedom *from the end*, which, in my view, is not inconsistent with the 'absurdist' philosophy of *Le Mythe de Sisyphe*, but rather constitutes the methodological premise of Camus's argument. The lyrical works define a mysticism without God that rejects the biologism and the 'immanent', naturalistic and sensualist interpretations of an earthly 'communion' and call the philosophical political understanding of action into question.

Critics have generally understood 'Communion' in erotic terms – 'le seul amour vraiment viril en ce monde (the only truly virile love in this world)' (*N*, p. 126)[19] – and Camus's 'nuptials' are considered to denote a return to an original union with nature by way of the sexual penetration and fusion of man with the earth's maternal womb, which annihilates conscience, thus, reducing the human to the status of an animal, to a raw sensory being-to-the-world.[20] However, placing 'Communion' beyond the 'servile' straitjacket of teleological reason and, therefore, displacing achievement, the 'nuptials' of the lyrical essays of 1933 and thereafter cannot be conceived as the reconstitution of an integral or 'natural' condition in the Aristotelian sense. Camus uses the term 'nuptials' to designate the solemn celebration of *consent* (I, p. 971) that has the power of *consecration* (*N*, p.126) and founds a new and higher form of life beyond the utilitarian chains of *ratio*.

I propose that Camus's writings of the 1930s be read in light of the author's Bergsonian concern for the widespread 'rationalisation' of the twentieth century (Soulez 1989, pp. 289 ff.) and, particularly, for two aspects of teleological reasoning that are of crucial importance in the author's political reflections: the power to justify actions (the 'reasons' for actions may very well not be true, and are not necessarily so[21]); and the rational calculability and predictability of political action (end-means logic). From the perspective of his own 'mystical' attempt at thinking beyond the bounds of Western teleological reason,[22] Camus, following in Bergson's footsteps, understands 'love' to be the expression of freedom, rather than an erotic regression to a pre-conscious state of animality.[23] In 'Été à Alger (Summer in Algiers)', the image of the lovers' sexual union exclusively refers to the 'mineral' world and not to the communion of man with nature; man's nuptials with the earth are consecrated by the smell of the carnal union that is consummated by the sun and the earth and provokes in man a process of aesthetic contemplation, (*N*, p.126).[24]

The Algerian nature of Camus's lyrical essays is that of a dynamic universe, the unity of sun/sea, sky/earth are understood, rather than in the spatial terms of fusion or completion, in a temporal or musical sense, similar to the rhythm that is characteristic of respiration (breath-in/breath-out; ascent/descent) (Mattéi 1997, pp. 277–94) or of a heartbeat (Werner 1972, p. 66). 'Communion' coincides with the subject's effort to 'tune' (*accorder*) his own respiration to the rhythm of the world's respiration (*N*, p. 106); this culminates in the ecstatic confusion that occurs between the poundings of the author's blood and those of nature's ever present heart (*N*, p. 112).[25]

Echoing the Bergsonian interpretation of Plotinus' *logos*,[26] Camus understands love as a 'chord' or 'harmony' that is attained through the aesthetic 'adjustment' of contemplation (I, p. 973), namely, through a mystic process that moves toward the obtainment of unity.[27] As he writes in 'L'été à Alger (Summer in Algiers)':

> Cette union que souhaitait Plotin, quoi d'étrange à la retrouver sur la terre? L'Unité s'exprime ici en termes de soleil et de mer. Elle est sensible au cœur par un certain goût de chair qui fait son amertume et sa grandeur. (Is there anything odd in finding on earth that union that Plotinus longed for? Unity is expressed here in terms of sun and sea. The heart is sensitive to it through a certain flavour of flesh that constitutes its bitterness and its greatness.) (*N*, p. 124)

From *La Maison Mauresque* to *Noces*, the union between the sea and the sun does not symbolise an organism, an entitative principle (*physis*), which the individual must 'return' to, but rather the beginning of a mystic contemplation, that liberates the subject from *ratio* by intensifying his/her internal life and awakening his/her conscience. In his lectures on Plotinus, Bergson compares this form of 'harmony' or 'love' to a dancer's performance (Mossé-Bastide 1954, p. 8); similarly, in 'Noces à Tipasa (Nuptials at Tipasa)' Camus draws an analogy between the nuptials with the Algerian nature and the performance of an actor: 'Dans un sens, c'est bien ma vie que je *joue* ici [...] (In a way, it is indeed my life that I am *performing* here [...])', (*N*, p. 108, my italics). The strange joy and feeling of satisfaction that seizes the author after one day of nuptials with the nature of Tipasa evokes a process of thinking and, more precisely, the forming of an aesthetic judgement, rather than a sexual appeasement:

> Il y a un sentiment que connaissent les acteurs lorsqu'ils ont conscience d'avoir bien rempli leur rôle, c'est-à-dire, au sens plus précis, d'avoir fait coïncider leurs gestes et ceux du personnage idéal qu'ils incarnent, d'être entrés en quelque sorte dans un dessin fait à l'avance et qu'ils ont d'un coup fait vivre et battre avec leur propre cœur. C'était précisément cela que je ressentais : j'avais bien joué mon rôle. (There is a feeling actors have when they know they've played their part well, that is to say, more precisely, when they have made their own gestures coincide with those of the ideal character they embody, having

entered somehow in a prepared design that they all of a sudden made live and beat with their own hearts. That was exactly what I felt: I had played my part well.) (*N*, p. 110)

The metaphor of the play-actor's performance, the beauty of which lies in the adjustment of the actor's body and feelings to an internal unitary principle, excludes the organicistic concept of fusional unity, as well as the 'idealistic' or romantic model of creation that is entailed in teleological reasoning. Applying Bergson's interpretation of *logos* as 'sympathy', 'love' or 'chord' to Plotinus' *Enneads* (I, 6),[28] Camus associates 'Communion' with a feeling of strong complicity with nature (I, p. 973), which increases the author's generosity and pity – 'je savais *aimer*' (I knew how to *love*') (I, p. 974, my italics).[29]

In an autobiographical fragment ('Tu vas mieux...') written between 1934 and 1936, Camus makes an analogy between the ecstatic union with the glorious Algerian nature and his being in the presence of his mother: 'Et comme devant toi, je me suis senti réduit à mes ultimes ressources (And as when I am in front of you, I felt that I was reduced to my last resources)' (I, p. 96). The author *tends* towards Communion with nature as he (re)*turns* to his mute and strange mother, who embodies the mystical halt (*arrêt*) of indifference; it is a moment of 'narrow and silent peace' (I, p. 971), which destroys the utilitarian chain of ordinary logic and dissolves lassitude (Chandra 1995, p. 118). Without beauty, riches, or complications of the spirit, the mother is 'pure as a crystal' (I, p. 95); her heart, body and mind are confused in indifference. Van-Huy and Tarrow interpret the maternal poverty (*simplicitas*) of indifference by reducing it to 'the natural and biological aspects of human beings, a link with the earth that stresses harmony and annuls the difference' (Tarrow 1985, p. 76); I suggest that the ecstatic *dénuement* ('denudement'), of which the mother is the emblem, evokes a spiritual process of liberation of thought from *telos*, namely, the purification from the all too human 'moral' constructions of reason. The image of 'dénuement' recurs in the language of the Mysteries and in Plotinus' *Enneads* to refer to the journey of the soul towards the One (*DES*, p. 1040), and conveys the mystic effort to become 'naked' and abandon the intellectual constructions of rational teleological thinking.

In Camus's 1933 lyrical essays, as well as in *Noces*, 'Communion' does not describe a reduction to sheer biological existence, nor does it describe the experience of being 'tied' (*rivé*) to the body's elementary feelings, which Lévinas, in his 1934 *Quelques réflexions sur la philosophie de l'hitlérisme*, detects at the core of the twentieth-century anti-humanist ideologies of race.[30] Camus's 'plenitude of indifference' coincides with 'cette extrême pointe de l'extrême conscience (this extreme point of the extreme conscience)', when 'tout se rejoint et se confond, cette pente de mon cœur et ce désir de mon esprit (everything merges and is confused, this inclination of my heart and this desire of my spirit)' (I, p. 96). The author is clearly referring to the mystics' 'spiritual desire', which brings thinking and love together in a unitary 'mystic intuition' (*intuitus*)[31] and frees thought from the determinations of reason (body/ spirit, subject/object, phenomenon/noumenon), culminating in *glorious joy* (N, p. 108).

Communion is described as an ecstatic moving-out-of-oneself (I, p. 970) in a mystic procession of intelligence that goes beyond mere reason and erodes the socially constructed Self (N, p. 112). It is not conceived as an active and violent self-assertion or annihilation, but rather as a passive *laisser-être*.[32] In *Noces*, the author is polished and consumed by the wind of Djémila, shaped to mirror the image of the blazing simplicity ('nudity') of nature itself which is surrounding him (N, p. 112), until he is able to stand beside and outside of his own Self, abandoned to the world (N, p. 107) in extreme 'denudement' (N, p. 113). In this 'mélange d'ascèse et de jouissances (mixture of ascesis and pleasures)' (N, p. 130), ecstasy coincides with the highest 'temperature' or degree of intensity of life when 'la chair devient *consciente* (the flesh becomes *conscious*).' (N, p. 131, my italics).[33]

The plenitude of 'Communion' is not understood to be a max-imisation, of the biological dimension (*zoè*) that is presumed to be the ultimate foundation and origin of being, or of an abstract universal principle (*archê*). Thus, with creation situated beyond *telos*, the ecstatic process evoked in Camus's lyrical pages does not define a technique of 'naturalisation' in the sense of an active return to a primordial, pre-rational end and completion. In *Les Îles* (1933), Jean Grenier's notion of 'plenitude of indifference' provides Camus with an example of a-teleological thinking that reaches beyond the nihilistic strive for reali-sation and perfection, which dislocates the achievement (in Gk. '*ergon*') that lies at the core of the organicistic model of contemporary political doctrines (Lacoue-Labarthe 1998, p. 109).

In the mid-1930s, Grenier traces in the notions of 'energy' (*energeia*) and 'activity', the common denominator of the early twentieth-century Nietzschean and Marxist voluntaristic theories, and detects in the demi-urgic aspiration of one leader or of a political party to radically *transform* man the distinctive feature of what he designates the contemporary 'totalitarian regimes' (Grenier 1967, p. 64).[34] In the same years, Camus refuses *telos* and replaces 'patience' and 'passivity' for the teleological notion of 'activity',[35] thus, taking his distance from the contemporary voluntaristic attempts at 'overcoming the human': 'Vanité du mot expérience. L'expérience n'est pas expérimentale.[36] On ne la provoque pas. On la subit. Plutôt patience qu'expérience. Nous patientons – plutôt nous pâtissons. (Vanity of the word experience. Experience is not experimental. One does not provoke it. One endures it. Patience rather than experience. We exercise patience – rather we suffer.)' (II, p. 796.)

Passivity and patience have the same root, *pati*, 'to suffer'; in the *Carnets* of September 1937, Camus notes a passage from Kierkegaard's newly translated *Rien philosophiques*:

> Le langage a raison dans le mot passion d'insister sur la souffrance de l'âme ; alors que l'emploi du mot passion nous fait penser plutôt à l'impétuosité convulsive qui nous étonne, et oublier ainsi qu'il s'agit d'une souffrance (orgueil – défi). *Id*. L'acteur (de vie) parfait c'est celui qui 'est agi' – et qui le sait, – la *passion passive*. (In the word passion the language rightly insists on the soul's suffering; while the use of the term passion evokes the convulsive impetuousness that surprises us, and makes us forget that it is a form of suffering (pride – challenge). *Id*. The perfect actor (of life) is the one who 'is acted', and knows it – *passive passion*.) (II, p. 835, my italics)

Much as Pascal's epigraphy to *L'Art dans la Communions* attests (I, p. 960), the relation between passion, passivity and suffering also plays a crucial part in Camus's early research for a method of thinking that evades the bounds of rationalism. Pascal illustrates the displacement of the Cartesian opposition between passion/obscurity and intelligence/clarity, situating his research of freedom past the limits posted by the teleocratic logic of philosophical and scientific reason.[37] In Camus's writings of the 1930s, 'passion' – also identified as the Pascalian 'heart' (*DES*, p. 1041) – defines a thought that delves deep into the suffering and tragedy of existence and abolishes the servile logic of reason (*telos*). Passion displaces the modern Cartesian notion of conscience (*res cogitans*) and replaces the active Subject of modern philosophical tradition with a passive mystical abandonment (*laisser-être*).

Teleological activity that is oriented towards achievement entails a type of movement or projection with which reason is able to foresee events, and *see* them through to their completion. As Hannah Arendt observes, 'the priority of vision for mental activities [...] remains absolutely decisive throughout the history of Western metaphysics and its notion of truth'. From Greek philosophy on, 'thinking has been thought in terms of seeing' (Arendt 1978a, p. 101). Intuition or contemplation have been thought of in terms of *vision* (*theorein*) of the truth, thus, contemplation and activity are closely related (Arendt 1998, pp. 225–7). In Plato's *Republic*, the philosopher is described as a 'lover of beauty' who retreats from the world – the dark cave of the myth – to contemplate the ideas that 'shine forth most' (*ekphanestaton*) and which are 'variations of the beautiful' (Arendt 1998, p. 225). In her analysis of the tradition of political philosophy that was inaugurated by Plato, Arendt links the metaphor of vision/seeing to the fabricative model of politics as artwork; when the philosopher decides to return to the cave and take charge of the realm of human affairs, it is the *vision* of Beauty that dictates the citizens' rule of conduct. The idea of Beauty despotically unites ('subsumes') and puts the dispersed multitude of deeds and words into order (Arendt 1998, p. 226). The philosopher, therefore, drags the idea of beauty into the cave to dispel the darkness and fragility of the human condition and transform it into the ideal blueprint or 'Good' with which to make political bodies.[38] The realisation of the mental vision is considered to entail a despotic, violent activity that dispels the suffering or incompleteness of that which exists by achieving its perfection or 'nature' (*physis*); the violence of the activity is inscribed in the irresistibility of the vision of the idea, which 'shines forth most'.[39]

The aesthetic contemplation Camus describes in his lyrical texts of the 1930s, rejects the 'servile' or utilitarian activity that is always projected *forward* in time and towards achievement (*EE*, pp. 70–1; II, p. 799). As he writes in 'Noces à Tipasa' (Nuptials in Tipasa), 'aux mystères d'Éleusis, il suffisait de contempler. Ici même, je sais que jamais je ne m'approcherai assez du monde. (All one had to do at the mysteries of Eleusis was contemplate. Yet even here, I know that I shall never come close enough to the world.)' (*N*, p. 107.) Following the methodological remarks in the opening lines of Camus's 1936 dissertation in philosophy on *Métaphysique chrétienne et néoplatonisme* (hereinafter *DES*), the reference he makes to the Mysteries introduces a 'change of level' in our interrogation (*DES*, p. 999), placing ecstatic contemplation *outside* the limits of teleology. Thus, 'Communion' with nature is conceived of as a 'miracle' or an effort to obtain liberation and rebirth (*DES*, pp. 1003–4). In a long note in *Carnets*, dated January 1936 (II, pp. 798–800), which he later reworks and incorporates in 'L'envers et l'endroit' (*EE*, pp. 70–1), Camus speaks of contemplation breaking the temporal necessity of ordinary thought ('science'), which is in itself oriented towards a finality in that it must come to an end and be completed.

By dissolving *telos*, the author 'is dead to himself' and is able to witness his own (re)birth (I, p. 799). In the 'return to nature' of Camus's lyrical writings, the emphasis on the beginning (Lat. *nasci*, 'to be born') of
a new form of life replaces the metaphysical understanding of 'nature'
as principal substance (Lat. *natura*) – 'et mon cœur s'en va à la rencontre de lui-même. (and my heart goes out to meet himself.)' (*EE*, p. 71.)
The reference to the 'heart', 'cette extrême émotion qui me délivre du
décor (this extreme emotion which delivers me from the scenery)' (II,
p. 799), is not fortuitous, but echoes the Pascalian contemplative effort
that delivers thought from the straitjacket of philosophical reason and
is able to find the 'vérité du cœur (truth of the heart)' in humility and
simplicity (*DES*, p. 1010).

I argue that Camus's lyrical essays challenge the identification of thinking with the vision of reason,[40] which lies at the core of Western ontology
and is expressed by the metaphor of seeing. In 'L'Été à Algers' (Summer in
Algiers), the Plotinian union manifests itself on earth in terms of sun and
sea, 'elle est sensible au cœur par un certain goût de chair qui fait son amer-
tume et sa grandeur (the heart is sensitive to it through a certain flavour
of flesh that constitutes its bitterness and its greatness' (*N*, p. 124). Insofar
as ecstatic 'Communion' exceeds the straitjacket of *telos*, it displaces the
fabricative logic of realisation that entails the use of pre*vision*, namely, the
fore*seeing* movement that characterises philosophical reason.[41] In 1938,
Camus notes in his *Carnets*: 'La pensée est toujours en avant. Elle va trop
loin, plus loin que le corps qui est dans le présent. Supprimer l'espérance,
c'est ramener la pensée au corps. Et le corps doit pourrir. (Thought is always
ahead. It goes too far, further than the body, which is in the present. To
suppress hope, is to draw thought back to the body. And the body must
decompose).' (II, p. 863.)

From his 1933 lyrical writings on, mystic liberation from *ratio* replaces
the traditional metaphor of seeing with that of touching or con*tact*, thus,
emphasising the ultimate unattainability of the '*mystica visio*' of the
Western *copulativa theologia*;[42] contemplation does not culminate in the
'return' to the undifferentiated totality of being (*maximum absolutum*).
Camus makes a distinction, which recurs in Christian medieval mystical
literature, between intelligence and analytical thought or 'reason' and
uses the notion of 'plenitude of indifference' to denote the most extreme
point of extreme conscience (I, p. 96) that lays beyond the 'differences'
proposed by rational thought (object/subject, body/spirit, etc.).

In ecstatic 'Communion', man *is* the world (I, p. 71), though not
in the orgiastic sense of a substantial fusion with this last, but rather
in the sense of the mystics' conscience that 'melts' the distinctions of

discursive reason. Communion abolishes the distance that is introduced between conscience and world by teleocratic thought, which is
'retranché du monde (removed from the world)' and projected in the
future (II, p. 800).[43] The dissolution of intellectual abstractions does not
coincide with the negation of intelligence *tout court* and, therefore, with
the annihilation of conscience and the reduction of the human being to
sheer sensory or bodily existence. Like the mystics' liberation from *ratio*,
the ecstatic 'indifference' of Camus's lyrical writings marks a temporal
unity (Lat. *nunc*, 'now') of *extreme* conscience in which intelligence
touches upon its limits and is 'present' (I, p. 96) – 'ce qui me frappe
à ce moment, c'est que je ne peux aller plus loin. Comme un homme
emprisonné à perpétuité – et tout lui est présent. (what strikes me in
this moment, is that I cannot go any further. Like a man imprisoned for
ever – and everything is present to him.) (*N*, p. 113.)

Camus's ecstatic rapture, in that it lays beyond the bounds of Western
reason, which is understood as fore*sight*, evokes the mystical 'presence'
(*presentia*) of a conscience that tends toward unity and that touches
upon the *murus absurditatis* ('wall of absurdity'). The leitmotiv of the
lyrical works, which is also the central issue of Camus's 1942 *Le Mythe
de Sisyphe*, is not the reconstitution of a primordial integrity through an
erotic fusion with nature, but rather the unattainability of perfect vision
or achievement. In mystical literature, the 'wall of absurdity', also defined
as *murus paradisi* ('wall of paradise') (Cuozzo 2000, pp. 68 ff.), is the
extreme limit with which human thinking comes in con*tact* in its effort
to move beyond discursive reason and reach toward the divine. This limit
cannot be transcended without the intervention of the Grace;[44] Camus
repeatedly resorts to the image of the *'paradis perdu'* ('paradise lost') or
the *'paradis défendu'* ('forbidden paradise') to emphasise the impossibility of ultimate achievement. The perfection of ontological participation,
evoked by the metaphor of seeing, is therefore precluded:

> Prisonnier de la caverne, me voici seul en face de l'ombre du monde
> [...] Mais le chant du monde s'élève et moi, enchaîné au fond de la
> caverne, je suis comblé avant d'avoir désiré. (Prisoner of the cave,
> here I am alone in front of the world's shadow [...] But the song of
> the world raises and I, chained to the bottom of the cave, am fulfilled
> before having even desired.) (II, p. 79–99)

In Camus's lyrical writings and in *Le Mythe de Sisyphe*, the metaphoric
constellation of 'contact' replaces that of 'vision' to emphasise the
limits to which human thought, imprisoned by the walls of absurdity,

is exposed. In the 1936 notebooks and essays, the metaphor of the prisoner bound inside the cave displaces the Platonic myth, declaring the impossibility of intelligence to go any further than it already has in penetrating the enigma. Camus merges two literary references that are pivotal to his reflections and confirm the continuity between his lyrical texts and the 1942 essay on the absurd: Pascal's *Pensées* and Aeschylus's *Prometheus Bound*.

A long quote from Pascal's *Pensées* is inserted in the section devoted to evangelic Christianity in the 1936 *DES*, where the image of the chains is introduced to convey the mortal condition of men:

> Qu'on s'imagine un nombre d'hommes dans les chaînes, et tous condamnés à mort, dont les uns étaient chaque jours égorgés à la vue des autres, ceux qui restent voient leur propre condition, dans celle de leurs semblables, et, se regardant avec douleur et sans espérance, attendent leur tour. C'est l'image de la condition des hommes. (Let us imagine a number of men in chains, and all condemned to death, where some are killed each day in the sight of the others, and those who remain, see their own fate in that of their fellows, and wait their turn, looking at each other sorrowfully and without hope. This is the image of the condition of men.)' (I, p. 1009)

In an autobiographical fragment of the same period ('Tu vas mieux...'), young Camus draws a parallel between the calm of a prisoner condemned to public execution and his own calm in front of the absurdity of being sentenced to death by tuberculosis. The ecstatic present of 'Communion' is inseparable from the lucid conscience of men's bound condition. Thus, mystical rapture is not conceived of as the loss of limits reached through the fusional unity with nature, but rather as the experience of freedom of thought and action from the hopes and intellectual constructions, namely, from the servile 'chains' of a teleological reason based on fore*sight* (I, pp. 95–6).[45]

Rational thinking, which by its nature entails a constant projection into the future, is traditionally represented by Prometheus, the father of the 'arts' or 'techniques' (*technai*) that are remedies for men's painful vision of their own termination. The hero of the Aeschylean tragedy gives two gifts to the mortals: fire for their survival, and *'blind* hope' so that men may *not see* their inescapable death.[46] In these gifts lies the error (*hybris*) for which Prometheus, the lover of mortals, must pay: bound and condemned to dreadful endless torment, this tragic figure embodies the fate of all human beings, who are, in turn, bound and condemned to 'malheur' (misfortune) and death when their entire being cries for joy and happiness (I, p. 96).

But Prometheus also has the courage to *see* his errors and look his own condition in the face. In the project of a foreword written around 1933–34, Camus relates courage to the Nietzschean notion of 'immoralism' as the refusal to cheat (I, p. 73). In 'Tu vas mieux...', the prisoner that is condemned to execution 'ne triche pas. Il sait bien qu'il ne va pas "payer sa dette à la société" mais qu'on va lui couper le cou. (does not cheat. He knows very well that he is not going "to pay his debt to society" but that they are going to cut off his head.)' (I, p. 95). Aeschylus's *Promethée enchaîné* (*Prometheus Bound*) figures among the theatrical works included in the openly anti-fascist cultural and political program of the *Théâtre du Travail*, Camus's amateur theatre company created under the auspices of the French Communist Party. The tragedy was adapted by the young actor and stage director and performed at the Padovani Baths in Algiers, in March 1937. A few years later, the young author hesitates between two titles for the second chapter of his first philosophical essay: 'Absurde et irrationnel (Absurd and irrational)' and 'Le Vautour (The Vulture)'. The vulture that devours Prometheus' liver recurs in Nietzsche's *Aurore* (*A*, I, 83),[47] and refers to the punishment of the hero's *hybris*; it does not signify the total annihilation of thinking, but rather it represents the humiliation of reason's attempt at *fore*sight, on which hopes are fed. The vulture brings human thought back to the 'chained' flesh (Lat. *humiliare* from *humus* 'ground' or 'earth'); as Camus writes in 'Le Désert (The Desert)', 'le corps ignore l'espoir. Il ne connaît que les coups de son sang. L'éternité qui lui est propre est faite d'indifférence. (the body ignores hope. It only knows the pulsing of its blood. Its own particular eternity is made of indifference.)' (*N*, p. 129.) And again in his notebooks: '[s]upprimer l'espérance, c'est ramener la pensée au corps. Et le corps doit pourrir. ([t]o suppress hope, is to bring thought back to the body. And the body must decompose)' (II, p. 863.)[48] This 1938 note ties together Prometheus' punishment and the mystics' *humilitas*, namely, the awareness of mortality and finitude that lie beyond the bounds of reason.

In the definitive version of *Le Mythe de Sisyphe*, the title 'Les Murs absurdes (The Absurd Walls)' replaces 'Le Vautour' (I, p. 1285, n. *a*). In the first chapter of his Absurd reasoning, Camus resorts to the mystics' distinction between intelligence and philosophical discursive reason in order to confirm his attack against the postulate of 'cette raison universelle, pratique ou morale, ce déterminisme, ces catégories qui expliquent tout (this universal reason, practical or ethical, this determinism, these categories that explain everything)' (*MS*, p. 233). In his view, thinking ('esprit') has nothing to do with the theoretical efforts of reason (*theorein*, 'to see'; and *Thèos* 'God' from *theorò* 'I see'), which deny 'sa vérité profonde qui est d'être enchaîné (its profound truth, which is to be enchained)' (*MS*, p. 233; Camus 1960, p. 24).[49] Camus goes as far as to define reason as an instrument of thinking and a comfort to the anxiety of an 'esprit arrivé aux confins (spirit that has reached the borders)' (*MS*, p. 238), bending over the horrifying limit of death 'passé lequel c'est l'effondrement et le *néant* (beyond which is decomposition and nothingness)' (*MS*, p. 260). Thus, like Prometheus's gift of *blind* hope to mortals, reason based on *fore*sight is a technique, or remedy, for the painful vision of the chains, which bind a humanity that is ultimately sentenced to death; reason, therefore, may be seen as an 'art' that creates new chains with its illusory constructions.

In the opening lines of *Le Mythe de Sisyphe*, Camus admits to two methods of thought: the method of La Palisse and the method of Don Quixote (*MS*, p. 222). These two figures powerfully displace the metaphor of vision and replace the famous discourse on method of Descartes, the philosopher of modern rationalism, with the 'balance between evidence and lyricism' (Ibid.). La Palisse represents the compelling, 'mathematical' evidence (*MS*, p. 230) of death and absurdity (*MS*, p. 222): 'Un quart d'heure avant ma mort, j'étais encore en vie. Ceci a suffi à ma gloire. Mais cette gloire est usurpée. Ma vrai philosophie est qu'un quart d'heure après ma mort, je ne serai plus en vie. (A quarter of an hour before my death, I was still alive. This was enough for my glory. But my glory is usurped. My true philosophy is that a quarter of an hour after my death, I will no longer be alive.' (II, p. 896.) The absurdity of death usurps the glory of the living human being, dispossessing him of his undisputed sovereignty (I, p. 95).

As Camus writes in the fragment 'Accepter la vie...' (1933), either to accept life or to revolt against it means to place oneself *in front of* and *outside of* life itself; but this is only an illusion and we are immersed in the pain of existence:

> [La vie] nous frappe, nous mutile, nous crache au visage. Elle nous illumine aussi de bonheur fou et soudain qui nous fait participer. C'est court. Ça suffit. Pourtant qu'on ne s'y trompe pas: la douleur est là. Impossible de tergiverser. ([Life] strikes us, mutilates us, spits in our face. It also illuminates us with crazy and sudden happiness that makes us participate. It is short. That is enough. Still, make no mistake: there is pain. Impossible to tergiversate.) (I, p. 985)

To accept life, namely, to want it and take it as it is, is the expression of a voluntarism that Camus dismisses as a ridiculous and sinister comedy (I, p. 985). In this early text, death is not considered original evidence, but makes its appearance with the violence of a silencing act that is committed against living beings and that deprives them of their own *rights*. In another short fragment, dated October 1933, 'Voilà, elle est morte (There! She's dead)', he writes:

> Elle meurt. Et je n'ai pas le droit de parler. [...] Je n'ai pas le *droit*, je n'ai pas le *droit*. [...] Mais si, j'ai le droit de crier, de me révolter. Puisqu'on me l'a tuée. Et qu'on m'a tué. Je l'aimais. On n'avait pas le droit de me l'enlever. Ou alors il fallait me l'enlever tout à fait. Et ne pas me laisser ce corps, cette pierre qui n'est plus elle que parce que je le crois, que je le dis. (She dies. And I do not have the right to speak. [...] I do not have the *right*. I do not have the *right*. [...] Yes, I do have the right to cry out, to revolt. Because they have killed her. And killed me. I loved her. They didn't have the right to take her away from me. Or else they should have taken her completely away. And not left me this body, this stone that is no longer her except because I believe it to be her, because I say it is her.) (I, p. 979)

The Promethean revolt fabricates the remedies that protect one from the vision of death and culminates in an aesthetic pessimism; echoing Nietzsche in another fragment, dated 1933, 'Perte de l'être aimé... (Losing the loved one...)', Camus writes that our life is our artwork (I, p. 983) and we are constantly projected forward in an incessant desire to believe in yet another 'lie' (I, p. 980), act another 'comedy' or 'game' (I, p. 982). But 's'il faut croire que vivre n'est pas autre chose que créer, il y a un singulier raffinement de cruauté dans ce geste qui suscite ce qui nous écrase. (if one must believe that living is nothing but creating, there is a singular refinement of cruelty in this gesture that gives rise to what crushes us.)' (I, p. 983; Camus, 1980, p. 162.) I argue that from the 1933 lyrical essays on, Camus uses 'Communion' to describe liberation from the vain anxieties that are related to such 'creations' or 'decors', namely, from the 'servile' expectations that govern our mundane activity. Ecstatic 'presence' does not coincide with the obliteration of the conscience of human misery and pain, but rather with a renewed awareness of our finitude – 'Notre royaume hélas est de ce monde. (Our kingdom, alas, belongs to this world)' (I, p. 96; *EE*, p. 71). Facing the absurdity of death frees thought from projection and anticipation, that is to say, from the creations of teleological reasoning, which distract

one from the painful 'certitude sans fond (endless certainty)' of death
(*MS*, p. 260).

In *Le Mythe de Sisyphe*, liberation from *telos*, understood as the mystics' freedom from the future and from the creations of philosophical
reason (*MS*, p. 259), dislocates the traditional metaphor of vision: being
'present' means to consider life 'sans la myopie de l'amant (without the
short-sightedness of the lover)' (*MS*, p. 260).[50] The literary character of
Don Quixote, the second figure that is used by Camus in defining the
method of absurd reasoning in *Le Mythe de Sisyphe*, is the epic illustration of the lover's short-sightedness:

> Oui, j'ai combattu des moulins à vent. Car il est profondément
> indifférent de combattre les moulins à vent ou les géants. Tellement
> indifférent qu'il est facile de les confondre. J'ai une métaphysique de
> myope. (Yes, I fought against the windmills. Because it is extremely
> indifferent to fight against windmills or against giants. So indifferent
> that one can easily confuse them. I have the metaphysics of one who
> is short-sighted.) (II, p. 896.)

Don Quixote represents the lover who is only capable of *seeing* his own
idea; Camus's Nietzschean aestheticism displaces the traditional constellation of sight/vision. Don Quixote is aware of his own short-sightedness;
therefore, he is free from the fetishistic belief in the objectiveness of
'blind' hope and of the 'dialectique savante et classique (learned and
classical dialectic)' (*MS*, p. 222) of a philosophical 'romantic' thought
that is constantly projected ahead in a distant time or space. From the
a-teleological perspective of indifference, the metaphysics of the myope
defetishises the 'ideals' of philosophical reason and sees them clearly for
what they are, namely, 'art' and lyricism.

According to David Sherman, Camus does not offer a methodology
(Sherman 2009, p. 41); the analysis of Camus's writings of the 1930s,
however, brings the young author's methodological interrogation to the
foreground, allowing us to detect in his rejection of teleological reason
and in his personal reception of a mystical 'method' of thinking, which
Camus identifies as lying beyond the bounds of *ratio*, a common thread
that runs through his lyrical essays and culminates in the *Le Mythe de
Sisyphe*. In the opening pages of his 1942 essay on the Absurd, Camus
defines the mathematical evidence of La Palisse and the lyricism of Don
Quixote as the only two viable *methods* of thought (*MS*, p. 222).

Camus conceives of contemplation as an *end*less mystical process that
rejects the ontological 'vision' of Truth, which he identifies as reason's

'prophetic' remedy against human suffering and finitude (*N*, p. 129). Thus, his lyrical essays challenge the notion of contemplation or 'theory' (from Gk. *theorein*, 'to see') that lies at the core of the Platonic–Aristotelian teleological model of action, and ground thinking itself in the suffering of men's mortal flesh, which evades beyond the fetishistic 'chains' of *ratio*. It is in light of these considerations that I propose we read Camus's replies to his friends Fréminville, who insistently invited him to join the Communist Party in 1934, and Grenier:

> Pour moi le communisme ne serait rien, s'il n'était une religion. (For me Communism would be nothing, if it weren't a religion.).[51]
>
> [...] Ce qui m'a longtemps arrêté, ce qui arrête tant d'esprits je crois, c'est le sens religieux qui manque au communisme. C'est la prétention qu'on trouve chez les marxistes d'édifier une morale dont l'homme se suffise [...] Peut-être aussi peut-on comprendre le communisme comme une préparation, comme une ascèse qui préparera le terrain à des activités plus spirituelles. En somme, une volonté de se dérober aux pseudo-idéalismes, aux optimismes de commande, pour établir un état de choses où l'homme puisse retrouver le sens de l'éternité. (That which has stopped me for a long time, and that which stops a lot of minds, I believe, is that Communism lacks a sense of religion. It is the Marxists' claim to build a morality in which man is self-sufficient [...] Perhaps Communism can also be understood as a preparation, an asceticism which will pave the way to more spiritual activities. In short, a will to shrink from the pseudo-idealisms, the commissioned optimisms, in order to establish a condition where man can retrieve a sense of eternity.)[52]

The emphasis Camus places on the religious 'sense of eternity' and the 'spiritual activities' that reach beyond contemporary 'romantic' or idealistic doctrines clearly connects the young author's idea of political engagement to the 'immoralist' questioning of modern rationalism in his 1933–34 writings. From the a-teleological perspective of his lyrical texts, 'eternity' coincides with the 'present' of ecstatic Communion with nature, thus, with liberation from the moral constructions of reason. In 'Le Désert' ('The Desert'), the frescoes of Giotto and Piero della Francesca are said to capture the eternal present of man's suffering flesh by freeing human mortal action from the temporal dominion of the finality and achievement, namely, from the expectation and anticipation of the future. 'Hell' is the word theologians have traditionally used to refer to the eternal present of suffering flesh that is without hope and expectation (*N*, p. 129). This must not be confused with the 'enslavement' of the human being to the primacy of the biological body, identified by Lévinas in the racist ideology of the Nazis on blood and soil.[53]

Moreover, Camus's 'ecstatic present', which is characteristic of 'Communion' with nature, is associated with greatness and with the mystics' *nobility* (*N*, p. 129) and emphasises the rejection of nihilistic or fetishistic servitude of the modern *homo oeconomicus*,[54] that Nietzsche identifies in the organisation of the contemporary Socialist party. As Camus writes in 'Le Désert', 'le chemin qui va de la beauté à l'immoralité est tortueux mais certain. Plongée dans la beauté, l'intelligence fait son repas de néant. (the path from beauty to immorality is difficult but certain. Plunged into beauty, intelligence feeds on nothingness.)' (*N*, p. 133.) In the ecstatic contemplation of beauty, intelligence erases 'man' (*N*, p. 134), namely, the moral constructions by means of which reason bestows sense upon existence, and exposes the *no*thingness (or non-objectiveness) that characterises these constructions.

Camus's *Noces* and, particularly, 'Le Désert' strikingly resemble Nietzsche's *Aurore*, which was written in the thinker's solitary intimacy with the sun and sea of Genoa (*EH*, 'Pourquoi j'écris de si bons livres' – 'Aurore', 1) and marks his campaign against morality. In Nietzsche's fifth book of *Aurore*, the mute beauty of the sea teaches man how to cease to be a 'man' (*A*, V, 423), elevating him *above* his own self, his errors and illusions (*N*, p. 135). Poet Blanche Balaine, who met Camus in Algiers around 1937, recalls Camus's predilection for *Aurore* at the time (Balaine 1999, p. 104). In 'Le Désert', the air of beauty is rarefied and its landscape, a desert magnificent to the heart (*N*, p. 134).[55] Camus's 'return to nature' recalls Nietzsche's criticism of Rousseau's philosophical concept of nature (*A*, V, 427): the contemplation of beauty leaves intelligence without a god to *achieve* it (*N*, p. 134), namely, it frees thought from the creations, constructs, visual illusions, and 'labyrinths' by means of which philosophical reason beautifies nature (*A*, V, 427).

Like the young people at the Padovani beach in Algiers, the Franciscans of Fiesole, immersed in natural beauty, strip themselves of their possessions, denude themselves in order to have greater life in the present, rather than for the next one (*N*, p. 133). They embody a 'futile' love and happiness (*N*, p. 135), that is to say, they are freed from the finalities and justifications of philosophical or moral reason.[56] In *Noces* and in the fragments of 'Sans lendemains' ('Without tomorrows'), dated between 1938 and mid-1942, 'futility' or *use*lessness denote the particular freedom from thinking that is characterised and dominated by finality (*telos*) and that rests *outside* of the nihilistic 'servile' logic of utilitarian reason.

The echo of Nietzsche's considerations on freedom in *Aurore* is especially apparent in the fragment of 'Sans lendemains' dated 17 March 1938, which Camus later reworks to include in *Le Mythe de Sisyphe* and which constitutes the link between his lyrical works and the essay on the absurd.[57] The young author relates the delusory 'postulate' of the agent's freedom of *being* (I, p. 1199) to the projections attributed to teleological reason, that 'enslaves' men and transforms them into 'fonctionnaires de l'esprit et du cœur (bureaucrats of the mind and the heart)' (I, p. 1199), cogs in a nihilistic machine that subjugates the value of life to the end or 'future' or achievement of human expectations. The continuity that exists between the methodological interrogation of Camus's lyrical writings, and in particular between the mystical method of liberation of thought from *telos* and the absurd reasoning of *Le Mythe de Sisyphe*, will be explored in further detail in Chapter 5.

In *Noces*, the beauty of Algerian nature calls the philosophers' Beauty into question and does not provide a model of morality to improve men and make them *better* (I, pp. 117, 122). According to Nietzsche, the moral desire to change and improve men is the sign of the negative judgement *ressentiment* has toward existence, which founds moral and political fanaticism. In Camus's lyrical pages, beauty offers a lesson of love and patience, inviting the human actor to abandon reason's blind hopes and to stay entirely within his 'passive passion' (*N*, pp. 112–13). Passivity entails a negation that is not a renunciation, namely, the rejection of the deceitful constructions of teleological thinking. The last pretends to satisfy the human hunger for truth (*N*, p. 112) and cheats intelligence by concealing the horrifying vision of death with picturesque creations.

In the contemplation of the beauty of Algerian nature, the human actor steps out of petty utilitarian logic of activity. The happiness or strange joy (*N*, pp. 108–9) attained through the extreme denudement and immersion in the natural profusion of sensual riches cannot be confused with the happiness of the modern 'last men', which lies in maximisation and achievement. Camus's love of life is inseparable from despair (*EE*, p. 67), in particular, from the revolt against *telos* (*N*, p. 137); it is only from this perspective, that the author's consent to life's pure flame acquires its tragic meaning, which is opposed and irreducible to contemporary 'naturalistic' or biologistic theories of life. In the early 1930s Camus's teacher Jean Grenier addresses these philosophical attempts to bring together – in an 'impossible marriage' – thinking, which ignores death, and life, which is bound to and must come to an end, as '*absolute* nihilism' and warns against the risks of their social and political application for European civilisation.[58]

In a note written in 1933 in the thetic claim to unity of human thought, namely, in its need for truth and achievement, young Camus also detects a *need for death*. Death puts an *end* to life, allowing it to form a unitary block (I, p. 957), but, at the same time, it affirms the irrevocable retreat of achievement, and dispossesses men of their life, particularly, of the final product of their incessant creative efforts (I, p. 983). In *Noces*, splendour, misery, and the profusion of life, found in the sensual communion with nature, on one hand, and, on the other, in the absurdity of pain and death, is the twofold temporal dimension ('envers'/'endroit') of a tragic thought that has evaded the logic of *telos* (*N*, p. 125) and displaces such delusory creations of reason as 'activity', 'free will', 'history' (*N*, p. 115).[59]

4
An Artist's Point of View

Dolorem exprimit quia movit amorem
(A. Camus *Carnets*, 1936)

In February 1935, a review of Max Scheler's *L'homme du ressentiment* by philosopher Bernard Groethuysen is published in the *NRF*.[1] This short text draws attention to Scheler's phenomenological approach, which is seen as a method of liberation from the 'servitude' to the so-called common sense prejudices and the constructs of scientific reason. The phenomenologist's viewpoint is said to free the world from the domination of the end (*'use'*), which values only such things that are perceived to be capable of obtaining prescribed achievement in a more or less distant future (*'lendemain'*). It is more than likely that Groethuysen's review brought Max Scheler's book to the attention of young Camus, who read it shortly thereafter.[2]

The influence the work on *ressentiment* has on the formulation of Camus's own thought is confirmed by his 1943 notebooks, which attest to the author's intention to use the reading notes of Scheler's book for an essay on revolt that would continue the philosophical investigation of *Le Mythe de Sisyphe* (II, p. 986). I suggest that *L'homme du ressentiment* is an essential source for Camus's writings of the mid-1930s and sheds light on the form and content of the young author's political commitment.

Max Scheler resorts to the notion of *ressentiment* as it is presented in Nietzsche's *Genealogy of Morals* to denote the subordination of life to a 'calculating' reason, which assigns a 'price' to life in terms of utility and efficacy and reduces the human being to a mere wheel in a machine, of which man himself is the creator (Scheler 1958, p. 187). Scheler identifies the origins of this particular mode of judgement in the negative

attitude of hatred and fear that is directed at the world and which gener-
ates the 'mensonge organique (organic lie)'; in other words, the falsification of an object's value on the basis of, and to what degree, this object
serves the disposition or temperament of the evaluating subject (Scheler
1958, p. 62). Whenever something is positively affirmed, estimated and
attributed value to, not for its intrinsic qualities but reactively, that is
to say, taking into consideration the existence of an external objective
and with the un-confessed purpose of depreciating an opposing value,
ressentiment submits reality to its 'servile' logic (Scheler 1958, p. 48).

Groethuysen calls attention to the phenomenological viewpoint
delineated in Scheler's book as an 'honest' way of considering things
as they are, that is, free from the servitude to the artifices of scientific
knowledge and the prejudices of common sense. The phenomenologist rejects the categories of use, 'tomorrow' ('lendemain'), calculation
and prudence; in other words, the teleological 'romantic' perspective
of *ressentiment*, which is unable to accept the world as it is and therefore negates it. The '*love* the world' that founds the phenomenological
viewpoint is illustrated by the artist, who 'sees everything and disposes
of nothing' and dwells in the world with which he has come to be rec-
onciled (Groethuysen 1935, pp. 309–10).

It is through Nietzsche's *Aurore* that Camus became familiar with the
distinction between 'romanticism' and 'artist's conscience'; however,
Groethuysen's respective identification of the artist with the phenomenologist and of his 'love of the world' with an 'anti-romantic' perspective are extremely likely to have brought the political dimension of the
artist to the young student's attention. Placing the artist's 'honest' viewpoint past the limits of the utilitarian 'servile' logic of modern thought,
Scheler challenges the categories of the dominant social-political
discourses (Scheler 1958, p. 66) and criticises the contemporary party
politics of both the right- and left-wing ideologies.

Upon Jean Grenier's suggestion, by the end of the summer of 1935
Camus joins the Communist Party and engages in 'active politics'.[3]
Political action appears to be a crucial issue in the discussions he had
with his teacher; the articles that Grenier published in the *NRF* between
1934 and 1935 attest to a growing concern for the appeals to 'fervour' and
'creation' in contemporary political discourses (Garfitt 2004, pp. 102–3;
Cornick 1995, p. 85) and question the possibility of a 'reasonable' political conduct opposed to the widespread political fanaticism of the times.
Frenzied and violent activity,[4] associated with the ideological affirmation
of total or absolute reason, is the issue taken up in Grenier's interrogation of the mid-1930s. Camus's reading of *L'homme du ressentiment* seems

to confirm the relevance of this problem for him and the development of his position at the time.

Scheler detects the claim of absolute reason, or the feeling of 'being (totally) right' ('avoir raison') in the contemporary concept of moral and political duty, which he believes to be based in *ressentiment*. In that it denotes a reactive attitude towards and a negative judgement upon the world, *ressentiment* may be illustrated by two spiritual typologies, the 'apostate' and the 'romantic' (Scheler 1958, pp. 19–22, 45 ff.). The apostate changes his 'faith' out of his love of negation, namely, of sheer antagonism towards his ancient beliefs; he illustrates a mode of thought that reactively secures ones' reasons, values, beliefs against the methodical exercise of doubt. By calling an unknowable factor x 'given' or 'truth', the apostate uses logic to place x beyond the reach of critical reason, thus removing it from any discussion that might call it into question. Modern philosophy and political ideologies incorporate the apostate's mode of thought that, in the capacity of opinions to *resist* doubt and avoid fruitful criticism, sees the proof that such beliefs are 'true' and 'real' (Scheler 1958, p. 47).

Scheler's pages on the apostate recall the considerations Nietzsche makes regarding the figure of the moral fanatic. In *Aurore*, the claim of absolute reason is founded on an 'intellectual vice', which consists in using the instruments of knowledge to falsify reality and 'sanctify' one's opinions for fear and hatred of criticism (*A*, V, 543). This mode of thought is exemplified by Kant's critique, which introduces a separation between pure and moral reason. According to Nietzsche, the Kantian moral edifice is demonstrated *in spite of* the evident 'immoralism' of nature and history; it is based on a negative or pessimistic judgement of the world[5] and on a contemptuous degradation of all that threatens the philosopher's reason (*A*, Preface, 4). Nietzsche associates Kantian rationalism to fanaticism and 'radical idealism' (*A*, Preface, 3) and uses the term 'romanticism' to designate this form of philosophical pessimism, which judges reality as ugly and morally *negative* and therefore attempts to 'evade' from it by means of imagination and ideas (*A*, V, 550). From Plato onward, philosophy is said to poetically divert thought from that which *is* and to beautify, through the use of all sorts of visual illusions, a world that is conceived to be arid and ugly (*A*, V, 427).

As I will demonstrate in detail in Chapter 5, Camus makes the difficult method of Nietzsche's 'honest' or immoralist thought his own and rejects 'radical idealism'; in 1942, he defines his essay on the absurd an act of fidelity and confidence in modern intelligence (I, p. 320) against the contemporary appeals for a 'return' to the Middle Ages, to nature, and to the primitive mentality. These contemporary appeals, proposed as solutions to the so-called European nihilism and, more specifically, to the modern loss of transcendent foundation, are considered by Scheler and Jean Grenier[6] to be among the 'romantic' attempts to negate intelligence and secure one's beliefs *in spite of* reality by means of 'radical idealism', which is the basis of moral and political fanaticism.

In his letter to Francis Ponge in 1943, Camus describes his *Le Mythe de Sisyphe* as a personal, although not original, attempt at thinking 'honestly' in the margins of modern nihilism (I, p. 887). In calling attention to the historical context, from which *Mythe de Sisyphe* springs and with which it critically confronts itself, Camus proves that he takes modern nihilism into account primarily as a socio-political question rather than as a metaphysical problem ('death of God'). I maintain that Scheler's phenomenological analysis plays a pivotal role in Camus's knowledge of the problem of nihilism between the late 1930s and early 1940s. The young author conveys his understanding of nihilism to be a specific evaluation and interpretation of existence that is ingrained in modern rationalism and subordinates the values of life to those of utility.[7]

Between 1936 and 1939, the influence of Scheler is apparent in *DES* and in Camus's lyrical essays. In *Noces*, Camus links his 'love of the world' to the phenomenological rehabilitation of an intuitive contact with things/reality just as they are, which Scheler openly places in opposition to the 'hate of the world', typical of the man of *ressentiment*. In Camus's lyrical works, which anticipate the epistemological considerations of *Le Mythe de Sisyphe*,[8] love has the appearance of the Algerian countryside 'tout entier livré aux yeux (completely accessible to the eyes)' (*N*, p. 117), wherein exist 'des pierres, la chair, des étoiles et ces vérités que la main peut toucher (stones, flesh, stars and those truths the hand can touch)' (*N*, p. 124). As he writes in 'Le Désert', nature without men is the only universe where *being right* has a meaning (I, p. 135); the ecstatic contemplation of nature brings the tragic limit of the absolute claims of reason to the foreground. The mystical negation of teleology does away with the resentful feelings of pride and contempt ('mépris') and culminates in the ecstatic outburst of feelings of generosity,[9] pity and goodness[10] (I, pp. 974, 96).

According to Scheler, modern philosophical rationalism 'falsifies' the immediate understanding of the world by submitting it to the teleology and utilitarian categories of *ressentiment*. This particular attitude permeates the contemporary political values of equality and justice, as well as the political doctrines, from Socialism to the Christian democratic movement and humanitarianism. In a letter to Grenier written in August 1935, young Camus echoes Scheler's criticism and expresses his concern for the 'false rationalism' linked to the 'illusion of progress' of the Communist doctrine, as well as for the notions of class struggle and historical materialism that are interpreted teleologically in view of the happiness and triumph of the working-class alone.[11] Scheler's methodological approach sheds light on the objections that Camus advances against the political programme of the PCF. By refusing to put a volume of Marx's *Capital* between man and life, Camus rejects the 'romantic' falsification of reality that replaces the subject's immediate presence in the world and to his fellow men with a doctrine. In his view, it is not the theoretical constructions, but rather life itself, the sensibility and origins of each single being, that lead to Communism.

The letter that Camus wrote to Grenier on 21 August 1935, concerning his decision to join the PCF, echoes, in some crucial respects, the argument of *L'homme du ressentiment*. First, Camus openly refuses the Marxist claim that morality can be founded exclusively on Man, which, in his opinion, reduces men and women's spiritual life to the biological concept of 'human species' or *natural* being. He believed that the Marxist theory shares the moral ideas of humanitarianism with the Radical theses of Édouard Herriot, those same ideas that Scheler criticises as the expression of an attitude of *hatred*, that brings about the isolation of the human being from the world and turns men and nature into the objects or means of domination and exploitation (Scheler 1958, p. 111). The aspiration to reach higher spiritual activities that go beyond the bounds of utilitarian rationalism runs through Camus's lyrical texts, from *La Maison Mauresque* to *Noces*. The author rejects the universalistic 'love of humanity' that is characteristic of modern humanitarianism in favour of a deep spiritual contact with the world and with his fellow men and women. In *Noces*, he points out how ecstatic communion with nature is not experienced in solitude, but denotes a spiritual form of love, a mystic *ascesis* that goes beyond reason and that the author shares with the ones he loves (*N*, p. 106).[12]

In 1935, Camus still conceives of the 'lack of religious feeling' within the Communist doctrine as an important drawback to political engagement in the Communist party (Camus and Grenier 1981, p. 22). But the Marxist criticism of the modern bourgeois 'progressivism' and the unmasking of the nihilistic teleology of modern economic and political thought are the basis of his non-orthodox rehabilitation of Communism, which subsequently culminates in his decision to join the PCF at the end of the summer of 1935. Camus conceives of Marxism as an '*ascesis*', or a preparatory stage that liberates action from the modes of knowledge typical of *ressentiment*. Although there is no evidence that he had read Marx's works around 1935, his position is reminiscent of Scheler's interpretation, in *L'Homme du ressentiment*, of the Marxian economic analyses.

In line with Nietzsche's *Genealogy of Morals*, Scheler identifies the teleocratic logic of efficacy to be the root of nihilism, which he detects at the core of the Liberal 'progressive' mode of evaluation. Founded on competition and regulated by the principles of Progress/Regression, the modern bourgeois mode of thinking relegates value to the end of a process of power accumulation (Scheler 1958, pp. 31–4); the value of each moment or 'situation' is derived reactively from the comparison with other competing moments, each of which exerts a constant effort to attain the highest rank of value and power. The identification of each single moment with an exchange value, a spendable commodity within a process of power accumulation that is potentially endless, culminates in the depreciation and devaluation of the world and of life. Thus, the criticism of modern nihilism coincides with the criticism of bourgeois rationalism, which informs the contemporary political assumptions of humanitarianism. On the teleological horizon of 'progress' and power accumulation, the positive value ('general Happiness') is the product of the political agent's work and depends on the *efficacy* of his actions; the actor is transformed into a *'moral proletarian'* at the service of the rational end-means concatenation within an horizon that is devoid of value (Scheler 1958, p. 144).

Camus's decision to join the PCF in 1935 seems to respond to a need to reclaim the concept of action from the clutches of the optimistic pseudo-idealisms, the basis of which Marx's criticism of Liberalism identified in the nihilistic logic of Western rationalism. Nonetheless, Camus is critical of the Marxist doctrine, in particular, of its teleological 'progressive' interpretations of class struggle and historical materialism,[13] and although he professes his political action to lean in favour of Communism, he preserves a pessimistic view of the Communist formulation of the social question.[14] As his friend Jeanne-Paule Sicard recalls, between 1935 and 1937 Camus propounds a Communist view that is sufficiently cleared of Marxist terminology and constantly looks for ways in which human misery may be fought.[15]

Rethinking participation beyond political 'romanticism'

Defended on 25 May 1936, Camus's dissertation in philosophy on Christian Metaphysics and Neoplatonism (hereinafter *DES*) is not an intellectual exercise that is totally unrelated to the political context and to the author's active commitment in the PCF. I propose that we read this philosophical text in light of Camus's Nietzschean criticism of modern rationalism, in that it provides a means of interpretation of his political thought and action in the convulsive period that preceded the outbreak of the Second World War.

DES is structured in four parts that are dedicated to Early Christianity, the Gnosis, Plotinus, and Saint Augustine. In the introductory pages, Camus demonstrates that he is essentially concerned with shedding light on the process that gives rise to a new civilisation, which, in his view, may be found in a change of 'level' or attitude towards the world that 'transfigures' pre-existing conceptual constellations (*DES*, p. 999) rather than in a substitution of systems or theories.[16] The influence that Scheler's phenomenological analyses had over Camus's investigation of the origin and sources of Christianity is apparent. According to the young student of Philosophy, the questions are posed on the emotional level of sensibility ('*sensibilité*') and approached from the specific view-point of the attitude one has towards the world (*DES*, p. 1000). The theoretical solutions or justifications that constitute Western philosophies in the proper sense cannot be understood without referring to this affective level.

Critics of Camus's early philosophical work have essentially focused on the textual sources of *DES* (Archambault 1972) and on the young author's 'obsession' for the issue of evil and of human suffering that he addresses in his treatment of the Gnostics and Saint Augustine (Archambault 1979; Caussat 1997); their analyses, however, have neglected the philosophical political dimension of Camus's 1936 dissertation, which, in my opinion, lies in the distinction made between the 'romantic' attitude and the artist's viewpoint. In *DES* Camus adopts the distinction Scheler makes and uses the term 'romantic' to refer to an emotional disposition of *hatred* towards the world that is associated with a negative moral judgement of the ugliness of the 'evil' world. Instead, the artist's attitude is defined as one of *love*, and is based on a positive aesthetic judgement of the world's beauty. The two perspectives are respectively illustrated in *DES* by the Gnostics and Plotinus.

In chapter II, Camus describes the Gnostics' theoretical solutions to the problem of evil as an illustration of a 'romantic' attitude (*DES*, p. 1056) and an expression of a pessimistic viewpoint (*DES*, p. 1029), upon which a moral position of contempt and negation of the world is founded. The Gnostics refuse to accept the world as it is and affirm an ascetic eradication of man from the evil creation, which culminates in the apocalyptic and revolutionary political theories of the world's destruction.[17] The pessimism of the Gnostics and their proud 'refusal to accept' are said to recall a truly *'modern sensibility'* (*DES*, p. 1029) – Camus is clearly alluding to the modern attitude that is explored by Scheler under the category of *ressentiment*, and the roots of which Nietzsche traces back to the eighteenth-century 'age of enthusiasm', of which the pessimistic judgement of the world's ugliness (in Nietzsche's opinion, typical of the philosophers) culminates in 'radical idealism'.

Camus demonstrates that he is especially concerned with the Gnostic's separation of reason (*logos*) from beauty that displaces truth and removes it to a place that is beyond the sphere of the sensory, where, instead, the aesthetic judgement is rooted. While for a Greek, beauty is both order and sensibility, 'economy' and object of passion, for a Gnostic the 'logical legislator' (*DES*, p. 1042) is abstracted from and opposed to the movement of life, which in its turn is conceived to be ugly and devoid of order and value (*anarchy*). The teleological reason inherent in the Gnostic Christian concept of history, for which this last is oriented towards Salvation, is opposed to the 'natural reason' of the Demiurge, which submits anarchic nature to an *evil* domination (*DES*, p. 1056). This concept of reason introduces a 'moralisation' of existence, specifically, an interpretation of the world in which this last is the arena of a struggle between Good (the Christ as Emancipator and Redeemer) and Evil (the Demiurge). Nietzsche criticises this moralisation in his pages on modern moral fanaticism (*A*, Preface, 3); the 'radicalism' or moral fanaticism that he detects in the contemporary revolutionary theories, from Robespierre and Saint Just to the nineteenth-century anarchist and communist doctrines, finds its root in a modern 'romantic' sensibility, of which the Gnostic attitude of contempt and hatred of the world are reminiscent.[18]

Plotinus' philosophical work seems especially to attract Camus's attention for the passionate combat the Hellenic thinker engages in against the Gnostics' 'romantic' theses (*DES*, p. 1056). According to Plotinus, the world can be explained *because* it is beautiful (*DES*, p. 1042); for him, beauty and truth are not separated. Plotinus is said to displace the extreme emotion that the artist experiences when faced with the world's beauty to the intelligible world, and opposes his 'aesthetic viewpoint' to the 'romantic' contempt that the Gnostics hold for the world (*DES*, p. 1056).

> Plotin pense en artiste et sent en philosophe, selon une raison toute pénétrée de lumière et devant un monde où l'intelligence respire. (Plotinus thinks as an artist and feels as a philosopher, according to

a reason that is totally pervaded with light and before a world where intelligence breathes.) (*DES*, p. 1055)

Plotinus *feels* like a philosopher in the sense that he 'transfigures' existence by casting the extreme emotion of *love*, which seizes an artist in his contemplation of the world, into the Greek forms of philosophical justification (*DES*, p. 1041). Camus resorts to the expression 'Mystic Reason' (*DES*, p. 1040) to describe the Hellenic's unprecedented theoretical solution, which (re)interprets the world from an artist's point of view (*DES*, p. 1042).

Plotinus' 'Reason' is neither the modern Cartesian 'mathematical reason' (*DES*, p. 1053) nor Plato's dialectical reason. In agreement with Nietzsche's criticism of the Platonic *'episteme'* ('science') (*A*, V, 427), Camus understands the Platonic dialectics to be a construct used for the purpose of bridging the gulf that is introduced by philosophers between the world and that which is conceived to be Good (*DES*, p. 1012). The author of *DES* shows his understanding of philosophy to correspond to the concept that is presented in Nietzsche's *Aurore*; Camus is clearly referring to Plato's concept of reason when he points out that, for Plotinus, science is 'une contemplation et un recueillement intérieur, non une construction (a contemplation and a meditation, not a construction)' (*DES*, p. 1041). Thus, the author of the *Enneads* does not think like a philosopher, but like an artist. Plotinus' love of the world pervades his theoretical effort, which re-evaluates the role of intuitive thought as opposed to the abstract 'reason' of philosophy (*DES*, p. 1059). His method of thought transcends the categories of traditional logic by resorting to metaphors that convey the tension between that which is sensible and that which is intellectual, in other words, the religious aspect of principles and their explanatory force (*DES*, p. 1059).

By defining Plotinian reason as 'mystic', Camus emphasises the continuity of the Hellenic's thought with the 'emotional themes' of early Christianity, in particular, the refusal of speculation and the emphasis on the dimension of the flesh ('la chair') as was experienced in the spiritual and carnal Communion with Christ (*DES*, p. 1015).[19] It is possible that reading Scheler's *L'homme du ressentiment* inspired Camus's decision to investigate early Christian metaphysics, from the Fathers to Saint Augustine. The phenomenologist rejects Nietzsche's criticism of Christianity as a monolithic phenomenon and distinguishes the morality of the primitive Christians from the later, especially, modern Christian morality; he calls attention to the first form of morality asserting that it provided an example of thought and conduct that was alien to bourgeois rationality and the utilitarian logic of *ressentiment*.[20] These considerations may have stimulated Camus to begin an exploration into alternative models or ways of thinking that evade nihilistic logic of Western reason. Plotinus defines a method of thought that is alternative and in opposition to the 'romantic' solutions of the Gnostics, who replace Christ's flesh, the mystic symbol of the suffering of humanity, with an abstract 'décor de kermesse métaphysique (scenery of metaphysical fair)' (*DES*, p. 1023).

For the Gnostics the world is ugly and in it no salvation may be had. The pessimistic view of the Gnostic philosophers culminates in the 'romantic' negation of this world and in the escape and evasion into the ideal. While the foundations of Eleusinian mysteries stemmed from the contemplation of the world's beauty, the philosophies of the Gnosis merge the Greek (Promethean) understanding of knowledge as a remedy to suffering together with the Christian notion of Salvation. According to the Gnostics, there is no such thing as *useless* suffering; every worldly event is justified within a teleological scheme, which transforms the world into the stage of a theatrical drama under the direction of a transcendent God (*DES*, p. 1036). From the 'romantic' perspective, drama and reality coincide (*DES*, p. 1032); Christian history is an anarchic stage, where values and truths are not contemplated but delayed, and then measured up against the achievement of the final end that is Salvation, which is projected to a point that is found *outside* of this world (*DES*, p. 1042). Camus emphasises that the attitude of contempt for the world inherent to the Gnostic teleological justification of existence and moral solution to the problem of evil was fiercely opposed by Plotinus.

The political dimension of the Gnostic 'romantic' theses, against which Plotinus' 'aesthetic' viewpoint passionately engages, is especially apparent in Marcion, whose doctrine culminates in the Christ's 'revolutionary' mission to achieve total destruction of the evil world (*DES*, pp. 1028–9).[21] The Gnostic pessimistic view of an 'anarchic' world devoid of all order and intelligence (*DES*, p. 1056) is strikingly reminiscent of the contemporary analyses of the 'religion' of Hitlerism, namely, of the Nazi so-called 'revolution' of biological life and 'rationalised romanticism' divulged in the *NRF*. It is plausible that Camus read Plotinus' *Enneads* all the while bearing in mind Nietzsche's criticisms of 'romanticism' or moral fanaticism, that Grenier and Scheler had detected in contemporary political ideologies. The Hellenic's Greek (Pre-Platonic) 'naturalism', which does not separate beauty from *logos* and which rejects the voluntarism that is inherent in the 'romantic' moral justification, is seen as an example of honest thought that lies beyond the limits of the logic of *ressentiment*.

Plotinus counters the position taken by the Gnostics by negating the antithesis between sensory appearance and intelligence, the dualism between spiritual principle and sheer matter of the metaphysical tradition; he propounds that there can be no such thing as a pure nature separated from human conscience. According to Camus,

> [c]e n'est pas l'apparence que Plotin recherche mais plutôt cet *envers* des choses qui est son paradis perdu. Et cette patrie solitaire du sage, chaque chose ici-bas s'en fait le vivant rappel. Voilà pourquoi Plotin décrit l'intelligence de façon sensuelle. (Plotinus is not searching for appearance, but rather for that *reverse side* of things, which is his paradise lost. And each thing down-here is the living recollection of that wise man's solitary homeland. That is why Plotinus describes intelligence in a sensual way.) (*DES*, p. 1042, my italics)

Influenced by Émile Bréhier's Bergsonian commentaries, Camus understands Plotinian intelligence as a temporal rather than spatial 'reverse side' that co-exists and is inseparable from the sensory and sensual 'right side' of the world.[22]

Contrary to the Platonic association of contemplation with a process of abstraction, contemplation in the *Enneads* is understood to be a process of liberation from the servile *ratio* of practical knowledge and habit; it is a spiritual concentration and purification of the senses, rather than from the senses, that leads the human soul, like a new Ulysses,[23] to reach the intelligible 'lost homeland' (*DES*, p. 1052).

Camus shows particular interest in Plotinus' method of non-spatial intuitive thought (*DES*, p. 1059), which rejects the philosophical principle of non-contradiction and replaces it with the religious principle of 'participation'. The *Enneads* are conceived by Camus to be the artist's expression of his *love* of the world; metaphors are used by Plotinus to convey the combination of the two 'indefinable' or extra-logical dimensions of feeling and concrete sensory evidence (II, p. 861) and express the dynamic tension of intuition, which transcends the fixed form of philosophical concept (Bréhier 1982, pp. 42–3). In a note written in the *Carnets* in 1938, Camus observes that metaphors are to Plotinus' 'mystic reason' what syllogism is to the philosophers' (i.e. Platonic–Aristotelian) reason[24] and he goes so far as to define the first an 'aesthetic' reason so as to distinguish it from the 'ethic' or moral reason of the philosophical tradition (II, p. 861).

In Camus's 1936 dissertation, the young author defines Plotinus' 'Mystic Reason' with a metaphor taken from his 1933 text, *La Maison Mauresque* (*DES*, p. 1042; I, p. 968). The textual relationship that Camus draws suggests that he associated his own artistic, openly anti-rationalist investigation with Plotinus' 'artist's point of view'. The author of the *Enneads* thinks as an artist and feels as a philosopher (*DES*, p. 1055); in 1936, Camus notes in his *Carnets*: 'On ne pense que par images. Si tu veux être philosophe, écris des romans. (One only thinks in images. If you want to be a philosopher, write novels.)' (II, p. 800.)

Early that same year, Camus took part in the collective creation of a play, *Révolte dans les Asturies*, of which he wrote the presentation and the opening stage directions[25]. The play, announced in the journal *La Lutte sociale* in April 1936, was to be performed by the Théâtre du Travail and bring to the stage the revolt of the Asturian miners, which had followed the victory of the coalition of the right in the 1933 Spanish General Election. This collective work evoked the dramatic moments of the miners' revolt: the armed insurrection of the workers against the abolishment of the social and political reforms introduced by the republicans between 1931 and 1933 and the accompanying occupation of various towns, including Oviedo; the organisation of the popular movement into a *social* revolution against the miserable condition of workers and their enslavement to the capitalist system through the replacement of money with 'work vouchers' and the creation of revolutionary committees that recalled the experience of the Paris Commune and the 1917 Russian revolution; and the defeat of the revolt and the bloody repression of the workers by the government troops of López de Ochoa which were supported by the Foreign Legion and the North-African *Regulares* led by Franco.

Révolte dans les Asturies must be situated in the historical and political climate of the February 1936 electoral success of the Popular Front, which followed the strong reactions in Spain and abroad against the brutality of the Francoist repression (Langlois 1981).[26] A singular aspect of this play that was never performed[27] is that in the stage directions Camus seems to cast his personal research of a popular art, deeply imbued with his political convictions and commitment, using the philosophical mould that he had already delineated in *DES*.

In defiance of the 'prejudice' that recurs in classical theatre of the opposition between actors and spectators, these last who observe and judge from the outside, Camus proposes a form of art in which the spectators would no longer be placed *in front of* or before the action, but would be immersed in the action itself and have to participate, each from their personal perspective ('[...] le fauteuil 156 voit les choses autrement que le fauteuil 157. ([...] seat 156 sees things differently than seat 157.)', I, p. 5). In the case of *Révolte dans les Asturies*, action culminates in the death of its actors; thus, it touches upon a form of greatness that is distinct to men and that Camus identifies with absurdity (I, p. 5). His stage directions echo another fragment ('Accepter la vie...')[28] in which Camus rejects the opposition between accepting life and revolting against it in that he considers it to be an illusory construct:

> Accepter ou se révolter, c'est se mettre *en face* de la vie. Pure illusion. Nous sommes dans la vie. Elle nous frappe, nous mutile, nous crache au visage. Elle nous illumine aussi de bonheur fou et soudain qui nous fait *participer*. C'est court. Ça suffit. (To accept [life] or revolt against it is to place oneself *before* life itself. Pure illusion. We are in life. It strikes us, mutilates us, spits in our face. It also illuminates us with crazy and sudden happiness that makes us *participate*. It is short. That is enough.) (I, p. 985, my italics)

This passage recalls his 1936 dissertation and, in particular, the distinction that Camus makes between the 'romantic' model of teleological reason of the Gnostics and the 'aesthetic' model of mystic reason of Plotinus. The Gnostics' revolt against evil creation or their 'refusal to accept' existence and their pessimistic view, which recall modern sensibility (*DES*, p. 1029), are the foundations of the 'romantic' vision of a teleological universe that Camus describes with his metaphor of theatre to underline its fictional character (*DES*, p. 1042).

It is no surprise, therefore, that the notion of 'participation' (*DES*, p. 1058), around which the young author develops his new concept of popular art, is repeated in *DES* to denote the Plotinian engagement against the Gnostic 'romantic' attitude of contempt (*DES*, p. 1057) and the Hellenic's tragic effort to think outside the established philosophical categories,[29] which place men in front of life, rendering them external spectators to a divine drama. Plotinus' 'aesthetic reason' is the expression of an 'artist's point of view' (*DES*, p. 1042) of the world; it is a way of interpreting existence outside the limits imposed by the nihilistic and fetishist logic of 'romanticism'.[30] Camus rejects the modern fatalism that reduces the living human being to a passive spectator and a mere cog within a teleological machine that capitalises value (Happiness) in a paradise that is not of *this* world. He writes in 'Le Désert': 'Le monde est beau, et hors de lui, point de salut. (The world is beautiful, and there is no salvation outside of it.)' (*N*, p. 135.)

A stranger to the world of *ressentiment*

During the period of his active militancy in the PCF, which comes to an end between August and September 1937, Camus's prolific activity within the Comité Amsterdam-Pleyel as the general secretary of the Algerian Maison de la Culture, as theatre director, playwright and actor with the *Théâtre du Travail*, and, subsequent to his break with the Communist party, with the *Théâtre de l'équipe*, attests to the close relationship that existed between his political commitment and art (Lévi-Valensi 1972). Camus refuses the so-called art 'in the ivory tower', that is separated from the social and political reality of its time, as well as the art that is put to the service of the power politics of the Fascist regimes; he perceives both conceptions of art to be two sides of the same 'nihilistic' coin of modern rationalism and of the identification of political action with efficacy and utility.

In the opening conference on 'La Nouvelle Culture méditerranéenne' held in honour of the newly-founded Maison de la Culture in February 1937, Camus envisages a new political constellation based on the notions of intelligence and life, which goes beyond force and the 'abstraction puérile et raisonnante (the puerile and reasoning abstraction)' (I, p. 568) of traditional power politics. Echoing Scheler's argument, he writes that 'la culture ne se comprend que mise au service de la vie (culture can only be understood in the service of life)' (I, p. 572), where life is opposed to the utilitarian logic of reason. The living Mediterranean culture that 'favorise l'homme au lieu de l'écraser (supports man instead of crushing him)' (I, p. 570) is born at the crossroads of the Eastern and the Western traditions (I, p. 569) and cannot be confused with the Fascist 'decadent' nationalistic and colonialist[31] revivals of the Latin myths. Camus identifies nationalism and imperialism to be the nihilistic products of modern rationalism, which separates the human being from the world (I, p. 571) and turns 'les paysages écrasés de soleil (the landscapes overcome by the sun)' into the abstract theatre *décors* of a violent will (I, p. 569).

The text Camus wrote for the 1937 conference on the new Mediterranean culture recalls the salient language and themes used in *DES*; his criticism of the Fascist arguments of self-redemption and politics of conquest (I, p. 571), in particular, is strikingly reminiscent of his analysis of the Gnostics' 'romantic' theses.[32] Camus affirms the primacy of the *spiritual* principle of 'man' (I, p. 566) over such abstractions as 'la Patrie' (the homeland), which justify the slaughter of men (I, p. 567), and he rejects the fetishistic reduction of the living being to a mere 'function' and a means to man's own creations and instruments of life – 'La politique est faite pour les hommes et non les hommes pour la politique (politics are made for men and not men for politics)' (I, p. 571).

Camus's considerations evoke Grenier and Scheler's disquieting diagnoses of the nihilistic 'fatalism' in contemporary political thought and call the concept of action of twentieth-century ideologies into question. Jean Grenier's essays, written between 1936 and 1938, on the contemporary revolutionary doctrines bring the voluntaristic self-redemptive faith in the realisation of a *'new* man' to the foreground. Camus's teacher calls attention to the plastic and 'dramatic' concept of man that is the basis of the contemporary 'Religion of Progress'; not only does he define Marx to be a 'professor of energy', who aims at transforming the world (Grenier 1967, p. 161), he also considers his faith in the 'new man' to be part of the utopias that are founded on the bourgeois optimistic belief in 'fatal', mechanical and continuous progress.[33] Grenier traces this faith back to 'la folie de la raison (reason's madness)' of the *Philosophes* of the Enlightenment and, more precisely, of the eighteenth-century moral fanaticism, which submits the exercise of intelligence to utility and turns reality into the arena of a moral struggle against *evil* opponents (*méchants*) the goal of which is the ultimate achievement and victory of Reason and Justice (Grenier 1967, p. 121). He emphasises the continuity between this form of rationalism and Lenin's Marxism and identifies the roots of nineteenth- and twentieth-century political fanaticism to be in the reduction of thought (*esprit*) to reason by the philosophers.

Anticipating Hannah Arendt's lectures on Marx and the tradition of political philosophy, Grenier's essays on political orthodoxy of the mid-1930s allocate the Marxist philosophy of History and dialectical materialism, as well as the opposition 'revolutionary *vs.* reactionary' philosophies, in the Western tradition, and, more precisely, consider it to be situated in the philosophers' 'reason'. Camus's teacher distinguishes politics of the extreme-left from the *metaphysics* of the extreme-left (Grenier 1967, p. 45) and he identifies the foundations of the last in what Nietzsche calls the 'radical idealism' of the eighteenth and nineteenth centuries.[34] In the 1935 essay 'L'intellectuel dans la société', Grenier openly rejects pernicious rationalism that culminates in political fanaticism; he warns against reducing the capacity of the human mind ('esprit') to Reason and against the nihilistic 'sacrifice' of human existence that is intrinsic to the Marxist 'rationalist mythology' (Grenier 1967, p. 127). In the same year, however, he exhorts Camus to take action by committing to a political party. It is more than likely that

Camus had Grenier's words in mind when, in a letter dated 21 August 1935, he promised to remain lucid (*'clairvoyant'*) and not to throw himself blindly into party action (Camus and Grenier 1981, p. 23); and reassured Grenier again, in July 1936, when he confessed the impossibility of not sharing and agreeing with his teacher's thoughts and position, particularly, concerning Communism (Camus and Grenier 1981, p. 25).

When we take into consideration Camus's 1937–38 cultural and political commitment favouring a 'new culture' we must take his criticism of rationalism and of the categories of the philosophical political tradition into account; the two cannot be analysed separately. His notes on Plotinus' 'aesthetic reason' of 1938 (II, p. 861) attest to his intention to challenge the philosophers' concept of reason from the artist's perspective that was delineated in the *Enneads*. The notion of beauty proves to have an essential part in his reception of Plotinus' thought, which, according to Camus, 'saves' the phenomena from the nihilistic logic of utility.[35] In his lyrical essays, *uselessness* is at the root of the author's revolt (*N*, p. 132); the ecstatic contemplation of the beauty of the Algerian nature rejects the abstract principle of 'Man' that is established by modern rationalism and humanitarianism, as well as the contemporary 'return' of the racial ideologies to animal life (blood and force) (I, p. 1432, n. 2); this ecstatic contemplation reveals the presence of a spiritual dimension of humanity that exceeds teleology and *use*.

These elements recur in the 1938 programme of a 'living' Mediterranean culture that Camus writes for the newly established journal, *Rivages*.[36] The author explicitly refuses all 'radical' or fanatic claims to reason and takes position against the 'powers of abstraction and death' (I, p. 870), namely, against the nihilistic justification of reason, that separates men from the world. His appeal to a common love of life and to a 'taste for a *disinterested* intelligence' that he links to a 'superabundance of life' (I, p. 869), decisively situates Camus's cultural programme under the banner of the Nietzschean criticism of the 'servile' logic of reason, for which men are enslaved to the end objective and to utility or interest.

Beauty is understood to be the key term of an alternative 'aesthetic' political constellation that lies beyond the hegemonic constellation of *ressentiment*; it replaces the traditional concept of freedom, which is associated to those of power and force, with a 'more subtle' notion of freedom (I, p. 870) that is identified with the artist's self-mastering. Camus's emphasis on 'une certaine barbarie (a certain barbarism)' (I, p. 870) – 'barbarian' being a *stranger* to the dominant *logos* – alludes, precisely, to the effort of thinking beyond the limits established by the logic and categories of Western 'reason' and to creating a new civilisation. In 'L'Été à Alger', begun in summer of 1937 and completed in 1938, Camus calls the Algerian people an authentically *creative* people of 'barbarians', who are, literally, strangers to the myths of the philosophical political tradition and, therefore, can affirm the 'greatness' (*grandeur*) of man that lies beyond the nihilistic devaluation of human life characteristic of Western civilisation (*N*, p. 124).

In *Noces*, beauty culminates in 'immoralism' (see Chapter 3), and it provides the possibility of obtaining a *greater* life, as opposed to *another* life, that is, one of poverty[37] and 'denudement'. In the novel *L'Etranger* (*The Stranger*), the figure of Meursault illustrates this very poverty and nudity: 'Il existe, comme une pierre, ou le vent, ou la mer sous le soleil, qui *eux ne mentent jamais*. (He exists, like a stone, or the wind, or the sea under the sun, *that never lie*.)' (Letter to Mr Hädrich (1954); I, p. 1269, my italics.) Meursault is the embodiment of the 'negative truth' of being and feeling (I, p. 215) that finds itself in opposition to the romantic constructions of reason;[38] he is a 'barbarian', who lives in a passionate relationship ('parenté') with things. He says what *is* and refuses to say more than what he feels, thus, his character recalls the phenomenological 'honest' perspective, evoked by Groethuysen's review of *L'homme du ressentiment* in the *NRF*.

Meursault is a stranger to contemporary nihilistic civilisation, which, as Camus notes in April 1938, is founded on the enslavement of the working people (II, pp. 849–50). In a fragment, entitled 'Sans lendemains' ('Without tomorrows') and dated March 1938, Camus explicitly traces the miserable condition of the modern 'slaves' back to the postulate of freedom, which *directs* life using the criteria of the 'future' ('tomorrow'), the realisation of predefined 'ends' and the affirmation of the 'self' (I, pp. 1198–9). The argument of human enslavement to the idea of one's own freedom (to *be*), in other words, of the fetishistic submission of men to a metaphysical 'lie', an all too human creation, that turns them into paltry functions of society's organisation ('functionaries of the heart and of the mind', I, p. 1199), brings to mind Nietzsche's remarks on the concept of freedom in *Crépuscule des Idoles* and *Humain, trop humain* (I. 'Des choses premières et dernières', 18), that Camus reads in the early months of 1938 (II, p. 857).

Camus considers the belief in the freedom of the will to be rooted in a false causal connection or the logical organisation of being, which subordinates men to the constant effort of calculating and measuring their very actions according to the parameters of success defined by certain specific ends (e.g., money, social position). The argument of

'Sans Lendemains' bears striking affinities with that of Georges Bataille's 'L'Apprenti-Sorcier' published in Paulhan's *NRF* a few months later,[39] confirming the influence Nietzsche's work had over the thoughts and the formulation of ideas of the two authors during the late 1930s.

Without ambition, or projects to reach or obtain a better economic and social position for himself – 'en tout cas toutes se valaient (in any case, they were all on the same level)' (*E*, p. 165) – Meursault is a stranger to this world and to its utilitarian logic. Ambition necessitates that one have preferences and that one project oneself into the future, while Meursault is perfectly *indifferent* to living in one way rather than in another. When his boss proposes a career in Paris to him, he sees no reason why he ought to change his situation; his only concern seems to regard upsetting the man with his reply (*E*, p. 165). Meursault reveals extreme sensitivity to the emotional reactions of his interlocutors; for instance, when Raymond addresses him as his 'friend', he does not mind being friends with a pimp ('Cela m'était *égal...*'), particularly because the man really wanted it (*E*, p. 159). He goes on to accept the task of writing a letter for Raymond that consequently leads to the episode of the prostitute's beating; he then agrees to go with Raymond to the police to bear witness in his favour simply to make him happy. Meursault does not mind marrying his lover, Marie, ('Cela m'était *égal...*') and accepts to do so just to please her (*E*, p. 165). This echoes the position Camus takes in 'Sans lendemains', where the writer makes a distinction between the feeling of loving someone from ('eternal') love, which he understands to be a social and metaphysical illusion (I, p. 1201). Meursault does not justify marriage, or the reason to marry, with love, which he considers to be a word without meaning (*E*, pp. 161, 165).

From Sartre's commentary[40] to more recent critical analyses of *L'Etranger*, the figure of Meursault has generally been interpreted as a *pre*-reflective or selfless 'natural man' (Sherman 2009, p. 64). It would be more accurate, however, to say that the Stranger thinks *outside* the bounds of logic, rather than to say that he does *not* think. Meursault thinks 'honestly' in the sense defined by Scheler and Nietzsche, that is to say, he thinks beyond the limits established by the nihilistic *telos* of modern thought.

Contrary to the opinions of those critics who label Meursault as 'impassible (impassive)', Camus prefers to use the word 'bienveillance (kindness)' (II, p. 961) to denote the Stranger's refusal of nothing. To refuse something would still imply that a preference for something exists ('it is *better* not to choose...'), thus, that one behaves according to a 'moral' scale of evaluation. But Meursault is a stranger to the 'romantic attitude' (I, p. 1202) of those men, who are subjugated to the nihilistic and utilitarian logic of 'tomorrow' and who are slaves to the idea of their freedom (career, situation, love). By describing the Stranger in terms of 'bienveillance', Camus places his hero beyond the confines of *ressentiment* and outside the limits put in place by the moral or 'romantic' justification of existence that defines contemporary civilisation.

In 'Sans lendemains', the belief in the modern concept of freedom distracts men from seeing that they are slaves of death (I, p. 1199). The absurdity of the mortal condition dissolves social and moral prejudices, those constructs of teleological reason that force men to organise their life in terms of function and partial objectives; death allows lucid men to fully seize their own life as a whole (I, p. 1201). In the second part of the novel, Meursault is confronted with the inescapable certitude of his death. Found guilty of the murder of an Arab and sentenced to capital execution, he learns the 'divine liberté du condamné à mort (divine freedom of he who is condemned to death)', which turns him into a 'stranger to his own life' (I, p. 1200).

According to René Girard, who interprets Meursault's trial using the perspective provided by Nietzsche's notion of *ressentiment* (Girard 1964), Camus takes sides against the judges, who sentence the protagonist to death; but if the hero is a positive innocent figure, as his author seems to imply, then his judges must be *guilty*. In my opinion, Girard fails to grasp the crucial influence Nietzsche's argument had over the composition of *L'Étranger*, which consists, precisely, in the radical criticism of the notion of 'guilt' as the product of a *false* interpretation. Girard fails to comprehend exactly what the essential question of Camus's thoughts was at the time; the focus of Camus's contemplations touches upon the particular creativeness of *ressentiment* and poses the question: for what *reason* must Meursault die?

The Stranger kills a man and he is sentenced to public execution on the grounds of a specific interpretation of his deed. In *The Genealogy of Morals* (on 'Guilt, Bad Conscience and Related Matters'), Nietzsche writes that in the face of the murderous and fatal deed of one of their fellow men, the ancient Greeks could not conceive of any other *reason* for such an act than foolishness – 'Some god must have deluded him' (*GM*, II, 23). Nietzsche observes that the Greeks preferred to have their gods take the guilt of the terrible deed upon themselves, and leave the responsibility and punishment to the actor, rather than *think evil* of their peer.

In the beach scene that concludes the first part of *L'Étranger*, the Sun, with its oppressing heat and light, blinds the protagonist, who presses the trigger of the revolver that kills the Arab. Questioned by the Court on the reasons of his murderous deed, Meursault himself can only reply, not without being aware of his own ridiculousness, that 'c'était a cause du soleil (it was because of the sun)' (*E*, p. 201). His peers, however, prefer to think *evil* of him and exclude him from humanity rather than to preserve him from a guilt that casts aspersions on him as a 'criminal'.

Meursault is defined as a man who 'refuses to justify himself'.[41] As a matter of fact, Meursault does attempt to justify himself, but the reasons he presents as a means to account for his *act* are different from those that are applied to judge *him*. In the speeches of the Prosecutor and the defender, who silence and crush Meursault under the moral construction of his culpability (*E*, p. 198), the shift of focus from the deed to the doer is distinctive of the 'reason' of *ressentiment*; it is from the act that reason derives the criminal nature of the *evil*doer. The discourses of the investigating magistrate, of the prison chaplain and of the newspapers illustrate a form of interpretation or 'justification' of action, the roots of which Nietzsche locates in *ressentiment*; he also identifies this to be a *false* causal interpretation, founded on such paradoxical ideas and 'fat words' (*GM*, III, 16) as '*guilty* nature' or '*criminal* soul'.

As Abbou observes,[42] Camus had become acquainted with these procedures during his activity as a journalist for *Alger républicain* and *Soir républicain* in 1938–39. The articles of this period attest to the young author's deep concern for the systematic mystification of language in political trials, racial slogans, moralistic preaching and sermons, as well as in the use of delation and violence under the right-wing local government, not to mention the openly fascist and racist politics of the mayor of Algiers.[43] The question repeatedly arising in the articles of *Alger républicain* and *Soir républicain* and in *L'Étranger* is precisely that of the murderous power that 'fat words' have; in other words, of the relation between death and the fabrication of the *evil*doer. By reading Nietzsche, Camus sustains that the 'criminal soul' is the end product of a logical error or 'intellectual vice' (*A*, V, 543), which is the basis of the contemporary moral and political fanaticism. In the second part of *L'Étranger*, the construction of Meursault's culpability, as it is portrayed in the words of the investigating magistrate, fully illustrates this will or need to prove the point ('radical idealism').

In *L'Étranger*, Camus does not question the murderous action of his hero, but rather the mystifying or falsifying devaluation carried out by those, who are supposed to be his fellow men, and who judge *him* (rather than his deed) from the moral perspective of *ressentiment*.[44] The agent is negated the role of peer, and his actions are justified from the vertical top-down perspective of contempt and hatred that expunges him from humanity and relegates him to the position of being '*below the human condition*' (I, p. 588).

Camus demonstrates that he is perfectly aware of the intimate connection suggested by Nietzsche in *Aurore* and in *Genealogy of Morals*, that exists between despising reason, that thinks *evil* of man on the one hand, and, on the other, subjugation to the 'fatal' logic of utility, that reduces men to mere functions of their own social and political constructs. Meursault is caught in the implacable mechanism of capital execution, in the cogwheel of the mechanical rite of the guillotine (*E*, p. 204), *because* of his culpability, namely, because of that particular causal interpretation that justifies his deeds as those of an *evil*doer in the eyes of those who condemn him. The judgement of guilt activates a machine that leads the living human being to death with 'insolent certitude' (*E*, p. 205). The 'mathematic' and violent dimension of this certitude is the basis of the horror of capital execution (II, p. 871). Meursault expresses the feeling that there is a disproportion between the sentence, that declares the 'truth' of his annihilation, and the execution of the sentence, namely, the fabrication of a death that eliminates chance and turns him from being an agent (peer) into nothing more than a passive subject or *patient* (*E*, p. 206).[45]

Nonetheless, the abysmal certitude of death also gives way to liberation. Death deprives the condemned man of all hope or projection of his life into the 'future', thus giving him a freedom of action that goes beyond the illusory idea of 'free will': '[...] libre d'agir parce qu'empêché d'être ([one is] free to act because one has been prevented from being)' (I, p. 1200).[46] The condemned man turns towards his death much as a mystic turns toward God (I, p. 1199), stripping himself of the constructs of reason.[47] Camus conveys the climate of this particular liberation by drawing an analogy that he later incorporates in his essay on the Absurd (*MS*, p. 259): like the slaves of antiquity, who did not belong to themselves, the condemned man enjoys the freedom of 'not feeling responsible' (I, pp. 1200, 259). The figure of the ancient slave is not intended to be an apology of humility,[48] on the contrary, he is an example of a condition that bypasses the feelings of guilt and responsibility, which are *ressentiment*'s most refined creations.

With an emphasis on freedom of action, Camus rejects the false causal interpretation that couples the deed with a responsible doer (*GM*, I, 13), and in contraposition to the moral justification of the doer's guilt expressed by those who would condemn the doer, he affirms that *the deed is everything*. The 'divine availability' of a man condemned to death coincides with his 'incroyable désintéressement à l'égard de tout, sauf de la flamme pure de la vie (incredible disinterestedness towards anything except the pure flame of life)' (*MS*, p. 260); in other words, it coincides with the spiritual liberation from the nihilistic and utilitarian *telos* of rationalism. Death is seen to disclose an unprecedentedly intense and hateful 'pouvoir de vivre (power to live)' (I, p. 1200): it is no surprise that the extreme desire of the 'barbarian' Meursault is to be received on the day of his execution by a large crowd shouting at him with hate (*E*, p. 213).

René Girard rightly defines the Stranger as a nihilist in the sense of the word as it is expressed in *Le Mythe de Sisyphe*. *L'Étranger* is the story of a man who does not 'play the game'[49] of moral fanaticism and does not submit to the logic of modern rationalism, which governs the political discourses and the public sphere. Meursault does not allow for his passions to *demonstrate* anything and lives his private, solitary and sensual life in the margins of the false justifications of moral reason. He does not lie in the same way in which, according to Nietzsche's *Crépuscule des Idoles*, philosophical reason lies, and he dies because of the judgement of those who prefer the *idea* they made of him rather than who he simply *is* (II, p. 814).[50]

The Stranger recalls the 'men of knowledge' that Nietzsche speaks of in the concluding pages of *The Genealogy of Morals*; the philosopher refers to them as Antichrists and nihilists (*GM*, II, 24).[51] Meursault embodies an honest, harsh thought that pushes the desire for truth to the extreme negation of the false constructs of *ressentiment* – 'Nothing is true, everything is permitted' (*GM*, III, 24). He represents the 'ground zero' of the negation of moral or teleological reason, a 'mystic' liberation from radical idealism. As Camus declared in 1954, the Stranger does not embody the catastrophe of morality *tout court*, but of the fetishistic relationship that is the foundation of the contemporary moral and political fanaticism in the contemporary 'universe of trial', be that bourgeois, Nazi or Communist (I, p. 1269).

But the 'point zéro' is also the starting point of a new process that *L'Étranger* and *Mythe de Sisyphe* are specifically intended to illustrate (II, p. 952). As Camus writes in 1938, everything begins with indifference (I, p. 1201); negation dislocates the *theorein* of tradition and challenges the nihilistic concept of action of political philosophies, revealing the way to reach a greater complexity, an a-teleological 'perfection without reward' (II, p. 952). In September 1942 he designates this 'point zéro' as a *'good* nihilism' (I, p. 320) in order to distinguish it from the nihilistic logic of modern rationalism, that abases the living human being and reduces him to a valueless function, a powerless cog within a 'fatal' machine of power.[52] In *Soir républicain*, a few months after the outbreak of the Second World War, Camus explicitly links the war's frenetic action of total destruction ('collective suicide') to a widespread 'fatalist' or fetishistic relationship of men to 'le monde fermé et machinal que nous avons construit (the closed and automatic world that we have fabricated) (I, p. 1372).[53]

The displacement of philosophical reason liberates action from the 'romantic' constructs of *ressentiment* and the servile logic that submits life to the final objective. In an interview in 1945, Camus declared:

> Je ne suis pas un philosophe. Je ne crois pas assez à la raison pour croire à un système. Ce qui m'intéresse comment on peut se conduire. Et plus précisément, c'est de savoir comment il faut se conduire quand on ne croit ni en Dieu ni en la raison. (I am not a philosopher. I don't believe in reason enough to believe in a system. What interests me is to know how to behave. And, more precisely, to know how one can behave when one believes neither in God nor in reason.) (I, p. 1276)

5
Commencement of Freedom

Beauté, mon pire souci, avec la liberté.
(A. Camus, *Carnets* 1941)

In February 1941, Camus completed his three works on the 'Absurd', the novel *L'Étranger*, the philosophical essay *La Mythe de Sisyphe*, and the first version of the play *Caligula*, after which he noted in his *Carnets*: 'Commencements de la liberté. (Commencements of freedom.)' (II, p. 920.) The three protagonists of these works, Meursault, Sisyphus and Caligula, portray three different perspectives from which the author investigates the relationship that exists between freedom and the criticism of modern rationalism.

Commentators, who have declared 'Camus's limitations as a philosophical thinker' due to an alleged lack of precision in his consideration of the meaning and definition of reason in *Le Mythe de Sisyphe* (Willhoite 1968, p. 33), fail to grasp the crucial role that his earlier considerations on Plotinus' 'aesthetic' or 'Mystic Reason' and his criticism of the 'ethic' reasoning characteristic of the contemporary historicist doctrines have played in developing his absurd reasoning (*MS*, p. 252). I maintain that Camus develops his personal 'style' of thought, in particular, through the influence the readings of Nietzsche and Scheler had upon him, and he defines his own 'aesthetic' position in *Le Mythe de Sisyphe* by situating his reflection along the margins of modern nihilistic logic as well as along the margins of the categories of the philosophical political tradition.

As Maurice Blanchot observed in 1943, *Le Mythe de Sisyphe* should not be regarded as an 'ordinary book' (Blanchot 1943, p. 70), and its author engages in a far more demanding issue than simply analysing and explaining the period of time he lived in by enumerating the various ways of thinking and feeling that were developed during the early twentieth century (Blanchot 1943, p. 66).[1] Interviewing Camus in 1946, Dorothy Norman insists on Sisyphus' endless 'struggle *against logic*'[2] and places Camus's absurd reasoning, of which the mythic hero is the embodiment, in the margins of the Western rationalist tradition, which may be represented on one hand by Descartes and, on the other, by Kant's *Critiques*. In Blanchot's words, the absurd is engendered by the coherence and logic of our mental mechanisms (Blanchot 1943, p. 66), namely, by the rational aspiration towards reaching a unity that *slips away* from us ('se dérobe') (Blanchot 1943, p. 67). Thus, Sisyphus' *struggle with logic*, or the relationship between rational logic and absurd ('illogical') logic, is the crucial issue and it is this 'originality of the absurd' (Blanchot 1943, p. 67), that situates Camus's thought at the periphery of that which was commonly understood as nihilism in the contemporary sociological and political analyses.[3]

In the 1930s, Camus brings this issue into focus by meditating on Nietzsche's criticism of 'moral' reason. He uses the term 'logic' to refer specifically to the causal interpretation of reason, the straitjacket by means of which existence is apprehended and given a sense and direction (*telos*). Between 1938 and 1942, Camus reads the French editions of Nietzsche's *Crépuscule des Idoles* (*The Twilight of the Idols*), and *Humain, trop humain* (*Human, All Too Human*) published by Mercure de France, and Geneviève Bianquis's translation of *La Naissance de la philosophie à l'époque de la tragédie grecque* that is published by Gallimard in 1938.[4] As the inventories of his private library attest, he also owned three translations of the philosopher's collections of posthumous fragments published in France in the mid-1930s with the titles: *Œuvres posthumes* and *La Volonté de puissance*.[5] He had plausibly read these works by 1941.

Crépuscule des Idoles and *La Naissance de la philosophie à l'époque de la tragédie grecque*, in particular, prove to be essential to Camus in the formulation of the argument he presents in *Le Mythe de Sisyphe*; the readings and the influence they had over him help to shed light on the originality of the absurd and elucidate the meaning of Sisyphus' 'struggle against logic'. In Nietzsche's 1872 text on the pre-Socratic thinkers, Heraclitus of Ephesus offers us the example of a 'divine' way of thinking, an all-contemplating intuition that is opposed to reason's representation of reality through concepts and logical combinations (*NP*, p. 56). The Ephesian philosopher is portrayed as the champion of anti-rationalism, who rejects the principle of non-contradiction, and negates the notion of a permanent Being that is related to the logical principle A=A. Because of his affirmation regarding the unity of the opposites, Heraclitus is accused by Aristotle of 'crime against reason' (*NP*, p. 57) or against logic (*NP*, p. 83). Beyond the defined categories and causal connections characteristic of reason, the idea that being *is* activity reveals the terrifying and uncanny intuition of a unique reality endlessly becoming (*NP*, p. 58; Nietzsche 2006, p. 64).

Camus read *La Naissance de la philosophie à l'époque de la tragédie grecque* after *Ecce homo* and *Aurore*, and probably in the same period that he read *Crépuscule des Idoles*; between 1938 and 1941, Nietzsche's early pages on Heraclitus are likely to have captured Camus's attention[6] and to have been interpreted in light of the criticism of reason that the German philosopher expresses in his 1880s works, especially, of the metaphysical notion of free will and the related concepts of crime and guilt.

In *La Naissance de la philosophie*, Heraclitus is said to reclaim the world's innocence from the Anaximandrean interpretation, which identifies becoming with the guilty emancipation from the true, immortal and eternal Being, to which it must return by paying for its unjust crime (*hubris*) with death (*NP*, pp. 49–50). The Ephesian's 'divine' thinking sees the world outside the separations that are created by reason between being and action, and between the active will and passive matter, that found the *moral* interpretation of existence. His philosophy does not rest on the pessimistic judgement that man ought not to exist and suffering and death are the punishment for the crime he committed against immortal Being (*NP*, p. 49), nor does he feel compelled, like Leibniz, to *prove* that this is the best of worlds (theodicy) (*NP*, p. 69).

For Heraclitus, wisdom is expressed by the eternally living fire, the boy-god Aeon, who beautifully and innocently *plays*, builds and knocks down; thus, tragic wisdom is placed beyond the teleological constructions of philosophical reason. According to Nietzsche, Heraclitus sees existence with the eyes of an aesthetician and his *logos* may be understood as an Artist's view of the world (*NP*, pp. 67, 69). This 'aesthetic' perspective that Nietzsche detects in the Ephesian's thought bears striking affinities with Camus's own considerations on Plotinus' 'aesthetic' or mystic 'Reason',[7] and confirms the issues raised by Scheler's *L'homme du ressentiment*.

Bianquis's translation of the Nietzschean text on the pre-Socratics, however, adds one essential element, a fragment from Nietzsche's *Die vorplatonishen Philosophen*[8] and cited in a note, that must be taken into account in order to fully grasp the philosophical political implications of the position Camus elaborates in *Le Mythe de Sisyphe*. Nietzsche observes that modern commentators have failed to grasp the crucial point of the distance that separates Heraclitus from Anaxagoras, which

lies in two opposite models of intelligence: respectively, those of contemplative intelligence ('intelligence *contemplative*' or *logos*) and of
productive intelligence ('intelligence *ouvrière*' or *Nous*) (*NP*, p. 68 n. 1.
Nietzsche 2006, pp. 70–2).

In order to explain the Ephesian's thoughts regarding the Fire/*logos*
that eternally *plays* and *contemplates* the order created by its divine
activity, Nietzsche resorts to describing an artist's creative act. He distinguishes it from the activity of a worker or artisan, which he evokes
to express the mode in which the Anaxagorean *Nous* creates the cos-
mic teleological order. Thus, Nietzsche makes a distinction between
two different ways of conceiving the world's rationality. At the heart
of teleology, the German philosopher detects a *productive* intelligence
that interprets existence using the model of the worker's activity;
Anaxagoras' intelligence is the Will, a force that knows, sets goals,
moves and creates (*NP*, p. 68 n.1; Nietzsche 2006, p. 72). The opposition
between material and immaterial, between inert matter and a soul that
wants and submits the first in order to reach its ends (*NP*, p. 68 n. 1), is
instilled in productive intelligence, which, according to Nietzsche, was
introduced for the first time in philosophical thought by Anaxagoras'
theory and was bound to become dominant in the Platonic–Aristotelian
tradition of Western metaphysics.

In *La Naissance de la philosophie à l'époque de la tragédie grecque*,
Nietzsche formulates an intuition, the political implications of which
are fully expounded upon by Hannah Arendt in the late 1950s, according to which the Platonic philosophical understanding of thinking or
contemplation is 'taken from the realm of fabrication' (Arendt 1998,
p. 225). Productive intelligence sees the worker's creativity through to its
end[9] and interprets existence or Becoming by introducing a separation
between being and acting, between the material and the immaterial,
passive shapeless matter and active 'free' will. In *Crépuscule des Idoles*,
these considerations are further developed in the sections on '"Reason"
in philosophy' and 'The Four Great Errors', where Nietzsche attacks the
concept of a spiritual principle or Will, conceived to be the cause of
(and separated from) action, which founds the basis of the philosophical
notion of agent or 'Subject'.

The moral justification of existence in terms of crime, guilt, and punishment is possible only by introducing the separation, belonging to productive intelligence, between will and action. According to the author
of *La Naissance de la philosophie*, the Anaxagorean teleological cosmos
is the 'representation' of a productive intelligence, which is incorporated in the Platonic–Aristotelian concept of 'reason'. In *Crépuscule des*

Idoles, Heraclitus rejects the metaphysical notion of Being and the anti-nomy material–immaterial as 'fictions' of reason and refutes the causal ('moral') interpretation as reason's 'falsification' of becoming.

The relevant element, that the earlier work *La Naissance de la phi-losophie à l'époque de la tragédie grecque* adds to Nietzsche's 'immoralist' remarks, lies in his definition of Heraclitus' 'divine' mode of thought as one that is not moulded on the categories and utilitarian logic of productive intelligence, but rather is understood in terms of aesthetic contemplation and judgement. The German philosopher resorts to the use of the analogy of the artist's activity as opposed to that of the manual worker in order to grasp the Ephesian's mode of thinking. Just as an artist is outside and above his work when he meditates, he is inside and one with his work when he creates; similarly, conflict and harmony come together in the Heraclitean Boy-God's endless game of destructions and (re)constructions (*NP*, p. 67).

In the 'aesthetic' justification of becoming, the 'drive to play' replaces the (moral) notion of *hubris*, which Nietzsche interprets to mean 'crime' and to be a sign of the presence of a teleological viewpoint that is alien to Greek thought before Anaxagoras. Heraclitus' *logos* is an artist's point of view (*NP*, p. 69): analogously to the genesis of a work of art, the conflict of a plurality (*polemos*) carries a *law* and a *right* within itself. This immanent *Dike* displaces the dominion of the will, which violently submits matter to a finality and form that is external and foreign to it, and replaces the notion of *organisation*, which belongs to fabrication, with the endless contemplation of the artist-creator.

Nietzsche observes that ancient wisdom (*sagesse*) consists in think-ing with contemplative intelligence, therefore, it rejects the productive intelligence that governs the worker's activity. Wisdom must not be confused with the Aristotelian notion of 'prudence' (*phronesis*), which is submitted to the utilitarian logic of a calculating reason (*NP*, p. 47); it coincides with the Artist's perspective, or ecstatic intuition of the *logos* (*NP*, p. 69), that simply knows *without calculating* (*NP*, p. 75). Thus, con-templation is not understood in the Platonic sense of *theorein*, namely, as the 'vision' of teleological reason that organises action as a means to obtain the final accomplishment of the end.[10]

Nietzsche identifies the Heraclitean notion of 'play' (*jeu*/ παιδιά) as being one of the highest examples of mystic ideas that is to be found beyond the confines established by the utilitarian logic of reason. Furthermore, by detecting the expression of Greek 'agonal' thought (from Gk. *agōn*, 'contest') in his 'illogic' notion of unity of the opposites, Nietzsche asso-ciates Heraclitus' 'aesthetic' perspective with a way of envisioning action that belongs to the ancient Greek political life (*NP*, p. 60). In another passage, devoted to the philosophy of Thales, Nietzsche connects the ancient notion of wisdom to the faculty of taste – the wise man is *sapiens*, 'one who tastes' (from Gk. *sapio*, 'to taste') and *sisyphos*, '[a man] of sharp taste' (*NP*, p. 46; Nietzsche 2006, p. 8). Opposed to the 'tasteless' science that is subordinate to the logic of utility and to the prudential calculation of one's interests, wisdom denotes a 'divine' or futile (*inutile*) knowledge free from the utilitarian 'servile' logic of reason.

It is no surprise that between September 1940 and February 1941 Camus chooses to entitle his essay on the Absurd *Sisyphus*[11] (II, p. 920). I have demonstrated that the rejection of *telos* and of the 'servile' logic of reason is a crucial issue for the formation of Camus's position between 1935 and 1939, from his lyrical essays to *DES* (see Chapters 3 and 4). The essay on the Absurd, which he begins to work on in 1938 and completes in 1941, specifically explores the emancipation of thought that is bound by the nihilistic teleocratic 'logic' of reason. In *Le Mythe de Sisyphe*, the commencement of freedom is placed under the category of 'futility'.

Sisyphus or Happiness in Hell[12]

In the Greek myth, on which Camus dwells in the last section of his 1942 essay, Sisyphus is condemned to ceaselessly push a rock to the top of a mountain whence it rolls back down of its own weight. This 'prolétaire des dieux (proletarian of the gods)', and 'travailleur inutile des Enfers (futile labourer of the Underworld)' is described by Homer as the *wisest* of mortals (*MS*, p. 301). Camus, like Nietzsche in *La Naissance de la philosophie à l'époque de la tragédie grecque*, associates wisdom with futility, in other words, with the emancipation from the utilitarian logic of reason. The mythic figure embodies the divine or 'aesthetic' viewpoint of the wise *sisyphos* (*MS*, p. 303), when, descending towards his endless torment, he contemplates it.[13] Looking back over his life, his memory's eye creates his own fate by unifying the series of unrelated actions that occurred during his existence in an artwork that is sealed by death (*MS*, p. 304). Like Oedipus, the tragic hero is *a blind man eager to see and yet knows that the night has no end* (*MS*, p. 304); contemplation dissolves the 'idols' of reason (*MS*, p. 303) and culminates in a judgement: 'All is well'.

Sisyphus' contemplation does not coincide with a redemptory vision of life, but rather with a mystic or 'aesthetic' liberation of thought from the dominion of *telos*; from this world it drives out a god, who has come into it with dissatisfaction and a preference for futile sufferings

(*MS*, p. 303). In Nietzsche's posthumous fragments and writings of the 1880s, dissatisfaction and the preference for futile sufferings are the sign of *ressentiment* and the negative judgement this has upon the world, in which reason's remedies, the 'false' constructs, hopes and moral justification of existence are rooted. In Camus's essay, the absurd man 'says *yes*' (*MS*, p. 304), which refers more to a way of thinking or taking things into account that is beyond *ressentiment* than the act of consenting *to* something. By judging that all is well, the wise man refuses to accept the negative 'moral' judgement that is typical of moral reason.[14]

In contemplation, the wise 'absurd' man (*sisyphos*) is emancipated from petty utilitarian logic ('the images of earth') (*MS*, p. 303) and from the fetishistic submission of life to the constructs of reason, of which Sisyphus' rock is the metaphoric representation. From a teleological perspective, *use*less and *hope*less work (*MS*, p. 301) is the most dreadful of punishments; but, in Sisyphus' infernal torment, teleology is dislocated. As Maurice Blanchot notes, with the work he does, the tragic hero illustrates the *opposite* of work itself, he is representing an activity that is *the contrary* of action (Blanchot 1943, p. 66). The mythic hero is a futile worker, the tragic 'illogical' figure of usefulness-and-uselessness. Like the contemporary workman, Sisyphus works at the same repetitive task without end and leads to no final accomplishment;[15] his entire being is exerted towards accomplishing nothing (*MS*, p. 302).

Camus's reconstruction of Sisyphus' torment brings to mind Nietzsche's criticism of the 'enslavement' of the modern workers, whose activity is regarded as a mere function of an economic system (capitalism) that is supported by the 'nihilistic' logic of contemporary rationalism (*A*, III, 206).[16] The workers submit their own activity and life to the category of *use/utility*, which then determines their 'price' within the utilitarian 'machine'. The author of *Le Mythe de Sisyphe* resorts to the term 'tragic' to distinguish the absurd man from the modern slave and to associate the particular contemplation of *sisyphos* with liberation from the nihilistic teleology of what Nietzsche calls the 'worker's intelligence'. When Blanchot writes that Sisyphus' activity is the contrary of action itself, he is drawing attention to the displacement of the traditional fabricative concept of action, understood as execution of the 'idea'. The absurdity of the workers' infernal torment lies in the fact that, in the contemporary nihilistic assembly line, the final achievement of their action *slips from them*. This which gives rise to the suffering of the agent and, therefore, his/her torment, is not the endlessness or futility of the action in and of itself, but rather the logic according to which s/he values his/her activity and life; in other words, the displacement or slipping away (*se dérober*) of the end – on the metaphysical level (loss of Truth), as well as on the practical level (alienation) – is a *problem* only from the perspective of productive logic and within a teleological model of action.

This is precisely what Camus writes in the draft of a preface to *Le Mythe de Sisyphe* in 1942: modern intelligence suffers from nihilism, namely, from the withering away of the Truth or foundation ('end'), because it cannot come to terms with absurdity, which exposes the fetishistic belief in the objectiveness and transcendence of these 'creations' of human thought. The contemporary slipping away of the end calls the *logic* of the Western tradition radically into question (II, p. 948). The solution to so-called European Nihilism can only consist in stepping out of teleology and the fabricative model of action, rather than resorting to the 'old solutions' that are still etched in the nihilistic logic of philosophical political tradition. Like Georges Bataille, Camus detects a connection between the category of 'use' and the modern nihilistic 'servitude' of human activity and life to the despotic dominion of *telos*.[17]

As Blanchot also observes, *Le Mythe de Sisyphe* may be read as a survey of the various viewpoints on the loss of Truth or the 'end' in the twentieth century; there is more to the essay than that, however. *Le Mythe* is an essay on the absurd rather than on absurdity (*MS*, p. 217), and an essay on freedom. More precisely, it is an attempt to define free thought and action beyond the confines of Western utilitarian logic.

Although it is developed around the negation of reason's meanings and ends, *Le Mythe de Sisyphe* is also a book that 'says *yes*'. Sisyphus represents the 'illogical rule' (II, p. 817) of the tragic unity of the contraries: an action that is the contrary of an action, work that is the opposite of work (Blanchot 1943, p. 66). As Camus notes, this myth is tragic because its hero is 'conscious' (*MS*, p. 302); the lucidity ('clairvoyance'), from which the wise man's silent joy stems (*MS*, p. 303), is the sign of the 'aesthetic perspective' in the sense of Heraclitus' 'divine' contemplative intelligence in Nietzsche's *La Naissance de la philosophie à l'époque de la tragédie grecque*, that goes beyond reason's negative judgement upon the world and its teleological solutions.

In defining the domain of the absurd as the domain of 'non-knowledge' ('*non-savoir*') (Blanchot 1943, p. 71), Blanchot draws attention to the affinity between the philosophical investigations of Georges Bataille and Albert Camus. The Bataillan term 'Non-Savoir' links the notion of tragic to a revolt against the world of labour and against the enslavement of man to the economy of use/end, that is expressed in the ordinary language and logic of the present (Morot-Sir 1982, p. 106). Both Camus and Bataille show themselves to be deeply influenced by Nietzsche's criticism of language, that is understood to be the 'crystallisation' of the teleocratic logic of reason, upon which the contemporary moral, economic and political systems are founded.

In particular, Camus's criticism of rationalism in *Le Mythe de Sisyphe* openly recalls Nietzsche's argument on '"Reason" in philosophy' in *Crépuscule des Idoles*, and, especially, his thesis of a relationship between language and philosophical reason, namely, between traditional logic and the fetishistic belief that a doer or 'ego' that intentionally *causes* a deed exists. In Nietzsche's posthumously published fragments that Camus reads in the two French editions of *La Volonté de Puissance*, this fetishistic relationship is the basis for the false theory of a 'free will', as well as the naïf psychological view of the will as the 'cause' of man's actions. Moreover, in the pages of *La Naissance de la philosophie à l'époque de la tragédie grecque*, this causal interpretation, based on the worker's teleological activity, ties together the metaphysics of Being and the logical principle of non-contradiction.

Nietzsche sees, in the fetishistic enslavement to reason of the modern 'last men', the question of nihilism primarily as a problem of language. Our grammar, concepts and logical connections are the product of reason's *use* or moral interpretation of the experience of absurdity; it is no surprise that, as Edouard Morot-Sir observes, both Camus and Bataille excel in the art of writing the essay, that is to say, in a 'discourse that is *against discourse*' (Morot-Sir 1982, p. 108, my italics). I suggest that the author of *Le Mythe de Sisyphe* is perfectly aware that the a-teleological viewpoint of the absurd needs to be expressed in a different language,[18] one that is closer to the mystical forms of Oriental thought than to the abstract conceptual formulas of the philosophical tradition of the West (*NP*, VII, XI). Before dwelling on the 'crime' against Aristotelian logic and philosophical reason that is perpetrated by Heraclitus' *logos* and his 'mystical' unity of the contraries, Camus had meditated on Plotinus' style of thought (*DES*, p. 1041). Like the Hellenic thinker, who resorts to metaphors to express a 'mystic Reason' that exists beyond the limits imposed by the Gnostics' teleological reason, Camus thinks in images[19] and writes essays that are 'metaphor from one end to the other' (Audin 1985; Audin 1991, p. 13). In *Le Mythe de Sisyphe*, the complex metaphoric constellation of the Absurd demands slow 'rumination' and constant re-evaluation from the reader.

In the 1942 essay, Camus attempts to radically call philosophical language into question and to think past the fetishistic pitfalls typical of rational logic. Metaphors displace the 'closed' concepts of traditional philosophical thought and 'struggle' with the principle of non-contradiction, evoking the 'slipping away' of truth or the end that is unveiled by absurdity. 'Le sentiment de l'absurdité au détour de n'importe quelle rue peut frapper à la face de n'importe quel homme. Tel quel, dans la nudité désolante, [...] il est insaisissable. (At any street corner the feeling of absurdity can strike any man in the face. As it is, in its distressing nudity, [...] it is elusive.)' (*MS*, p. 226; Camus 1960, p. 16.) Yet, the feeling of absurdity is not the absurd. This last denotes an 'attitude de l'esprit (attitude of the mind)' (*MS*, p. 227) that sheds its distinct light upon the world, namely, one that displaces teleology and replaces the *moral* justification of reason with that which in Nietzschean terms is called an 'aesthetic justification' of existence.[20] The 'originality of the absurd' (Blanchot 1943, p. 67) lies in the effort of defining free thought and action in the margins or beyond the limits of the Western philosophical language and logic.

In *Le Mythe de Sisyphe*, the feeling of absurdity, for instance, of a man confronted with death, begins a process of 'liberation' (*MS*, p. 259) that culminates in the tragic consciousness of the wise man (*sisyphos*). Around 1938, Camus reads Nietzsche's *Crépuscule des Idoles* and meditates on the relationship that exists between freedom and death and that is grasped in the notion of 'conscious death'.[21] As the end 'slips away' from reason, the absurdity of death dissolves the hierarchies and the notion of 'free will' (*MS*, p. 258), which Nietzsche traces back to the teleological model of 'productive intelligence'.[22]

The consciousness of absurdity reveals the possibility that one may reach beyond logic; it coincides with the artist's perspective of the ancient *sisyphos* that rejects teleology and 'says *yes*', restoring the majesty of life beyond the impoverishment of nihilism and the depreciation that occurs with 'moral' justification of existence (*MS*, p. 256). To the negative judgement that is characteristic of *ressentiment*, Camus opposes the positive judgement of Sophocles' blind Oedipus, 'All is well' (*MS*, p. 303).

The author links ancient wisdom to modern heroism and introduces the example of Kirilov to illustrate this connection. Dostoyevsky's character of *The Possessed* also concludes that 'All is well', and his argument elucidates the absurd man's a-teleological perspective: 'If God does not exist, *I am god*' (*MS*, p. 292, my italics). If the transcendent principle of Platonic–Christian metaphysics (God/Being/Truth) does not exist, it cannot be a matter of filling the (empty) space of the Master/Creator. To be *god* is to evade the servile logic of productive intelligence and to acquire the 'divine' aesthetic perspective of contemplative intelligence.

Kirilov fancies that Jesus, at his death, did not find himself in Paradise. Were Christ to have to endure his time on the cross without end, his torment would be *useless*; the Christ would be tortured for nothing, just as is Sisyphus and each victimised and crucified human being (*MS*, p. 293). Jesus' *end*less divinity disrupts the traditional notion of God that belongs to the fabricative model of thought. Kirilov does not identify divinity with the *God*-man of Western tradition, but rather with a *perfect* man or man-*god*, where perfection is not understood in teleological terms, but in the 'aesthetic' terms of a 'perfection *without reward*' (II, p. 952, my italics) that is free from the servitude of achievement and from the crime/punishment logic of *moral* reason. The Passion, which without the Redemption of Kirilov's man-*god* is literally *use*less, challenges the teleological model of metaphysical thought, on which the vertical relationship of dominion (master/slave) and the political concept of power are founded.

Existing beyond the utilitarian logic of productive intelligence, the perfect man embraces the artist's divine and immanent perspective, which perceives beauty to be in the innocent 'game' of creation, rather than in the final execution of the act that will lead to reaching the final objective. From his a-teleological perspective, all work, whether it be conquest, love or artistic creation, may very well *not be* (*MS*, p. 299). Tragic 'divine' thought rejects the concept of Being, the idea that 'I am', as well as the individual's 'freedom *to be*' (*MS*, p. 258); these are rational postulates that ground the moral belief in an active will, that, like a worker, freely directs and organises his deeds and life in view of the realisation of pre-defined objectives. Sisyphus' infernal torment emphasises the eternity of futile and endless work in the present.

From *Noces* to *Le Mythe de Sisyphe*, hell symbolises the temporal dimension of the suffering flesh that exists beyond the metaphysical constructions of moral and political philosophy ('Being', 'free will', 'self', 'subject'). Strictly speaking, the absurd action is not a form of production, but an ephemeral creation 'sans lendemains (without tomorrows)' (*MS*, p. 255), that is to say, a creation that evades the vision ('theory') of teleological or anticipatory reasoning projected upon the future. Thus, the negative thought that inspires the absurd creative attitude coincides with an *ascesis* (*MS*, p. 297) that lies beyond the bounds of teleology. The difficult wisdom of the absurd creator, who works and creates *for nothing* (*MS*, p. 297), resides in the simultaneous performance of two tasks: negating and magnifying. Rejecting the moral justification of philosophical reason, the absurd man, like the Heraclitean *sisyphos* in *La Naissance de la philosophie à l'époque de la tragédie grecque*, refuses such concepts as 'immortality', 'sin' and 'guilt'; he magnifies the innocence and beauty of the world and of human action beyond the straitjacket of *telos*. The absurd creator embodies the 'divine' availability of a man without recourse, who feels innocent, and the irreparable innocence of his existence *permits him to do everything* (*MS*, p. 255). The 'aesthetic' viewpoint of Oedipus, Sisyphus, and Kirilov culminates in the words of Ivan Karamazov, 'Everything is permitted' (*MS*, p. 294), that is to say, in nihilism.[23]

Nothing is possible, everything is permitted

In August 1938, Camus notes in his *Carnets* that the only possible freedom is a freedom in the face of death.[24] A truly free man chooses to accept all of the consequences associated with death, including the revaluation of all traditional values of life. Ivan Karamazov's 'Everything is permitted', he adds, is the only expression of a '*consistent* freedom' (II, p. 857, my italics), but only on the condition that one gets to the bottom of the formula. This is precisely what he attempts to do in the chapter on 'Absurd Freedom' in *Le Mythe de Sisyphe*.

The continuity between his 1938 writings and his investigation on the absurd is confirmed by a series of terms that situate Camus's exploration of 'absurd freedom' beyond the bounds of traditional conceptual analyses – 'the hell of the present'; the retreat of abstract evidence in the face of lyricism; and the '*transfiguration*' of spiritual conflicts that become embodied and recover 'l'abri misérable et magnifique du cœur de l'homme (the miserable and magnificent shelter of man's heart)' (*MS*, p. 255; Camus 1960, p. 46). The author resorts to the Nietzschean term 'transfiguration' to denote a change in the way reality is interpreted that liberates thought from the servile prejudices and common rules of discursive reason, just as the reference to the mystics also confirms (*MS*, p. 259).

Camus follows in the footsteps of Nietzsche's *Crépuscule des Idoles* and his aphorisms in *La Volonté de Puissance* on nihilism, and relates the absurd or 'consistent' freedom and the 'transfiguration' of values that this freedom entails to the negation of the existence of a true 'objective' knowledge. 'All thought is anthropomorphic' (*MS*, p. 231):[25] to understand the world is to imprint it with the unifying categories or artifices of reason (*MS*, p. 231) that 'divert' the eye and mind from the painful vision of a strange inhuman world by introducing a familiar order made *in the image of reason*. Echoing the Nietzschean criticism of Cartesianism (*VPI*, II, 88, 98), Camus also rejects the illusion of the 'self', conceived of as a unitary internal being that is subject to[26] or the *cause* of thoughts (*MS*, p. 232). Thus, he displaces the starting point of modern philosophy and refuses the psychology of the so-called 'objective mind' (*MS*, p. 225). The idea of a 'free will' or 'soul', capable of directing one's actions and life in view of pre-defined ends or of a future realisation (*MS*, p. 258), is a postulate of reason that separates being from action and creates a 'false' causal connection between single unrelated phenomena (*MS*, p. 232).

The problem with the teleological interpretation of reason is that that which is traditionally called 'freedom' coincides with the enslavement of human life and actions to the achievement of the final end or objective. The modern man is a slave to the illusion of a 'free will', and this illusion binds him to a logic of *utility* and achievement (*MS*, p. 258), thus reducing his life to a mechanism or a mere function in the rational chain of means and ends. To take the metaphysical concept of freedom seriously is to generate 'fonctionnaires de l'esprit et du cœur (bureaucrats of the mind and the heart)' (*MS*, p. 259; Camus 1960, p. 51); in *Crépuscule des Idoles*, these last are called 'perfect men', but it should be noted that Nietzsche's 'perfect men' are the opposite of Kirilov's 'perfect-man' (*MS*, p. 293).

Camus, clearly influenced by his readings of Nietzsche, ties the question of freedom to the question of God – 'Savoir si l'homme est libre commande qu'on sache *s'il peut avoir un maître*. (To know whether or not man is free requires that one know *whether man can have a master or not*.)' (*MS*, p. 257, Camus 1960, p. 49, my italics.) The question is not about knowing whether man has a master, in other words, whether or not God is dead, but rather whether he can have one at all; thus, it is a question of *logic*.

La Naissance de la philosophie à l'époque de la tragédie grecque and *Crépuscule des Idoles* bring to Camus's attention the relationship that exists between the fetishistic enslavement of modern men and the vertical structure of dominion of the master/will over the slave/matter as a relationship that is inherent to the fabricative logic of thought and action of philosophical reason. In *Le Mythe de Sisyphe*, the Absurd designates an 'aesthetic' or tragic way of thinking that lies beyond productive logic, which is introduced along with the fiction of an objective Being or truth by reason's teleological interpretation of the world. In the formula 'Nothing is true, everything is permitted' (*VPII*, III, 108–9), extreme negation does not consist in the affirmation that the space of the transcendent principle is empty ('God is dead'[27]), that the post of master of creation is left vacant, and, therefore, is there for man to assume the position. The 'slipping away' of the end calls the fabricative logic that lies at the core of reason's interpretation of reality and the 'servile' fetishistic submission of man to his own creations into question. Beyond the limits of *telos*, the question of whether man has a master or whether man is the master can no longer be asked. Therefore, extreme negation, and the only consistent freedom possible, can only occur when one *steps outside* of the vertical relationship of dominion that exists between the master and the slave.

For Camus, no true knowledge is possible (*MS*, p. 233); lucid thought evades the belief in the objectiveness of an artifice, by means of which, for centuries, men have apprehended not the world in and of itself, but the projections and forms of the world that their own reason has introduced ('fetishism') (*MS*, p. 229).[28] Reason is an 'instrument' of thought for the purpose of anaesthetics (*MS*, p. 252) and a specific mode of interpreting the world. Camus uses the term 'reason' to refer to all forms of teleological thinking, from habit to logic, science and philosophy that bestow a direction ('*sens*') upon life through the fabrication of stage-scenery to mask the density and strangeness of the world and to heal the anxiety and suffering of a senseless existence with hope (*MS*, p. 231).

Therefore, Camus writes to Francis Ponge, in 1943, and asserts that the feeling of absurdity is the 'dying world' (I, p. 887), namely, the retreat of reason's moral interpretation of the world: 'ce divorce entre l'homme et sa vie, l'acteur et son décor, c'est proprement le sentiment de l'absurdité (this divorce between man and his life, the actor and his setting, is precisely the feeling of absurdity' (*MS*, p. 223). The feeling of absurdity does not coincide with the negation of the world, but rather with the retreat of the '*dying* world', in other words, of teleology.[29] The metaphor of 'divorce' reshapes the negative acceptation of the term 'absurdity', which in the common understanding of the word is associated with sheer non-sense or loss of (rational) meaning (Audin 1991, p. 19). Absurdity dissolves the causal connections typical of teleological thought and its appearance coincides with the retreat or 'slipping away' of the 'reason *to* live' that, like a 'screen' or 'stage-set', conceals the senselessness of life. The feeling of absurdity coincides with the negation of the objectiveness of these creations ('settings'), by means of which men have made the world familiar (*MS*, p. 223).

The theatrical metaphor, which introduces the argument in the first chapter of *Le Mythe de Sisyphe*, plays a crucial part in Camus's 1942 essay. As a matter of fact the first element to be treated metaphorically is not the absurd, but suicide (Audin 1991, p. 16): 'Se tuer, dans un sens, et *comme au mélodrame*, c'est avouer. C'est avouer qu'on est dépassé par la vie ou qu'on ne la comprend pas. (In a sense, and *as in a melodrama*, killing yourself amounts to confessing. It is confessing that life is too much for you or that you do not understand it.)' (*MS*, pp. 222–3, my italics.) To commit suicide, Camus adds, is to confess that life is not worth living. The unexpected comparison with melodrama, traditionally used to refer to a degenerate form of tragic theatre, identifies suicide with a magniloquent and inauthentic act (Audin 1991, p. 16).

Camus's use of this theatrical metaphor is unexpected but not unwarranted. In a posthumous fragment dated 1888, and published in the first volume of *La Volonté de Puissance* (*VPI*, I, 249), Nietzsche also resorts to the metaphoric constellation of theatre to refer to the notion of free will and its relation with the feeling of power. The German philosopher dismisses the concept of freedom of Western metaphysics as a 'theatrical attitude' that is based on the assumption of the will as the active *cause* of perfection, namely, on a 'false' construction or a fiction created by reason. Nietzsche's use of the theatrical metaphor in the posthumous aphorisms – it is more than likely that Camus read *Volonté de Puissance* in the late 1930s – sheds essential light on the argument presented in *Le Mythe de Sisyphe*. Through the image of 'melodrama' the act of taking one's life is associated with the causal interpretation of reason, in particular, with the fiction of a free agent, who is capable of intentionally causing his thoughts and acts. Suicide is the confession that life is too much for the agent, that s/he cannot understand it and, therefore, 'it is not worth the trouble' (*MS*, p. 223). The theatrical metaphor emphasises the teleological or fabricative model of thinking and acting that lies at the core of this notion, and underlines the fictional character of the idea of a free subject, capable of directing his/her life towards the achievement of prefigured ends as sheer illusion.

In the opening lines of *Le Mythe de Sisyphe*, suicide is defined as the only truly serious *philosophical* problem (*MS*, p. 221). Camus proves to be concerned primarily with the logic that is involved in the act of taking one's life. The theatrical metaphor anticipates the answer to the pivotal question that is posed in the essay: does death follow any particular logic (*MS*, p. 225)? Traditionally understood as an extreme act of individual freedom, suicide is etched into and is a part of the texture of teleology, thus, it is inserted into a context of 'servile' logic. The agent prefers to will *nothing* than not to will anything at all, namely, to intentionally put an end to his life whenever it does not satisfy the objectives, values and expectations of the anticipating subject. Thus, behind the illusion of freedom, the suicidal act exposes the fetishistic enslavement of man to the end(s) or objectives dictated by teleology, and confirms rather than invalidates the fabricative model of thought and action that, as its logical consequence, culminates in the annihilation of life.

It follows that the other question, whether the absurd *commands* death (*MS*, p. 225), can only be answered negatively. Camus places absurd thought beyond the limits and *against* the dominant way of thinking ('royal road') of reason (*MS*, p. 235). He cites Zarathustra to define an 'aesthetic' perspective that frees the world from its servitude to an eternal will/master and restores the innocence and ancient nobility of the world by rejecting reason's moral justifications. It is no surprise that Camus relates the absurd to contradiction, antinomy, anguish or impotence that evoke Heraclitus' innocent universe *outside* the straitjacket of teleological thinking in *La Naissance de la philosophie à l'époque de la tragédie grecque*. The affinity he has with the Heraclitean 'aesthetic' perspective is confirmed by the three metaphors he uses to define the absurd in the first part of *Le Mythe de Sisyphe*:

> L'absurde est essentiellement un divorce. [...] l'absurde n'est pas dans l'homme (si une pareille métaphore pouvait avoir un sens), ni dans le monde, mais dans leur présence commune. Il est pour le moment le seul lien qui les unisse. [...] La singulière trinité qu'on met ainsi à jour n'a rien d'une Amérique soudain découverte. (The absurd is essentially a divorce. [...] the absurd is not in man (if such a metaphor could have a meaning) nor in the world, but in their presence together. For the moment, it is the only bond uniting them. [...] The singular trinity that is brought to light in this way has nothing to do with the sudden discovery of America.)' (*MS*, pp. 239–40)

Camus's notion of Absurd displaces the categories of traditional logic, as well as the 'objective' viewpoint of reason. The Absurd cannot be conceived of as an entity or a fact that can be conquered by reason just as the continents of America in the fifteenth century were conquered by the European explorers. The analogy suggests that the Absurd evades the metaphysics of Being and the correspondence theory of truth of philosophical reason. Camus associates absurd thought to the 'aesthetic' viewpoint of the wise man (*sisyphos*) and situates the Absurd beyond the confines set in place by teleology, thus, he places the 'divorce'/'bond' between man and the world outside and against the traditional dualisms of rational thought.

The Absurd may be conceived of in the sense of Heraclitus' *Logos*, namely, as a *relation*.[30] In another passage, Camus defines this distinct negative relation ('divorce') as the contradiction that binds the desire for unity and achievement of human thought and the singularising retreat of the world together (*MS*, p. 253).[31] Camus, in the second part of

Le Mythe de Sisyphe, significantly refers to the figure of the play-actor to illustrate this specific contradiction *in existentia* (*MS*, p. 275). The actor's body carries the tragic knowledge of its limit, where human aspiration to achieve and live every possible experience encounters its mortal refutation. A monotone single model that is passed on from hero to hero, the body of the play-actor is the illogical *one-and-many* and the living negation of the philosophical concept of Being (*MS*, p. 274).

Although Camus acknowledges thetic aspiration as being constitutive of thought (*MS*, p. 231), this nostalgia for unity and clarity *does not prove* that a unifying immutable principle (i.e. Parmenides' One) actually *exists*. The absurd 'honest' thought refuses to draw such conclusion and steps outside the boundaries posed by traditional logic, of which the Aristotelian syllogism is the representation. The absurd rejects the causal justification of reason that attempts to 'leap' over the wall of absurdity by deducing the existence of the true Being or Principle from the human desire for immutability and truth.[32] In the fifth book of *Aurore*, the logical connection that is made between passion and truth is denounced by Nietzsche as a 'vice of the intellect' that culminates in the victory of the 'sanctified lies' of moral fanaticism (*A*, V, 543). I suggest that Camus's effort to define an absurd way of thinking that reaches beyond the logic of reason is closely related to the criticism of what Nietzsche calls contemporary 'radical idealism'. His 1938 notebooks and the novel *L'Étranger* attest to his early concern for the generalised 'volonté de prouver' (desire to prove), that forms the basis of reason's moral justification of existence and is detected by Nietzsche in contemporary political radicalism (see Chapter 4). According to Camus, the methodological question 'What does that prove?' embodies the essential movement of absurd thought (*MS*, p. 294).

These considerations allow us to further define the absurd 'struggle against logic' (II, p. 676) as a struggle against moral and political fanaticism. The moment it is recognised, absurdity is the most harrowing of passions (*MS*, p. 234), but it *proves* nothing. Camus's argument against the intellectual leap or 'philosophical suicide' of 'universal, practical or moral reason' (*MS*, p. 233) clearly recalls Nietzsche's criticism of the 'false' argument ('radical idealism') which derives the reality of one's opinion or idea from the intensity of one's belief in it (*CI*, 'The 'Improvers' of Mankind', 1). Moreover, the author of *Le Mythe de Sisyphe* is aware of the relationship that is outlined by Nietzsche, in *Crépuscule des Idoles* and in his posthumous writings, between reason's moral justification of existence, which interprets life by submitting it to its utilitarian logic, and the negative judgement that human reason bestows upon the world and man. Camus does not ignore the political implications of this negative judgement on which the moral aspiration to change both by making them *better* is founded; his teacher individuated this ambition in contemporary power politics, particularly, in the right- and left-wing ideological claims to revolution.

As early as 1936, in his essays on political orthodoxy, Jean Grenier had called attention to the totalitarian aspiration to completely *transform* man.[33] In his 1942 essay and then again in the articles he wrote for *Combat*, Camus takes a strong position against the contemporary voluntarisms of his time and replaces the teleological concept of *transformation* with the 'superhuman' effort of the absurd consciousness to *transfigure* existence (*MS*, p. 297). Absurd thought rejects *telos* and with it the forms of domination (master/slave) inherent to the fabricative model of thinking and acting that philosophical reason has incorporated and introduced into the world (*VPII*, III, 111). To get to the bottom of Ivan Karamazov's 'Everything is permitted' is, precisely, to negate those forms of dominion and consider them 'settings' or 'fictions' of reason, the logic of which necessarily implies the '*use*ful' transformation of man and world. To get to the bottom of the formula also requires that the body, affection, creation or action and human nobility are *transfigured* (*MS*, p. 255), namely, that they are interpreted anew and beyond the bounds of traditional ('nihilistic') utilitarian logic.

The absurd introduces the contradictory or 'illogical' notion of *use*less action. The absurd conqueror declares: 'Il n'y a qu'une action utile, celle qui referait l'homme et la terre. Je ne referai jamais les hommes. (There is but one useful action, that of remaking man and the earth. I shall never remake men.)' (*MS*, p. 279.) After defining an absurd or 'aesthetic' way of thinking that reaches past the limits set by teleology in the first part of *Le Mythe de Sisyphe*, Camus devotes the following pages on the absurd man to illustrate an *action-that-is-not-action*, in other words, an action that evades both the servitude to the final objective and the use that characterise the traditional fabricative model. Absurd thought is 'sterile' (*MS*, p. 267); it negates fetishistic submission to the logic of productivity, which is incorporated in ordinary language and modes of thinking. This allows the author to affirm the primacy of action over the moral interpretation of reason, which submits action to 'free will'.

The absurd 'negative thought' recovers the divine availability of human thought and action (*MS*, p. 258) that exists outside the categories of the philosophical political tradition. In *Le Mythe de Sisyphe*, Camus reinterprets the traditional notions of action, freedom, and happiness from an a-teleological perspective and outside the categories imposed by the fabricative model of the Will/demiurge. I propose that we attempt to understand the emphasis Camus places on the effort (II, p. 849), tenacity (*MS*, p. 226), and courage to live without appeal in the absurd 'waterless deserts' without hope (*MS*, p. 225), in an extra-moral 'agonal'[34] sense that is consistent with the 'aesthetic' perspective of the absurd. The absurd replaces the violent manipulation of the worker and his teleological 'at last' with the 'once more' (repetition) of the artist's effort or the athlete's discipline (*MS*, p. 267); the moral category of improvement of the teleological ethics of quality is replaced with the notion of repetition, which is the basis of the absurd ethics of quantity – absurd men do not strive to be *better* and different (*MS*, p. 282).[35] The absurd liberates action from the master/slave relationship of dominion that is intrinsic to the teleological model of reason and (dis) places human conduct, moving it beyond the reach of *dictated* traditional morality (*MS*, p. 265). Camus imagines the absurd man to be an 'adventurer of the everyday', who, by the sheer amount of experiences acquired in time, would 'break all records' and win his own code of ethics (*MS*, p. 261). An ethics of quantity is the only code of conduct that is consistent with the 'aesthetic' perspective conveyed by absurdity. Absurd men illustrate an 'economy' of life that rejects the negative judgement of *ressentiment* and the moral categories of better and worse that are rooted in *ressentiment* itself (*MS*, p. 280), and 'say *yes*'.

But if the Absurd negates reason, it cannot be understood as a 'return to nature' in the sense of the unleashing of human boundless instincts.[36] The 'everything is permitted' of the immoralist revolt against reason culminates in *ascesis*.[37] Camus associates this term, used in ancient Greek times with reference to sports (from Gk. *askēsis*, 'training'), with those of 'life style' and 'example' (II, p. 951) in order to define the 'aesthetic' constellation of absurd conduct.[38] In a note written in 1942 (II, p. 949), Camus interprets the Nietzschean notion of the Eternal return as a repetition of the highest moments of humanity and the ephemeral re-enactment of the great '*exempla*'[39] in a myriad of lives, loves, deeds. In *Le Mythe de Sisyphe*, the three absurd figures of the seducer, the play-actor and the conqueror illustrate the absurd revaluation and ennoblement of the world and of the single living beings as opposed to the despotic *reductio ad unum* characteristic of rational and metaphysical thought (*MS*, p. 270). The Absurd rejects the negative judgement rooted in the 'romantic' evasion or 'leap' outside of that which is encompassed by the moral '*ought* to be' ('As they are, things are not satisfying') and glorifies the plurality and variety of that which offers itself up to be lived.

This two-fold movement of negation and affirmation is fully captured in Pindar's epigraphy to *Le Mythe*: 'Ô mon âme, n'aspire pas à
la vie immortelle, mais/ épuise le champ du possible. (O my soul, do
not aspire to attain the immortal life, but/ exhaust the limits of the
possible.)' (*MS*, p. 217.) It comes as no surprise that the absurd man is
represented by the figure of the traveller, who endlessly runs through
('parcourt') and exhausts ('épuise') that which exists (*MS*, p. 274) rather
than aspiring to attain the impossible. Camus draws a link between
aspiration and hope, and places this connection on the scale of projections that bring the end of the foresight of thought nearer. Revolt
is not able to aspire and is, therefore, considered to be one of the few
philosophical positions that is consistent with the *end*less perspective
of the absurd (*MS*, p. 256). The negation of reason's logic and categories
excludes the possibility that perfection may be projected outside of
this life and world into a 'future' qualitatively different from and *better*
than the present (*MS*, p. 260); thus, revolt entails a positive judgement
on existence – it 'says *yes*'. From the tragic perspective of the absurd, to
exhaust the limits of the possible means to live all that is there to be
lived and to live (it) as long as possible. Life is freed from the fetishistic
or servile constructs of reason, which identifies the possible with that
which does not (yet) exist and awaits to be realised.

As mentioned, the question of nihilism is primarily a question of language. As Camus observes in his review of Brice Parain's *Recherches sur la
nature et la fonction du langage*, nihilism is a matter of knowing whether
our language is a lie or the truth; in other words, whether a language
may be conceived outside of a space filled by a god that guarantees the
(transcendent) meaning of words (I, p. 901). With his 'Nothing is true...'
or 'Everything is a lie...' (*VPII*, III, 108–9), Nietzsche calls into question
the relation between traditional language, Western logic and the forms
of dominion intrinsic to reason's moral justification of existence, of
which God is the representation.

Like Parain, Camus is aware that if nothing is true (death of God), then
our traditional language is meaningless and *everything is possible* (I, p. 907).
But this formula, in his opinion, is not consistent with the absurd 'slipping away' of Truth; it is the expression of an equivocal use of language
(I, p. 901), for which freedom is seen as an extreme form of servitude.[40]
In the phrase, 'Everything is possible', the super-human exhortation to
be God is submitted to the fabricative logic and vertical relationship of
dominion characteristic of teleocratic thinking, of which ordinary language is the crystallisation; the phrase is interpreted as the invitation to
assume the position and function of Master vacated by God.

In the early 1940s, the political implications of this 'equivocal freedom' of men from traditional authority (I, p. 901) are clear to Brice Parain and Georges Bataille,[41] as well as to Camus, who explicitly relates the belief that 'Everything is possible' to the creation of the stupid and cowardly gods of Hitlerism (I, p. 901; II, p. 12) and, more generally, to the twentieth century cult of action. Camus is obviously not referring to the absurd or 'aesthetic' model of action that is embedded in Kirilov's idea of man-god and in Karamazov's 'Everything is permitted'. Camus makes a distinction between 'Everything is permitted' and 'Everything is possible' as two opposite conclusions, that the 'absurd' or honest men and the Nazis respectively draw from what he calls the twentieth century *'metaphysics of the lie'* expressed by the Nietzschean phrase 'Nothing is true' (*LAA*, p. 25).

The author of *Le Mythe de Sisyphe* demonstrates that he calls into question not the premise, but the logic that lies behind the phrase 'Everything is possible'. In the fourth *Lettre à un ami allemand*, addressed to a German friend/opponent on the eve of the Liberation of Paris, Camus writes:

> Vous n'avez jamais cru au sens de ce monde et vous en avez tiré l'idée que tout était équivalent et que le bien et le mal se définissaient selon qu'on le voulait. Vous avez supposé qu'en l'absence de toute morale humaine ou divine les seules valeurs étaient celles qui régissaient le monde animal, c'est-à-dire la violence et la ruse. Vous en avez *conclu que l'homme n'était rien* et qu'on pouvait tuer son âme, que dans la plus insensée des histoires la tâche d'un individu ne pouvait être que l'aventure de la puissance, et sa morale, le réalisme des conquêtes. (You have never believed in the meaning of this world, and you derived from this the idea that everything is equal and that good and evil are defined according to one's will. You supposed that in the absence of all human or divine morals the only values were those that govern the animal world, that is to say, violence and cunning. You *concluded that man was nothing* and that one could kill his soul, that in the most senseless of histories the aim of the individual could only be the adventure of power, and his morals, the realism of conquests.) (*LAA*, p. 26, my italics)

In Camus's opinion, the nihilism of Hitlerism, with its emphasis on the active will as a demiurge and also on the annihilation of the living human being subjugated to the end-means mechanism characteristic of 'political reason' or realism, is etched into the very fabric of the Western Logic.

The absurd rule of conduct and Nazi power politics are two opposite positions that are derived from the same principle ('Nothing is true'), but only the first is consistent with the premise and has got to the bottom of Karamazov's formula, therefore, has rejected reason's nihilistic teleology. The nihilism of the absurd 'Everything is permitted' places itself in the margins of a more widespread *inconsistent* nihilism, of which Hitlerism is the extreme expression. The phrase, 'Everything is possible', is rooted in a logical error, namely, in a mode in which, through words and thought, the absurdity of existence is appropriated by teleological reason. The traditional way in which language itself is used and developed serves the lies and hatred embedded in the weave of Western logic and perpetuates 'fatalism', namely, the fetishistic subordination of life to the economic and political constructs that turn the living human agent into a powerless cog, a *nothing* (*nihil*) in the end-means machine, and into an expendable 'fonctionnaire de l'esprit et du cœur (bureaucrat of the mind and the heart)' (*MS*, p. 259). Thus, from the absurd perspective that negates the servile logic of *telos*, 'rien n'est possible mais tout est donné (nothing is possible, but everything is given)' (*MS*, p. 260).

Jean Paulhan's literary criticism,[42] the work of Francis Ponge,[43] and Brice Parain's historic philosophy, as opposed to the Historicist philosophy of contemporary Hegelianism, are three examples of an interrogation on language that radically call into question the *logic* of the philosophical political tradition, along with the political uses of language that this tradition allows. These reflections on language are closely connected with the reality of the time, in that they seriously take into account and consider what Paulhan calls the contemporary 'mal du langage (language sickness)' (Trundle 2007, pp. 10 ff), in other words, the widespread radicalism or 'radical idealism' in contemporary, and especially, political discourse. Camus has the investigations of these authors in mind, when he writes that 'mal nommer un objet, c'est ajouter au malheur de ce monde (to poorly name an object, is to add to the tragedy of this world)' (I, p. 908), and connects the 'depraved' use of words and logical connections to the suffering of human beings.

The negative and 'honest' thought, expressed in *Le Mythe de Sisyphe* as well as in the works of the aforementioned authors, is said to be an attestation of a certain fidelity to intelligence (I, p. 320) that reaches beyond the sphere of the 'intellectual vice' of radicalism (*A*, V, 543). Camus goes so far as to define the absurd phrase of Nietzsche and Karamazov, 'Everything is permitted', as a '*good* nihilism' (I, p. 320) and detects in Francis Ponge's *Parti pris* the illustration and definition of this form of nihilism: 'Le bon nihilisme est celui qui conduit au relatif et à l'humain (Good nihilism is one that leads to that which is relative and human)' (I, p. 887).

'Good' nihilism liberates the agent from the servitude to a murderous and terroristic *telos* ('fatalism'[44]) that has been crystallised in the words and causal connections of the Western philosophers' use of reason. Camus writes to Ponge in 1943, 'la volonté de l'absurde, c'est le monde nouveau (the will of the absurd is the new world)' (I, p. 887); the *'new* world', or the *'new* man' are not understood as the end-products of a transformation, but rather they denote a 'transvaluation' or 'transfiguration' of existence that may be found beyond the limits imposed by teleology. The nihilistic phrase, 'Everything is permitted', indicates a change in the way life is interpreted and the way in which a new 'price' is attributed to life (*MS*, p. 256) that goes beyond the disparagement and contempt that characterise reason's justification of existence, as well as the social and political discourses and structures of dominion that are founded upon such justification. As Camus points out in his 1944 'Sur une philosophie de l'expression', it is not so much a question of having to rebuild (*reconstruire*) the world as it is a question of having to rethink (*repenser*) it; this may be done by questioning the language in which existence is known and communicated.[45]

The possibility of transfiguration, namely, of a reinterpretation of that which falls outside the categories of reason, lies in art. For Camus, just as for Parain and Bataille,[46] there is something more to each word than the object it designates, yet this something more is not *enough* (I, p. 907). Language does not satisfy the thetic aspiration of human thought; it does not achieve the objective or end and nor does it attain the Truth (I, p. 904). Neither true nor false, language expresses the tragic contradiction of being useful-and-futile; its 'terrible inefficacité (terrible ineffectiveness)' is the sign that it exceeds or 'transcends' the utilitarian and nihilistic logic that, to date, has traditionally governed ordinary existence (I, p. 908). Similarly to Parain, Camus believes that the refusal to 'lie' coincides with the refusal to *arrive at a conclusion* (I, p. 907); an 'honest' thought stops at the margins of ontology and refuses to *prove*, or to derive Being from the nostalgia of transcendent foundation. The definition of an absurd or 'good nihilism' brings the question of the 'radical' mode of thought and speech to the foreground and is inseparable from it. Based on a logical error, this 'radical idealism' provides a foundation for contemporary moral and political discourses and culminates in fanaticism.

The political relevance of these issues is confirmed around 1945 by Georges Bataille's project to write a report on the relationships between literature or art and politics for *Actualité*; it was to include contributions by Camus, Blanchot, Monnerot, Parain, as well as an extract from Jaspers' *Nietzsche* that dealt with politics.[47] As Camus notes in 1944, the question of language cannot be reduced to a Byzantine exercise on grammar, but is inseparable from social criticism (I, p. 909) and concerns the emancipation of thought and action from the servile yoke of Western utilitarian and annihilating logic. The author of *Le Mythe de Sisyphe* especially insists on the social and political dimension of the contemporary attempts at calling language into question. The intellectuals of the *NRF* are opposed to the Surrealists, who, in Camus's view, derive anarchy or boundless freedom and calculated 'disorder' ('*démence*') from the negation of reason (I, p. 909).

The works by Parain, Ponge, Paulhan and himself illustrate an honest thought that extracts internal discipline (*ascesis*) and a 'new classicism' from the Nietzschean 'metaphysics of the lie'. Their 'good' or consistent nihilism does not culminate in an apology of instincts, but in a 'parti pris d'intelligence' (I, p. 910), a choice that favours intelligence over and as opposed to radicalism and fanaticism, or terror. It is no surprise that the elements of their intellectual engagement also define Camus's own commitment as a journalist: 'Le goût de la vérité, une leçon de modestie qui termine une analyse scrupuleuse, servie par l'information plus étendue [...]. (the taste for truth, a lesson of modesty that terminates in a scrupulous analysis, served by the most extensive information)' (I, p. 910).

In his 1950 commentary of Nietzsche's *La Volonté de Puissance*, 'Nietzsche et le nihilisme', which was published in *Les Temps Modernes* and later included in *L'Homme révolté*, Camus confirms the Nietzschean parentage of the 'good' or consistent nihilism of the absurd in *Le Mythe de Sisyphe*. The method of revolt is identified with the negation of teleology, thus, with the 'liberation' of the world from the moral justification of reason that subjugates it to divine will. The death of God has no other meaning than the methodical negation of constructs of reason such as unity and finalism, which liberates existence from the dominion of the Judge (*HR*, p. 116), who values and condemns that which exists in view of that which ought to be. Insofar as nihilism is identified with the inability to believe that which exists and the impossibility to live that which is there to be lived, reason's moral interpretation of existence is not a restraint or remedy for nihilism, but rather its *raison d'être*. According to the philosopher-diagnostician, nihilism is rooted in the negative judgement that is held on the world by *ressentiment*, which lies at the core of all forms of 'idealism' and teleology (*HR*, p. 119).

Nietzsche is seen to displace his authentic morality outside of the figures of domination (Master/God) of reason and to base it on the phrase 'Nothing is true, everything is permitted' (*HR*, p. 118).[48] Divinity is placed beyond the limits of reason, thus beyond the confines dictated by fabricative logic, and can be detected at the core of the notion of apocalypse. '[Nietzsche] devinait le visage sordide et calculateur que cette apocalypse finirait par prendre [...] ([Nietzsche] guessed the sordid and calculating aspect that this apocalypse would finally assume)' (*HR*, p. 116; Camus 1971, p. 57). Camus traces the roots of the modern concept of history back to the moral interpretation of reason; this last introduces the teleological idea of judgement, of punishment and reward and turns nature into a (meaningful) history and gives birth to the idea of 'human *totality*' (*HR*, p. 119). The author's criticism of totalitarian ideologies is condensed in these few lines; it was developed in the third part of *L'Homme révolté* that was devoted to 'Historical Revolt' and confirms the crucial part played by Camus's interpretation of Nietzsche in the analysis of his own time.

The text on 'Nietzsche et le nihilisme' does not add anything new and original to Jaspers' interpretation of Nietzsche's thought on nihilism and politics; however, it brings Camus's methodological approach into full focus and is essential in shedding light on his political thought, which openly calls the categories and logic of political philosophy into question. Associated with the liberal theories on totalitarianism of the 1940s and 1950s, in particular, with Raymond Aron's definition of the contemporary ideologies as 'secularised religions', Camus's analysis of the rational and irrational forms of State terrorism in *L'Homme révolté* has been accused of lacking the clarity of method and theoretical rigour of contemporary political theorists (Pisier and Bouretz 1986, p. 274). It is my opinion that one must keep in mind and take into consideration the fact that Camus does not attempt a historical-political analysis of twentieth-century regimes, but endeavours to make a philosophical investigation into the logic that governs the way contemporary men think, speak and act. Camus's attempt cannot be understood without taking his lifelong interrogation on nihilism as a primary political issue into account, nor can the method of thought that he formulates in *Le Mythe de Sisyphe* be ignored; it is important to remember that Camus, in 1950, explicitly relates his 1942 essay to Nietzsche's criticism of philosophical reason.

The nihilism of the traditional morality of *ressentiment* is the absurd man-god's gravestone; it results from the 'secularisation of the sacred' (*HR*, p. 119), in other words, it descends from the victory of logic over the absurd and the subjugation, domestication and extermination of that which is 'non-thought' (*'non-pensé'*) and 'un-spoken' (*'non-parlé'*) according to the categories of reason (Blanchot 1954a, p. 856). In the eyes of the 'profane' world of utility, the absurd is the senseless and the 'sacred', the illustration of which is the tragic figure of Sisyphus (Blanchot 1943, p. 66). As Blanchot observes in his 1954 'Réflexions sur le nihilisme', the problem of nihilism, or more precisely, of the unprecedented nihilism of destruction and sterile violence of the twentieth century, lies in the effort to bind the absurd and force it to abide by the mechanisms of the logic of our 'happy reason' (Blanchot 1954a, p. 852). In other words, nihilism is the invisible work of Sisyphus that lies at the heart of and under the cover of reason, the tragic hero having become a servant, a bureaucrat and police officer of reason (Blanchot 1954a, pp. 856–7).

Sisyphus' infernal torment represents the dispossession of death, this last being understood by reason as the end of human life, as well as the limit to and the power of life itself. The absurd hell describes a 'region' or limit where man has no longer or not yet reached a state of *power* and where human beings have fallen below the 'dignity' of death (Blanchot 1954a, p. 857). Blanchot suggests that the destructiveness of nihilism lies in a 'connivance' that exists between the Absurd and logical reason that culminates in systematic extermination or *end*less death that characterises the twentieth century. In his 'Réflexions sur le nihilisme' and in 'Tu peux tuer cet homme', Blanchot openly bases the contemporary nihilistic 'absolute power', defined as the power *of* death (Blanchot 1954b, p. 1064), in human beings' absurd dispossession of the end or limit that is represented by (their) death. The absurd is that which is 'sacred', also identified with the 'nudity' or 'extreme baseness' of human life (Blanchot 1954a, p. 857); it is the sacred upon which thought and history lay the foundations of the beginning of civilisation and their measureless violence. Thus, in Blanchot's analysis, the Absurd indicates the *limit* of absolute power over death, a low 'naked' state of being ('the vermin') that is both included in and excluded from the logic of reason, and that must be suppressed (Blanchot 1954b, p. 1060) in order to build a *world*.

Inconsistent or destructive nihilism calls the relationship between Absurd and power into question. Camus explores this relationship through the figure of Caligula in his homonymous tragedy of the early 1940s (see Chapter 6). When Blanchot identifies the absurd with the 'nudity' of a life that is placed below the dignity of death and, therefore, is killable, he neglects the essential point of Camus's argument in *Le Mythe de Sisyphe* and in his later writings. That 'killability' is inconsistent with the absurd principle, 'Everything is permitted'; that nudity is the extreme product of reason's teleology. What Blanchot fails to acknowledge, and is extensively emphasised by Giorgio Agamben, is the crucial link that exists between the fact that certain human beings have become '*homines sacri*', that is to say, men or women that can be killed without committing homicide (Agamben 1995, pp. 126–7), and the fact that they are *found guilty* and banned from the living political community of people.[49] Camus's Absurd cannot be understood, as Blanchot seems to suggest, as the impossible *commencement* of the 'world' that was erected by reason; in other words, the Absurd is not a sort of indefinable Hobbesian 'state of nature' that must be suppressed in order for the community of men to exist. Sisyphus is found guilty and punished for his *crime against reason*. The absurdity of his condition lies in the punishment and in the banishment itself, the infernal endless torment, which is at the same time etched into and expelled from the teleocratic logic of crime and punishment.

The banishment from the 'royal road' of reason is what begins the process that culminates in the hero's tragic consciousness of the Absurd. The Absurd is no longer subjugated to the banishment (e.g., the punishment of the rock); it implies a change of perspective that refuses the 'nudity' and 'killability' of the outcast, insofar as it negates the servile teleological constructs of reason that the banishment creates. Blanchot rightly observes that negative thought of the Absurd involves utter powerlessness (Blanchot 1954b, p. 1061). In his endless repetition, Sisyphus 'says *yes*', but in his absurd positive judgement he does not affirm anything; in order to start a revolt against his condition, he would have to at least become a *slave* (Blanchot 1954a, p. 858). Consciousness of the Absurd, however, frees the tragic hero from the logic that subjugated, condemned and banished him. The negation of the end established by reason (*telos*) abolishes both contempt and the possibility to revolt – and, without the possibility to revolt and without contempt, who can remain a *slave*? (*MS*, p. 258).

Thus, the question is not whether the phrase 'Everything is possible' is logically derived from the Absurd – it has been demonstrated that Camus would answer that it is not – but whether the Absurd provides the 'reasons' needed to oppose this murderous inconsistent or 'radical' nihilism. As Camus observes in his 1950 'Nietzsche et le nihilisme', the negation of the metaphysical concept of a divine will does away with the vertical relation of dominion that is rooted in the teleological interpretation of reason. Men cannot be judged in the name of anyone/anything that exists above them (*HR*, p. 117). The moral values of the judge are replaced by the 'aesthetic' or a-teleological values of the creator (*HR*, p. 123).[50]

In Nietzsche, the rejection of reason leads to a *higher* morality, one that pushes the traditional relationship of obedience off the hinges of the teleological model of action. The statement 'Nothing is true, everything is permitted' does not culminate in the totalitarian (inconsistent) phrase 'Everything is possible', but rather in the impasse implied in the statement *'Nothing* is permitted' (*HR*, p. 121). Camus is fully aware that contemporary politics are the stake and that the outcome lies in the distinction and in the conflict between two opposed declinations – fabricative and contemplative – of 'creation'. However, Nietzsche's lucid diagnosis of European nihilism does not provide the instruments needed to diminish or halt the murderous tendencies of twentieth-century power politics, which turns his announcement of the Over-man to initialise the systematic fabrication of 'sub-men' (*sous-hommes*) (*HR*, p. 125).

As Camus observed in his notebooks as early as 1943, 'l'absurde est *réellement* sans logique. C'est pourquoi on ne peut *réellement* pas en vivre (the absurd is *really* without logic. This is why one cannot *really* live it)'. Either the absurd is negated (suicide), or it negates itself by revealing a principle of satisfaction (II, p. 1005). To live of the absurd is *to make use* of it, and the tragedy of *Caligula* powerfully illustrates the murderous 'desertification' that results from such use that, according to Camus, results in the negation of both life and the absurd:

> L'absurde, c'est l'homme tragique devant un miroir (Caligula). Il n'est donc *pas seul*. Il y a le germe d'une satisfaction ou d'une complaisance. Maintenant, il faut supprimer le miroir. (The absurd, is the tragic man in front of a mirror (Caligula). Thus, he is *not alone*. There is a seed of satisfaction or indulgence. Now, the mirror must be suppressed.)'
> (II, p. 995)

6
The Absurd and Power

Celui qui a conçu ce qui est grand doit aussi le vivre.
(Nietzsche)

In March 1941, a few weeks after completing the manuscript of *Le Mythe de Sisyphe*, Camus notes in his *Carnets*: 'L'Absurde et le Pouvoir – à creuser (cf. Hitler). (The Absurd and Power – to be investigated (cf. Hitler)' (II, p. 921). The Italian anti-fascist intellectual refugee from France, Nicola Chiaromonte, recalls meeting Camus in Oran that year, before fleeing to the United States. It is not difficult to imagine the political tenor of the conversations between these two men, whose friendship back then was sealed by an ecstatic love and admiration of the sea. Hitler had just occupied Greece and Chiaromonte was obsessed with the idea that humanity had reached its lowest point, that history was senseless and the only thing that made sense was the part of the living human being that is irreducible to history. 'Camus told me then that he was writing a tragedy about Caligula, and I tried to understand what could attract a modern writer to such a subject. Unfettered tyranny? But contemporary tyranny did not seem to me to have much in common with Caligula's' (Chiaromonte 1977, p. 52).

Caligula was not intended to be an historical investigation of the contemporary forms of government; the text of *Le Mythe de Sisyphe* suggests that Camus was primarily concerned with exploring the relationship that exists between the *logic* of power and the 'illogical' perspective that the Absurd embodies.[1] His tragedy tackles the question of *how* men can be free (I, p. 442) and calls the relationship between free action and power of the Western tradition into question.

According to Georges Bataille, *Caligula* challenges the traditional categories of political philosophy by exploring the inhuman lyricism or the murderous power of poetry (Bataille 1947, p. 8). Caligula is the Emperor-Poet, who puts the negation of the servile logic of reason into action; thus, he is the tragic incarnation of what the author of *L'expérience intérieure* calls the 'sacred' or the 'impossible'. In Bataille's view, Caligula embodies the 'uselessness' of art that has been endowed with limitless power, which dissolves the petty politics of security. The emphasis on the criminal excesses of the Emperor's boundless passion, which transgresses the laws of reason, however, relegates this tragic figure to the traditional concept of tyranny; Bataille seems to confirm Chiaromonte's perplexities regarding the capacity of Camus's tragedy to capture the unprecedented character of Nazi politics.

In the 1944 version of the play, Camus openly rejects the moral interpretation of Caligula's madness, which identifies him with the traditional figure of the tyrant as a '*blind soul*' (I, p. 362). The use of the metaphor of seeing to express the act of thinking in the philosophical tradition identifies tyranny with the negation of reason, therefore, with a 'blind' and boundless passion. But for Camus's hero, the tyrant is not alien to the nihilistic logic of reason, by sacrificing men to his personal ambition or idea, the action of the tyrant is 'enslaved' to teleology, which lies at the core of political realism. On the contrary, Caligula rejects both honour and power as his objectives, he is free from productive logic, in which the metaphoric constellation of vision is rooted.

Camus inserts the reference to the tyrant in act III that, in the 1941 version of the play, is entitled 'Divinity of Caligula' – the echoes of *Le Mythe de Sisyphe* are apparent, particularly, those pages on the absurd freedom of the contemporary man-god. In act III, Camus identifies the concept of power with the vertical relationship of dominion that is associated with the figure of God/Sovereign/Master. Insofar as the last is an illusory construct of teleological reason, power becomes a matter of drama; every man can exert the gods' 'ridiculous profession' without apprenticeship, 'il suffit de se durcir le cœur (all he has to do is to harden his heart)' (I, p. 421). Camus merges the two Nietzschean metaphoric constellations of theatre and craftsmanship together and ascribes power to the teleological or moral interpretation of reason.

Caligula ridicules the concept of power (I, p. 451) by exposing the fiction of teleology and the fetishistic relationship of man to his own creations; in the opening scene of act I, the tragic hero embodies the absurd or 'aesthetic' perspective of the Heraclitean Infant-Artist that is depicted in Nietzsche's *La Naissance de la Philosophie à l'époque de la tragédie grecque* and evades the servile logic of reason. The death of Caligula's sister and lover, Drusilla, exposes the fictional characteristic of the teleological interpretation of existence, as well as of the moral and political hierarchies erected by reason; Camus's hero affirms that nothing is important (act I, scene X), everything is on the same level (act I, scene VII), and all actions are equivalent (act III, scene VI).[2]

From the a-teleological perspective of the Absurd, all deeds are beyond the measure of good and evil, and, outside the bounds represented by reason's moral justification of existence, 'play' ('*jeu*') is the only 'honest' way of dealing with the great issues of human existence. Camus entitles the second act of the 1941 version of his tragedy, 'Jeu de Caligula (Caligula's game)'. The tragic Emperor recalls Heraclitus' Infant-Artist both physically (CAC4, p. 14) and in the 'illogical' consistency of his words and acts, as is transmitted by Suetonius. Insofar as his Nietzschean laughter unveils the fetishistic mode of thought that supports the traditional structures of authority, Caligula embodies the *limits* of man, namely, that which Blanchot defines as the human 'region' or experience (Absurd) that evades teleology and is no longer and not yet *power* (Blanchot 1954b, p. 1061).

But Caligula is the absurd man, who refuses the enslavement to logic *and* he is also Emperor, namely, the depository of absolute power. Jean Grenier observed the contradictoriness of this figure (Camus and Grenier 1981, p. 51), which must be ascribed to the fact that the tragic hero is at the same time within and outside of the limits established by teleology and merges two irreconcilable dimensions, the 'aesthetic' or 'illogical' perspective of the Absurd and the productive logic of power.

Camus's *Carnets* attest that, as early as 1941, the author had already questioned the particular contradiction that exists between the Absurd and Power and had demonstrated an apparent concern for the contemporary political situation (II, p. 921), which had brought him to seriously reconsider the problem of action. In act I of *Caligula*, the Emperor-Artist (I, p. 392) negates the petty reasons of ordinary life and begins a monologue in front of the mirror that brings the pivotal question of *Le Mythe de Sisyphe* to the foreground: can one live with 'empty hands', in other words, can one live without hope (I, p. 393)?

In the opening scenes, Caligula places himself beyond the confines delimiting reason and into the *end*less and powerless universe of 'play'; when the tax inspectors recall him to his official duties, however, the absurd man re-enters the nihilistic game so wilfully played by his administrators and agrees to follow the rules dictated by the 'servile' logic of interest, which governs the finances, public morals, foreign politics, the army and the laws (I, p. 395). Bataille does not seem to notice that it is Caligula's passionate and immoralistic 'instinct to play', in other words, his 'divine' freedom from *utility* that makes him condescend to play the game of reason.[3] Caligula consents to espouse the utilitarian point of view of the 'functionaries of the spirit and of the heart' (I, p. 1199) and to act according to the logic of modern thought – 'Si le Trésor a de l'importance, alors la vie humaine n'en a pas. (If the Treasury is of some importance, then human life is of none)' (I, p. 335). Thus, Bataille fails to associate the stifling logic that governs the tragedy with Caligula's determination to take the 'servile' utilitarian reason to extremes.

Beyond good and evil, the nihilistic devaluation of human life that is intrinsic to the moral interpretation of reason is conceived to be merely one more 'game' among others (I, p. 336). Caligula is not an idealist in the Nietzschean sense (CAC4, p. 33); he ridicules the belief in the objectiveness of the all too human economic, political and moral constructs. But he consents to act consistently with the fetishistic logic of modern thought and declares his pedagogic intent demonstrating to his subjects and functionaries how much the logic that they 'freely' profess to and that enslaves them to the economy of utility will cost them (I, p. 396; I, p. 336). Echoing Zarathustra's exhortation on the final page of *Crépuscule des Idoles* ('The Hammer Speaks'), Caligula wears the harsh mask of the creator in the absurd innocent universe; but the moment he decides to be *logical*, he replaces Nietzsche's hammer with the sword, in other words, he replaces creation with terror.

While the novel has allowed Camus to bring the issue of intelligence and the logic of *ressentiment* into full focus, the relevance that the issue of action acquired in the early 1940s justifies the author's recourse to expressing himself through tragedy.[4] The absurd rejection of the teleological model of what Nietzsche calls 'productive intelligence' brings the primacy of the deed to the foreground and calls for a reconsideration of the traditional model of political action.

By identifying Caligula's absurd freedom with the negation of the rational order (*telos*), thus, with a transgression of law and 'measure', within which crime and horror are necessarily present (Bataille 1947, pp. 6–7), Bataille seems to neglect that in *Le Mythe de Sisyphe* Camus rejected all attempts to derive criminal and deadly actions from the absurd premise 'Nothing is true, everything is permitted' as error or intellectual vice. The Absurd does not *command* death (MS, p. 225); this point is made even more clearly in the 1944 version of *Caligula*. Camus revises act I, scene IV, and introduces a dialogue between the Emperor and his servant Helicon, in which Caligula declares his 'besoin de la lune, ou du bonheur, ou de l'immortalité, de quelque chose [...] qui ne soit pas de ce monde (need of the moon, or happiness, or immortality, of something [...] that is not of this world)' (I, p. 331) – in one word, his need of the *impossible*.

The death of Caligula's lover becomes the sign of a truth that makes the impossible necessary for him: 'Les hommes meurent et ils ne sont pas heureux. (Men die and they are not happy.)' (I, p. 332). Caligula's desire to make the impossible possible is the logical consequence of two judgements: 'The world, as it is, is unbearable' and 'things as they are do not seem satisfactory to me' (I, p. 331). In a world where 'Nothing is true', the Emperor's logical attitude is rooted in his extreme desire for truthfulness (I, p. 332). Caligula fuses the belief that existence is unbearable together with the observation that one has no right to suppose that a 'hereafter' or a 'thing in itself' ('the divine') exists; thus, he illustrates what Nietzsche, in his posthumously collected texts calls 'radical nihilism' (*VPII*, III, 103).

Caligula's claim regarding truth is still embedded in *moral* reason. His murderous action appears to be the logical consequence not of the Absurd, but of a moral interpretation of existence (act I, scene XI), that culminates in the phrase, *'Everything is possible'*. The Emperor identifies the *use* of power with making the impossible possible (act I, scene IX); everything begins with the logic of the public Treasury (I, p. 339) and culminates in the world of trial. All men are subject to the Emperor's absolute power and they are sentenced to death as *guilty*; they are spectators and victims that are invited to *the most beautiful of spectacles* (I, p. 339; I, p. 401) – Caligula's murderous action, which echoes Tertullian's spectacles of cruelty that Nietzsche evokes, may be ascribed to the God-like perspective of *ressentiment* that, in turn, is destructive of the living community of men.

Caligula bestows a negative judgement upon men and the world and submits both to a superior, 'moral' will to change things, namely, to make them *better*. In the closing lines of act II, in the 1941 version, Camus explicitly bases the Emperor's murderous 'play' on contempt (*'mépris'*) (I, p. 358; I, p. 417), which is the sign of a nihilistic interpretation of life and kindles Caligula's obsessive objective of realising the impossible. His desire to actively *transform* the order of the world (act I, scene XI, pp. 338–9) is such that his reasoning is incorporated in the productive logic of reason that Camus places in opposition to the contemplative or 'aesthetic' perspective, which is represented by absurd love (I, p. 339; I, p. 401).

It is no surprise that in the preface to the American edition of his plays, dated December 1957, the author defined *Caligula* a 'tragedy of intelligence' and the 'history of a superior suicide', of the most human and tragic of *errors* (I, 447).[5] The terminology used is similar to that of *Le Mythe de Sisyphe*, and the error or logical 'suicide' is that of moral fanaticism. Camus uses the term 'intelligence' to refer to the Absurd negation of reason's categories and interpretations ('morality') and of men's fetishistic submission to their own creations and constructs. Caligula joins the productive logic of power and the 'aesthetic' perspective of the Absurd together; his negation of all transcendent foundations ('everything is lie'), however, is associated with a hypertrophic affirmation of the will as the only *cause* of truthfulness and action – he wants everyone to live in truth (I, p. 332). Thus, the Emperor's action falls at the same time within and without the moral interpretation of reason.

As an expression of his Nietzschean friendship, Georges Bataille offered to Camus a copy of his book *Sur Nietzsche*, published by Gallimard in 1945, with a dedication: '[...] la morale pourrait-elle être poussée trop loin? ([...] could morality[6] be pushed too far?)' (Favre 2004, p. 204). In October 1944, Bataille had begun collaborating with *Combat*, the newspaper created during the Résistance,[7] of which Camus was editor in chief. His two articles on 'Nietzsche est-il fasciste?' and 'La littérature est-elle utile?' develop and discuss the opposition that exists between freedom and servitude and identify man's 'divine freedom' in the *uselessness* of human work, art and action, in other words, in their refusal of the petty logic of utility that governs politics (Bataille 1988a, 1988b).[8] But what happens if this logic, which both authors identify with traditional 'morality', is pushed to its extremes? I propose to read Camus's tragedy, *Caligula*, as his own answer to this question.

In a 1938 note, Camus declares that the world has become deserted because Caligula *thinks* (II, p. 864); but in 1944, the author seems to argue that the world has become deserted because Caligula thinks *erroneously* ('pense *mal*'). During the six years between the first draft of the play and the first presentation in Paris, in September 1945, Camus had read Grenier's *Essai sur l'esprit d'orthodoxie* and Nietzsche's *La Naissance de la philosophie*, which bring the connection that exists between the teleological productive model of thinking (the philosophers' 'reason') and political action, understood as the *transformation* of man and the world, to his attention. In the 1944 version of the tragedy, Caligula 'plays' the role of Western 'romantic' reason, that submits life to the 'servile' and nihilistic logic of interest (the Treasury). Camus particularly insists on the pessimistic moral judgement that is the basis of the Emperor's desire to transform man and the world and to realise the kingdom of the impossible on earth (I, p. 339).

By asserting that Caligula's logic is rooted in contempt (*mépris*)[9] (I, p. 358; I, p. 417), Camus is suggesting that we are no longer dealing with the absurd mode of thought, but rather with the distinct mode of thought specific to *ressentiment*. Reminiscent of Scheler's pages, Camus endows Caligula with the will and the power to give men 'the gift of equality' that places everything on the same level (I, p. 339). The Emperor does so by abasing and condemning his subjects and declaring them *guilty*; Caligula's freedom of action is that of a God-Judge, rather than of a man-god as it is presented in *Le Mythe de Sisyphe*. Caligula understands free action in voluntaristic terms (I, p. 442), therefore, in teleological terms. His freedom of action is based on the illusions created by reason, first of all, that of a masterly 'active' will and sets the nihilistic devaluation of life, which is inherent in the utilitarian logic of Western thought, into motion. Therefore, '[elle] n'est pas la bonne ([it] is not the good one)' (I, p. 443).

Perfect absurdity exceeds logic; thus, it is silent (*HR*, p. 68). As Blanchot notes with extreme subtlety in his reflections on nihilism, absurdity in its pure negative form is essentially *un-thought* ('*non-pensé*') and *un-spoken* ('*non-parlé*') (Blanchot 1954a, p. 856) and, therefore, it coincides with a 'region' of human experience that is solitary and *world-less* (Blanchot 1954a, p. 858).[10] All attempts made by reason to control this 'region' leads off in two opposite and opposed directions, i.e., the nihilistic pleasure of negation, illustrated by Caligula, and a relative and provisional position (*HR*, p. 68), which coincides with the absurd thought of *Le Mythe de Sisyphe*.

Caligula is the exemplification of the great adventurer of the absurd (*HR*, p. 68), who *thinks* and takes absurdity ('the impossible'), which exceeds logical thought and traditional language (*logos*), in charge.[11] Camus's two manuscript versions of the Introduction to *L'Homme révolté* (III, pp. 1239, 1243) confirm this: 'D'une certaine manière l'absurde qui prétend exprimer l'homme dans sa solitude le fait vivre, comme Caligula, devant un miroir. (In a way, the absurd that claims to express man in his solitude makes him live, like Caligula, in front of a mirror.)' (III, p. 1241.) Camus is perfectly forthright about the fact that the problem with this form of radical nihilism does not lie in absurdity but in Western teleological or moral reason. As Tracy Strong notes, the image of the mirror in *L'Homme révolté* symbolises the desire for permanence and unity (Strong 2000, p. 129), in other words, it indicates the thetic claim associated with human thought (III, p. 1242). But to live in front of the mirror is the manifest sign of radical idealism, the 'intellectual vice' (*A*, V, 543) that 'leaps' from this all too human desire into the affirmation that a principle of unity and permanence exists. Caligula takes that 'leap' ('superior suicide') and affirms that 'Everything is possible'; by doing so, he brings on stage and enacts the negation of what Camus considered to be the essential legacy of the absurd phrase, 'Everything is permitted', that is to say, the abolishment of the moral judgement of guilt/punishment (II, p. 991) and the refusal to abase one's fellow men by submitting them to the God-like perspective of contempt.

Contempt is key to Camus's analysis of Hitlerism in the editorials printed in *Combat*. In 'Le temps du mépris' ('The Age of Contempt') of 30 August 1944, he resorts to André Malraux's word to effectively characterise the regime of systematic degradation and destruction of souls (CAC8, p. 158). The connection that exists between contempt and the utilitarian logic of Western rationalism is apparent in two editorials (17 and 20 September 1944) that Camus devotes to the situation of the German people:

> Ce peuple qui a tant détesté l'individu, a pris de l'individualisme la part la plus basse, celle qui met un homme au-dessus des autres au mépris de toute conscience. (This people that so detested the individual has taken up individualism's most base aspect: the elevation of one man above all others in contempt of all conscience.) (CAC8, p. 200)[12]

In the editorial of 15 September 1944, Camus summs up the sacrifice of the happiness of a thousand peoples, which was treated as a trifle when *compared* with the power of one great individual, Hitler, and he calls attention to the enslavement of art, philosophy and morality ('honour') to the law and common final objective of success (CAC8, pp. 188–9). Camus clearly ascribes Hitlerism to be the result of the logic of *ressentiment*; his analysis of the relationship between the German people and the Führer recalls Scheler's discussion regarding the two types of man: the strong or arriviste and the weak man of *ressentiment*. These figures are caught in a competitive system in which the individual's sense of self worth results from an endless *comparison* with others and in which being more than and above anyone else becomes the finality of all action. Scheler resorts to Nietzsche's term *ressentiment* from *The Genealogy of Morals* to demarcate this disposition to 'measure' one's own value against that of others, and he links it to an attitude of contempt or looking *down* upon the values and opinions of others that culminates in the negation of 'conscience'. We know that, in 1943, Camus reworked his reading notes of *L'homme du ressentiment* in his 'Remarque sur la révolte', which he wrote between 1943 and 1944 and published in *L'Existence* in 1945 (II, p. 986). The editorial of *Combat* places Nazism's systematic negation of human 'conscience' or 'soul' in opposition to 'intelligence, courage, and truth of the human heart' (CAC8, pp. 142, 182),[13] and ascribes 'anthropometric virtue' to the most heinous part of human reason (II, p. 494).

Camus particularly insists on the teleological aspect of Hitler's policies, which he perceived to be frenetically oriented towards success/ achievement and to entail the systematic 'enslavement' of living men to the abstract final objective of success and (future) power (CAC8, pp. 188–9). Hitler had acted in the name of the German people; the people had delegated the burden of thought to this 'great individual', who chose power over happiness (CAC8, p. 189) and identified right with might (CAC8, p. 200). Thoughtlessness, humiliation and the negation of dignity and honour lie at the core of the greatest achievement of Hitlerism: the fabrication of a total political unity or 'unconscious unanimity' (CAC8, p. 196).

As a matter of fact, Camus does not identify thoughtlessness with the total absence of reason, but rather with a distinct mode of thought that rejects 'constructive reflection' and refuses freedom because it 'hates criticism' (CAC8, p. 196), namely, with radical idealism. Subjecting existence to the 'servile' rationalism of moral and political fanaticism, the German people ignore freedom and refuse the 'revolutions that emancipate man' (CAC8, p. 196).[14] It is extremely likely that Camus was familiar with Hermann Rauschning's argument in *La Révolution du Nihilisme* (*Die Revolution des Nihilismus*). In this book, which was published by Gallimard in 1939 and reviewed in the *NRF* in February 1940, the German exile, who was in Hitler's entourage in the early phases of the Nazi rule, calls attention to the 'ordered destructiveness' of the new and unprecedented revolutions of the twentieth century in Germany and Soviet Russia. In both, he detects *misuse* of the human desire for order on a vast scale (Rauschning 1939, pp. 19–20).

In his articles, Camus's emphasis on the 'realism' of Nazi politics, which joins the irrational revolutionary movement with a cold and calculating pursuit of power and dominance, recalls Rauschning's theses (Rauschning 1939, pp. 18–19); when he discerns that Hitler (just like Caligula) has an unconcealed contempt of the common people, which he does not serve but uses (Rauschning 1939, p. 23), as well as the hostility to individualism and personality, pure science and art (Rauschning 1939, p. 28). The Nazi 'revolution of nihilism' is conceived by the German author to be the final achievement of the traditional, anarchist and communist understanding of revolution or mass revolt; it deems violence to be the basic element for changing the social order and carries the reduction of the human being to the animal or instinctual dimension of force[15] to completion (Rauschning 1939, pp. 19, 27–8). In addition to the 'nihilistic moral foundation' of extreme brutality, hatred, vengeance, envy, licentiousness, robbery, lying (Rauschning 1939, p. 47), Rauschning notes the 'eternal moralizing' that is characteristic of the revolution (Rauschning 1939, p. 46) and draws a parallel with the emotionality of the defence of 'virtue' that was distinctive of the French Revolution; thus, he links terrorism to the moral justification of violence, which identifies the opponent in that which is considered to be the public enemy and, consequently, *evil*. Rauschning detects a logical connection between these modern revolutions and nihilism, which he understands to be the total rejection of theory in favour of absolute dynamism and which he ascribes to moral scepticism. The last is responsible for the destruction of 'past categories of thinking and evaluation' (Rauschning 1939, p. 22), namely, for the cynicism and lack of principle that determines the effectiveness of revolutionary action.

Camus's understanding of the nihilistic revolution of Hitlerism differs from Rauschning's in one essential respect: the origin of this murderous nihilism does not lie in scepticism, but rather in rationalism or, more precisely, in the 'utilitarian' logic of realism, which drives the modern competitive system of evaluation to extremes and as a consequence crushes men under a machine of efficacy and dominion (CAC8, pp. 188, 190). In 1944, by suggesting that there is a parallel between Hitler and Caligula's *'jeux fixes'* in the mirror, Camus draws attention to the mediocrity of the Führer, who is consumed with his obsessions (*idées fixes*) (CAC8, p. 189), and brings the nihilistic logic that lies at the core of the concept of power into full light. As he observed in the editorial of 29 September 1944, this 'servile' logic reduces man to nothing more than a mere function that is at the service of the final achievement of an end objective that lies outside of himself and culminates in 'the most tragic and theatrical of suicides' (CAC8, p. 216), in *collective suicide* (CAC8, p. 201).[16]

In the Introduction to *L'Homme révolté*, Camus explicitly attributes the twentieth-century attempts to justify death – from self-sacrifice or martyrdom to 'collective suicide' and terror (*'logical* murder') (*HR*, p. 66) – to '(absolute) nihilism'. He uses this term to refer not to the absence of belief in superior values and transcendent meaning, which is frequently denounced in contemporary conservative political discourses, but rather to denote a specific logical argument, which 'legitimises' suicide and murder through its *indifference* to life. Echoing Nietzsche's *La Naissance de la philosophie*, Camus defines this to be 'une logique *besogneuse* aux yeux de laquelle *tout s'égalise*' (*HR*, p. 66 my italics), an industrious logic (Fr. *besogne*, 'work') that equalises everything. This 'industrious' teleological mode of thinking, which in *Le Mythe de Sisyphe* determines the suicidal act, bears 'the values of suicide', namely, the illusion of having a free active will and the primacy of efficacy and success,[17] to their extreme terroristic consequences, and is the basis of a form of politics of fear and contempt in which human beings are reduced to simple means that are at the service of a frenetic, endless activity of power accumulation.[18]

Camus openly mentions Nietzsche, who diagnosed nihilism by revealing the teleological model of productive intelligence ('reason') that may be found at the core of the Western philosophical tradition and rejected the fixed stance (objectiveness) of the illusory mirror of moral justification (*HR*, p. 68).[19] The tragic philosopher's criticism of rationalism and modern enslavement is seen to pave the way for the absurd revolt that breaks the mirror of logic (*HR*, p. 69) and rejects the vertical relationship of domination (master/slave) that lies at the core of teleological *ratio*.[20]

Camus has Heraclitus's Infant-Artist in mind (see Chapter 5) when he affirms that the replacement of the traditional concept of action with 'play' is one of the consequences of the absurd phrase 'Everything is permitted', which restores the innocence of Becoming (III, p. 1240).[21] As *Caligula* masterfully illustrates, however, the acceptance of murder is inherent to the perspective of 'play': all action, including murder, is indifferent and, consequently, *possible*.[22] Negation is replaced by destruction and the nihilists are replaced by assassins. The absurd thought makes *tabula rasa* of the servile logic and principles of tradition, but it provides nothing that could be of *use* to solve the significant questions of the twentieth century (*HR*, p. 69). In Nietzsche, the powerlessness of absurd thinking involves worldlessness.

Blanchot sees the absence of the world, in particular, of plurality and communication, to be the essential feature of the solitary 'region' of the Absurd (Blanchot 1954a, p. 858). In his view, the endless and powerless effort of Sisyphus of pushing a stone up the infernal slope is the illustration of the incommunicable nudity or inhumanity of the absurd. The worldless dimension of the absurd explains, in Blanchot's opinion, the hiatus that persists between this original experience and the onset of revolt. In order for revolt to take place, one must at least be a slave and take action for some shared and communicable value; Sisyphus, however, has nothing to revolt for and, therefore, he is not a *slave* (Blanchot 1954a, p. 858).

In *Le Mythe de Sisyphe*, Camus observes that Sisyphus' face, which toils so close to the stone, is already rock itself (*MS*, p. 303). But this 'inhuman' hero only describes the starting point of absurdity and not the awakening of the absurd 'conscience' that follows the initial feeling of despair and culminates in the absurd joy of the judgement 'All is well' (*MS*, p. 303). The author distinguishes the hero's endlessly repeating toil of pushing the stone, which is powerless and worldless, from the moment when, descending the slope in the pause from his painful labour, Sisyphus *contemplates* his life. Neglected by Blanchot and later commentators, this distinction is essential in order to shed light on the meaning of Camus's exhortation to break the 'fixed stance' of the mirror. This appeal to break the fixed stance of the mirror signifies the rejection of the servile logic of productive ('industrious') thought and the 'transfiguration' or reinterpretation of existence outside the categories defined by moral justification and from the 'aesthetic' perspective of *contemplative* intelligence.

This a-teleological thought 'liberates' man and the world from the vertical structure of domination (master/slave) that Nietzsche traces back to the metaphysical, moral and political constructs of reason. The absurd phrase 'Everything is permitted' marks the negation of the God-like perspective that is incorporated in reason's justification of existence. In his moment of contemplation, Sisyphus steps outside of the perspective of *ressentiment* that looks *down* on man and the world; he becomes the 'master of his days' (*MS*, p. 304), not of men. By slipping out of the productive logic of *telos*, however, the mythic hero also strips himself of the 'solitude supposé' ('alleged solitude') that logic restores to him (*RR*, p. 326; *HR*, p. 68). Powerlessness and worldlessness may be found only in absurd sensibility and in teleological thought (*HR*, p. 69).

The error of the twentieth century lies in reason's claim to base action on absurdity; this last is assumed to be as an overruling and pre-eminent emotion that is separated from the living human being (*HR*, p. 69). The idea of 'breaking the fixed stance of the mirror' has no other meaning than to recognise that the feeling of absurdity cannot be removed and considered separately from the 'mouvement vécu (lived movement)' of existence (III, p. 1242) and does not express the totality of living men and women. Contemplation, or absurd thinking, breaks the fixed stance of logic, which claims to take absurdity in charge by reducing man and world to monotone functions or 'abstractions'.

This is confirmed by Camus's notes for *La Peste* (*The Plague*), the novel that he writes between 1942 and 1946, where the deadly epidemic is identified with the war that Hitler spreads throughout Europe in September 1939. The brutal invasion of the war/plague marks the retreat of the beauty of the world and of its 'glorious faces' (II, p. 884) and the separation of men and women, who are 'imprisoned' in a worldless solitude without intimacy and communication.[23] The plague negates the human communication between intelligence, heart and flesh (II, p. 276); it marks the violent and violating reduction of living human beings to the levelling logic of domination.

Against this logic, which Caligula illustrates,[24] the 'aesthetic' thought of the Absurd recovers the 'mille petites voix émerveillées de la terre (myriad wonder filled little voices of the earth) and the 'appels inconscients et secrets, invitations de tous les visages (unconscious, secret calls, invitations from all faces)', which constitute the tragic and mortal 'unity' of the absurd man's *world* (*MS*, p. 304). What Camus seems to be implying is that the possibility of a living communication ('world') between men and women that goes beyond contemporary murderous nihilism lies in the 'aesthetic' or contemplative intelligence of the Absurd. In *Le Mythe de Sisyphe*, this contemplative thought is illustrated by Oedipus, who, blind and desperate, realises that the cool touch of his daughter's hand is the only bond that links him to the world; this leads him to pronounce the absurd phrase, 'All is well' (*MS*, p. 303). Sophocles' tragic hero is the anti-Caligula, who replaces the monotonous vision of the man reflected in the mirror with the plural dimension of *con*tact, literally, 'to touch' (*tangere*) 'together with' (*con-*).[25]

In the closing lines of act I of *Caligula*, all the memories and faces are erased (I, p. 340) and replaced by the image of the Emperor, who dominates the polished surface of the looking glass. Caligula represents the figure of the contemporary conqueror or adventurer, also identified with the man of action and the revolutionary (II, p. 493), who, in the great spectacle of nature, sees only himself (II, p. 492). He is the leveller who refuses the plurality and differences that lie in existence and, thus, negates absurd freedom – 'J'exterminerai les contradicteurs et les contradictions. (I will exterminate contradictors and contradictions.)' (I, p. 336.) According to Camus, it is inherent to the logic of the conqueror's attitude that he becomes executioner and police officer (II, p. 493). This attitude is one of 'hatred of the world', and this 'servile' logic, which abases existence and reduces it to the singular dimension of force and domination, is identified with 'ce qu'il y a de plus misérable dans la raison (that which is most ominous in reason)' (II, p. 494).

In 1948, the attitude of the conqueror is placed in open opposition to that of the artist, whose thoughtful consideration ('pensée réfléchie') has the characteristics of the 'aesthetic' perspective of the absurd as is illustrated by the blind Oedipus and the 'happy' Sisyphus (*MS*, p. 304). This alternative mode of conceiving of the world and living human relations, is reminiscent of Nietzsche's remarks on the Heraclitean contemplative intelligence and is confirmed by Camus's distinction between 'unity' and 'totality', which marks the end of the twentieth-century 'aestheticisation of politics' under totalitarian systems and coincides with the elimination of all differences. Unity, as it is revealed in the contemplation of beauty and in the artist's aesthetic judgement, is understood to be a 'harmonie des contraires' ('harmony of the contraries') (II, p. 493). It is in this 'artist's viewpoint', through which the absurd man contemplates the unity of his life outside of the categories and logic established by reason (*theoria*) and says *'yes'*, that I suggest we find the necessary premises to understand Camus's notion of revolt.

Combat with nihilism

Revolt, which lies at the core of the experience of the absurd, is brought to the foreground by breaking the mirror of logic (*HR*, p. 69; III, p. 1242). In 'Remarque sur la révolte', written between 1943 and 1944, Camus observes that a man who revolts is one who says *'no'*, '[m]ais s'il refuse, il ne renonce pas: c'est aussi un homme qui dit *oui* (but if he refuses, nonetheless he does not renounce: he is also a man who says *yes*)' (*RR*, p. 325). The 'no' of revolt coincides with the refusal of the nihilistic system of universal guilt that enslaves men; but, if it frees human thought and action from the moral justification of self-satisfied reason, it is not a renunciation. Here, Camus is probably making a reference to Nietzsche, whose *ascesis* he describes not only as a 'dénuement arbitraire (arbitrary destitution)'[26] but also as a renunciation (*HR*, p. 68).

Camus calls Nietzsche's solitary freedom into question as early as 1943–44.[27] He identifies *amor fati* with the absurd negation ('no') of the philosophical hatred of the world (*odium fati*), but this culminates in total acceptance ('yes') and in the divinisation of the world (*HR*, p. 124). Thus, the 'love of fate' that accepts everything, in which Bataille detected the highest expression of Nietzsche's understanding of freedom, renounces revolt. Camus seems to imply that the philosopher's solitude is inherent in the logic of domination, which the absurd conscience rejects, but that Nietzsche, with his notion of the will to power, does not entirely abandon.

Oedipus and Sisyphus say *'yes'* and they do not renounce, namely, they do not accept the reduction of human experience to the mono-tone *ratio* of power. Logic is the expression of an attitude of contempt that humiliates man and levels the values that are attributed to life in favour of those of interest, efficacy, utility. Therefore, logic goes *too far* (*RR*, p. 325). A positive or non-derivative value is entailed in the action of revolt that cannot be reduced to a re-active movement of demand ('revendication') nor can it be traced back to *ressentiment* (*RR*, p. 328). Camus defines revolt as a movement of *love* and uses this expression in the sense that Scheler employed in the third chapter of his *L'Homme du ressentiment*, primarily to distinguish it from the 'hatred of the world' that characterises humanitarianism (Scheler 1958, p. 111, n. 1).

The association of revolt with love, in the specific acceptation that the term acquires in Scheler's phenomenological analysis, has the precise intention of placing revolt outside and beyond the productive model of rationalism, assigning it to a different 'economy' of life that evades the 'masked nihilism' of Western logic. In the chapter on humanitarianism that is the source of Camus's argument, Scheler calls attention to two distinct declensions of love in early Christian morality (*Agapè/caritas*) and in the Platonic–Aristotelian tradition (*eros/amor*) (Scheler 1958, p. 69). The last relegates love to the sensory sphere of desire or need, which it perceives to be distinct from and inferior to the rational sphere (logic, law, justice, measure); *eros* coincides with a dynamic principle and 'method' to organise and move existence towards the attainment of perfection and plenitude (Being/*Nous*). It is not difficult to recognise in this that which Peter Sloterdijk calls 'erotodynamics' (Sloterdijk 2007), the finalistic 'economy' of productive thought.

In Scheler's opinion, the moral reflections of early Christendom, as may be exemplified by the work of Saint Augustine, postulates a dif-ferent understanding of love that dissolves the teleological structure of the '*sovereign* Good', dissociates love from need and from the biological sphere of 'nature' or sexual instinct, and identifies love with 'divinity' and with the spiritual dimension of the human being that exceeds or is situated beyond the bounds of reason (Scheler 1958, pp. 68–9). The rejection of the utilitarian 'economy' of *eros* lies at the core of Scheler's criticism of Rousseau's identification of love with pity. He sees a rela-tionship between the revolutionary heart of Rousseau's moral and political philosophy and the 'mechanism of a necessary illusion', an 'emotional hallucination', that he calls sympathy and which consists in the *artificial* insight into and absorption of the feelings of another human being (Scheler 1958, p. 114). Similar to the argument presented in *Aurore*, Scheler bases the revolutionary doctrines that were influenced by Rousseau's vindication of compassion or pity[28] on a radical idealism ('mechanism of a necessary illusion') and calls attention to the nihilistic logic that supports it. He identifies the humanitarian 'general love of man' with the desire for 'universal happiness' that inspires only those acts that are *useful* to the achievement of the common good.

Camus makes Nietzsche's and Scheler's theses that Rousseau's humanitarian pathos had a negative philosophical political influence on the revolutionary doctrines of the eighteenth to the twentieth centuries his own. He defines Rousseau's political philosophy as the logical product of radical idealism, namely, of an intellectual vice that advances the postulate of 'general will' and, by identifying this last with 'universal reason',[29] places it beyond the reach of constructive critical thinking ('new God', *HR*, p. 159). Thus, according to Camus, Rousseau's political theory is an integral part of the Western rationalistic tradition. Rather than rejecting the logic that underlies Hobbes's theory of social contract, Rousseau's theory takes it to extremes (*HR*, p. 158); he identifies the people with a sovereign political entity and conceives of freedom as a total submission of men to the postulate of general Will, thus, for him political action is necessarily incorporated in the traditional relationship of domination that is characterised by the Sovereign/Master/God.

Camus is essentially concerned with bringing the connection that exists between radicalism, moral or political fanaticism and power to the foreground. He defines Rousseau as the precursor of contemporary fanaticism, which actively dissolves opposition and neutrality by 'moralising' the realm of human intercourse. Under the law of moral reason, nothing is done without a *cause*; in other words, every deed is subjected to teleology and, therefore, fabricates its martyrs, ascetics and saints (*HR*, p. 159). In accordance with Scheler, Camus detects the utilitarian perspective of nihilism[30] or 'hate of the world'[31] in Rousseau's love of man; he, however, makes a distinction between the 'sanctified lie' of the general will on which Rousseau's civil faith is founded on and the 'foi émérveillée et généreuse (the astonished and generous faith)' of the insurgent people, who in the France of 1789 and in the Russia of 1905 and again in 1917 respectively tore down the scaffold of their standing political order and declared torture and the death penalty to be abolished (*HR*, p. 160 and note).

'Hatred' and 'love of the world' are not understood to be human feelings that are imposed upon nature, but rather two distinct modes of thinking or interpreting reality; the first may be associated with the nihilistic productive logic or 'reason' and the second is associated with the a-teleological ('aesthetic') contemplative intelligence, which *Le Mythe de Sisyphe* attempts to define. I suggest that, throughout Camus's articles published in *Combat* from 1943 to 1946 and his 'Remarque sur la révolte', these two modes of thought delineate two alternative political constellations, the traditional 'utilitarian' constellation of power, the basis of which may be found in the vertical relation of domination (master/slave; executioner/victim) and in the nihilistic logic of efficacy, and the constellation of revolt, which is articulated on the notions of 'generosity', 'honesty', 'courage', 'greatness', 'honour' and 'respect'.

In 'Remarque sur la révolte', Camus proves to be particularly concerned with placing revolt beyond the limits imposed by the nihilistic logic of modern political philosophy. Thus, he notes that revolt against the oppression and humiliation of another man or woman cannot be founded on sympathy or an illusory 'psychological identification' with the feelings of another. By rejecting the 'subterfuge par lequel l'individu sentirait en imagination que c'est à lui que l'offense se dresse (subterfuge with which the individual would feel in their imagination that the insult is directed against him) (*RR*, p. 327), Camus frees the concept of revolt from the utilitarian logic that lies at the core of the modern humanitarian 'love of man' and, by doing so, calls attention to a different, *'disinterested'* love of man and the world.

The apparent Kantian flavour of his remarks in 'Remarque sur la révolte' and throughout his editorials in *Combat*, where *disinterestedness* recurs as one of the key elements of the political programme of the journal (21 October 1944) and as the pivotal point of Camus's idea of social justice (24 November 1944), should not mislead us. The author makes similar, if not the same, criticisms of Kant's moral philosophy as Nietzsche and Scheler;[32] he understands the 'strange love', of which revolt is the expression, to be a gesture of 'folle générosité (insane generosity)' that gives everything to living men and women here and now[33] and liberates action from the 'servile' logic of calculation and capitalisation of human resources (material, intellectual, emotional) that is developed through the application of the concepts of interest and investment (*HR*, p. 322).[34]

It is no surprise that in the editorial of 9 February 1945 Camus identified the fight against the Nazi enemy with the fight against monetary powers (CAC8, p. 443).[35] Through the reading of Nietzsche, in particular *Humain, trop humain*, the author traces the policies of power and terror of Hitlerism and the bourgeois capitalistic system back to one common nihilistic logic, that may be symbolised in *Caligula* by the Treasury, which levels or 'equalises' all men. Cast in the conceptual

mould of compensation, 'equality' is the fulcrum of the moral judgement of guilt and of the idea that punishment is a form of retribu-
tion, according to which, in the Western tradition from Anaximander
onward, he who inflicts injury must *pay his debt* either to the Eternal
Being or to Society.

The definition of equality necessarily implies that the 'measurement'
and ranking of the value of human existence is based on the scale of
power;[36] in Nietzsche's genealogical analysis, the feelings of fear, contempt, as well as the pleasure of cruelty that human beings feel when
inflicting pain or in seeing pain inflicted upon others, are seen to incorporate this logic of compensation and equilibrium of 'weight' (value).
This logic is responsible for the twentieth-century 'human crisis',[37]
which, in Camus's view, is the extreme consequence of the 'measurement' and the fetishistic reduction of human existence to power and
domination. By abstracting man from the living movement of existence
and assuming him to be a function that depends on and is made for success, this logic coincides with the 'logique souveraine et fatale (sovereign
and fatal logic)' (II, p. 741) of the productive 'industrious' reason upon
which moral and political realism is founded. Hegel's 'dreadful principle'
for which man is made for History and not History for man (II, p. 741),
may be considered the emblem of this teleological reasoning, which in
turn is the mark of the nihilistic 'hatred of the world' and culminates in
the contemporary 'age of fear' (CAC8, p. 608). In the article he published
in *Combat* on 19 November 1946, Camus focuses on fear as a specific
technique used to 'level' existence to the servile mode of thinking and
relating to the world and to others in terms of efficacy and power; bound
doubly to 'equality' and therefore to domination, fear negates the acts of
communication and persuasion (CAC8, p. 611).

Radical idealism, which founds the fanatic's belief that s/he is absolutely right, delivers the living human being entirely over to *telos* ('history'). For Camus, as well as for Bataille and Simone Weil, however, there
exists a part of man that is as true and real as the rational side and is
irreducible to the 'historic' or teleological straitjacket. This part, which
may be rediscovered in the contemplation of the beauty of the world and
of people's faces,[38] is considered to be *useless* and powerless by traditional
rational thinking, that is to say, it goes beyond domination and force.

Camus was fully aware that the concepts of power and domination
did not exhaust all of the possible 'interpretations' of the world and,
especially, of political action. He had read *Humain, trop humain* and was
familiar with the aphorisms of 'Le voyageur et son ombre'; in 'Sagesse
des Grecs' ('Wisdom of the Greeks'), Nietzsche calls attention to the will

to dominate as an all too human feature, which is antecedent to the pleasure of equality, whose dangerous effects on the political order were well known to the Greeks. By sanctioning a space, the 'arena', where men could deplete their will to win and exert their dominance over others in musical or athletic competitions of equals, the Greek State affirms an understanding of political action that is a stranger to the logic of domination/equality and must be preserved from the threats of this inclination (*HTH*, II, 'Le voyageur et son ombre', 226).

Throughout his articles and editorials of *Combat* after the Liberation, Camus applies a strong negative connotation to the terms 'politics' or 'political', specifically in reference to the political practice codified in France under the Third Republic, which he traces back to the nihilistic constellation of rationalism or 'realism'. The combat of the Résistance fighter, however, testifies to a freedom that is irreducible to the voluntaristic logic of dominance and, as Camus repeatedly emphasises in his *Lettres à un ami allemand*, of political action that, although it refuses the logic of *ressentiment*, all the same steps into war and takes up the arms of violence to defend this freedom.

This freedom finds its roots in the artist's attitude of love and coincides with the absurd certainty that 'Everything is permitted', which, as Camus notes in his *Carnets* in 1943, entails 'qu'on ne juge plus les autres (that one no longer judges the others)' (II, p. 991), in other words, that one steps outside the relationship of domination that the role of the Master/Judge represents. In the same year, he confirms his firm refusal of the concept and practice of collective judgement and the need to reintroduce 'innocence' into public relationships (II, p. 1002). This does not mean that he refuses judgement *tout court*,[39] but rather he replaces moral justification, and the structure of domination that it entails, with 'aesthetic' judgement. This is the crucial challenge that emerges in Camus's articles and editorials published in *Combat* during the months that followed the Liberation and it explains why he chose the following fragment from Nietzsche's aphorism 'Les moyens pour arriver à une paix véritable' ('The means to real peace') (*HTH*, 'Le voyageur et son ombre', 284) for the epigraphy of the collection of his political articles of 1944–48 published in June 1950 under the title *Actuelles*: 'Il vaut mieux périr que haïr et craindre; il vaut mieux périr deux fois que se faire haïr et redouter ; *telle devra être un jour la suprême maxime de toute société organisée politiquement*. (Better to perish than to hate and fear, and better to perish twice over than to make oneself hated and feared – *this must one day become the supreme maxim of every politically organised community*.)' (II, p. 375, my italics).

The texts published in *Combat* attest to the author's refusal of the logic of nihilism, the presence of which he discerns in political philosophies[40] and in moral fanaticism ('fatalism'). The question of nihilism coincides with the issue of Western civilisation:

> [...] il s'agit de savoir pour nous si l'homme, sans le secours de l'éternel ou de la pensée rationaliste, peut créer à lui seul ses propres valeurs.[41] Cette entreprise nous dépasse tous infiniment. Je le dis parce que je le crois, la France et l'Europe ont aujourd'hui a créer une nouvelle civilisation ou à périr. (The question is whether man, without the help from the eternal or from rationalist thought, can create his own values. This enterprise is infinitely larger than us all. I say this because I believe it: France and Europe today must either create a new civilization or perish.)' (CAC8, p. 308)

Considered to be one of the great voices of the mystique surrounding the Résistance, Camus's writings for *Combat* clearly exceed the *topoi* of the French Résistance literature and attests to his effort to rethink and reconsider the concepts of action and politics outside the bounds of the teleological perspective of hatred and fear and present them from the 'aesthetic' perspective of love and freedom. The political position of *Combat*, which was manifest in the article 'De la Résistance à la Révolution' ('From Resistance to Revolution') of the first public issue of the journal in liberated Paris (21 August 1944), is openly based on a 'transfiguration' or revaluation of politics.[42] Like Sisyphus, the men of the Résistance, after years of torment and combat to defend their 'humiliated honour', have acquired a 'superior knowledge' (CAC8, p. 142)[43] that inspires their daily moral and political obligations and is the seed of all rebirth and renewal (CAC8, p. 199). 'Intelligence', 'courage', 'generosity', the 'truth of the human heart', constitute this type of knowledge that evades teleology and is the basis of a form of 'politics, meant in the noble sense of the word' (ibid.). The editorials 'Le sang de la liberté' ('The Blood of Freedom') (24 August 1944) and 'La nuit de la vérité' ('The Night of Truth') (25 August 1944) confirm the continuity that exists between the *good* nihilism of *Le Mythe de Sisyphe* and Camus's political reflections, with his constant emphasis on the flesh ('la chair') and the heart,[44] the human greatness and the 'great virile fraternity' of men and women.[45]

In August 1944, human greatness, namely, the rebel's decision to be stronger than his condition, is the constituting principle of Camus's concept of what peace will or ought to be after the Liberation. The only way man is able to overcome ('surmonter') an unjust condition is to be *just* himself (CAC8, p. 153); the parallel to Sisyphus, whose lucid 'conscience' makes him superior to his fate (*MS*, p. 302) and of the absurd conqueror is manifest. From the a-teleological or 'aesthetic' perspective of the absurd, to vanquish and to overcome mean to overcome oneself (*MS*, p. 280), namely, to be conscious enough of one's own strength to be sure that one will live constantly at that level, which exceeds and goes beyond the limits established by the logic of domination. In opposition to the modern conquerors that are portrayed by Malraux, Camus's 'absurd conqueror' illustrates the amazing greatness of human 'intelligence', which replaces the realist equation of reason and force or frenzy that lies at the heart of revolutions (*MS*, p. 280).

To overcome oneself means to rein in the exercise of one's force, to make oneself harmless when one is most fearful, not through calculation ('compensation') but through a high sentiment or spirit, which evades the nihilistic logic of domination and, thus, is situated beyond the reach of fear and hatred. This is the way towards achieving a true peace that, in conformity to Nietzsche's position, Camus imagined and propounded after the Liberation. As confirmed by his 1948 speech, 'Le témoin de la liberté', the absurd decision to be *just* in the face of an unjust condition, thus, to step outside the logic of 'compensation' that lies at the core of moral and political fanaticism, inspires the artist's political commitment. It consists in refusing to do harm by causing fear and suffering and in *seeing* or recognising the opponent rather than negating him as one's enemy (II, p. 491).

The absurd phrase, 'Everything is permitted', is the foundation of the rebel's mode of thinking and relating to the world; it rejects collective moral judgement, brings 'innocence' to social intercourse and does away with the modern humanitarian concepts of sympathy and altruism by affirming that the living human being cannot be reduced to the logic of reason (II, p. 1002).[46] In *Combat*, Camus invalidates the method of political realism (7 October 1944) and the productive or teleological model of political action, on which the twentieth-century 'optimistic' revolutions are founded, and proposes that morality be introduced to the practice of politics (CAC8, p. 240). In the editorial 'Le sang de la liberté' ('The Blood of Freedom') (24 August 1944), the blood that has been shed for the liberation of Paris symbolises the terrifying birth pangs of a revolution (CAC8, p. 150), but the metaphor of Marxian memory of traditional revolutionary movements is belied and gives way to the 'original theory' of a new 'pessimistic' or 'relative' revolution, a revolution 'without metaphysics' (CAC8, p. 198).

Revolt testifies to a freedom from power, politics and domination and links political action to greatness and *moral* justice; this 'generous' moral justice is based on the rebel's 'taste for honour', which is inseparable from a tremendous internal discipline (CAC8, p. 295)[47] and from a *disinterested* passion for human happiness that breaks the fetishistic economic and political chains.[48] In the editorial 'Morale et politique' (4 September 1944) Camus calls 'Revolution' the elimination of that which has been traditionally understood as politics and its replacement with morality (CAC8, p. 171). In other words, 'revolution' coincides with 'transfiguration' – as he writes to Brice Parain, '[ce] qui caractérise notre siècle, ce n'est peut-être pas tant d'avoir à reconstruire le monde que d'avoir à le repenser. (that which characterises our century, may not have so much to do with rebuilding the world than having to rethink it.)' (I, p. 909.)

In his letter to Bonnel, the absurd razes to the ground the moral interpretation of reason, which Camus traces back to the mode of evaluation of *ressentiment* ('hatred of the world'). The absurd is described as the effort to live 'beyond good and evil', namely, outside the traditional concept of morality and the nihilistic logic of efficacy and power. But, living means always to evaluate (I, p. 321): the absurd does not exclude an extra-moral form of revaluation of existence, namely, a form of value judgement that ignores the contempt that is traditionally held of man and the world (CAC8, p. 352). In opposition to the absolute claim of moral reason that levels existence to the relationship of domination, the artist embodies an alternative perspective, one that refuses to consider life to be secondary and to be a mere function of such human constructs as politics or economy (II, p. 744). The artist rejects the alternative, it is 'either the victims or the executioners'[49] – the executioner is someone, who, *for a living*, makes an attempt on the mystery of life and flesh (II, p. 490) and, thus, he is the expression of a nihilistic machine that crushes or reduces living beings to mere wheels. Camus expresses his artist's point of view in 'The Human Crisis', the text presented at Columbia University in 1946, where he formulates a political agenda that brings the creation of a space to the foreground intended for reflection and communication against radicalism and fanaticism. The last is possible only by ridding the world of terror, beginning with the global suppression of the death penalty. Doubtless our life belongs to others and it is proper that we give it to others when that is necessary; our death, however, belongs to ourselves alone. This is Camus's definition of freedom and the work of legislators and makers of constitutions. (II, p. 744)

7
Between Sade and the Dandy: Conclusion

> Dans nos ténèbres, il n'y a pas une place pour la
> beauté.
>
> Toute la place est pour la beauté.
>
> (R. Char)

In 1949 Camus was invited to develop his considerations on post-war Europe in a series of conferences in South America. He affirmed, in 'Le Temps des meurtriers' ('The Age of Murderers'), that Europe suffers from murder and abstraction and that these are the two manifestations of the same 'disease' (III, p. 353) that is caused by the 'virus of efficacy' (III, p. 356). He then examined how Europeans contracted this collective plague and investigated the ways to overcome it.

'Le Temps des meurtriers' recapitulates the French writer's scattered political remarks and confirms the internal consistency of his thoughts and opinions. Camus maintains that the 'plague' of terror(ism), which characterises the contemporary politics of efficacy and intimidation, infects men through thought and the act of *thinking erroneously* (III, p. 353). A murderer is someone who falls prey to his own delusory reasoning ('qui pense *mal'*) and subjugates every existing thing to the 'sovereign logic' of efficacy or utility (III, p. 356). This logic is seen to be deeply ingrained in the particular way of conceiving of political action or creation, the aim of which is to unify or to 'correct' the world by means of force and violence in the name of goals that have been previously stated in a specific theory (III, p. 358); it is not difficult to recognise the teleological model of 'productive intelligence' that, in *La Naissance de la philosophie à l'époque de la tragédie grecque*, Nietzsche detected at the very core of the Western philosophical tradition.

131

Camus goes even further and links the 'anthropometric virtue' of reason (II, p. 494), which 'measures' everything on the scale of efficacy and power, to the dematerialisation of objects and of men and women in the contemporary 'artificial' society where financial economy has prevailed over traditional forms of capitalistic economy and has replaced the land and gold with abstract symbols (IV, p. 251). This society, which mystifies and dissolves existence and 'prostitutes' words to the 'sovereign logic' of interest, reached its paroxysmal point in the twentieth century with extermination camps and the atomic bomb. Throughout his writings of the late 1940s and 1950s, Camus is extremely firm in his denouncement that the form of 'enslavement' of modern workers, diagnosed by Nietzsche at the end of the nineteenth century, is determined by the exact same 'sovereign logic' that governs the concentration and extermination camps.

Productive intelligence, of which calculating or utilitarian reason is the expression, interprets the world to be the Will's sphere of action and subjects nature and the lives of human beings to the violent domination of the end or achievement (success). Camus anticipates Hannah Arendt's argument in Part II of her 1951 *Origins of Totalitarianism* ('Power and the bourgeoisie') when he identifies total destruction ('nihilism') with the reduction of living men and women, as well as all things, to mere functions within a utilitarian system that removes the very last obstacle – the 'carnal truth' of existence – that stands in its way and limits its potentially endless accumulation of power.

Camus admits that his concept of nature is of Greek inspiration and specifies that he does not refer to the Aristotelian construct but rather to the concept of natural life characteristic of the pre-Platonic or tragic philosophers (III, p. 363). Nature is not conceived of in exclusively organicistic terms; it can neither be reduced to 'matter' nor to mere sexual instinct, but rather it denotes that which exceeds history and reason (III, p. 358). In other words, Camus identifies nature with a different 'economy' of life that attests to the impossibility for the rational 'economy' of efficacy and power to exhaust all aspects of existence; thus, he openly replaces productive or teleological reason with aesthetic or contemplative intelligence.

The 'Greek mind' Camus refers to ignores the idea of the 'original sin' that characterises the moral or teleological interpretation of existence and calls to mind the Heraclitean 'divine' way of thinking that is described in Nietzsche's *La Naissance de la philosophie à l'époque de la tragédie grecque*. In a note in his *Carnets* that was written in 1950, Camus places the Greek mind in opposition to the revolutionary mind, where, in this last, the (negative) moral judgement is instilled and actively subjects political action to the 'sovereign logic' or the logic of domination of *useful* murder ('meurtre utile', III, p. 355) – 'L'esprit révolutionnaire refuse le péché origine. Ce faisant, il s'y enfonce. (The revolutionary mind refuses the original sin. By so doing, it plunges into it.)' (IV, p. 1100.) Camus transforms Socrates, the 'enemy' of the Nietzschean will to power, into a 'deponent of freedom', who rejects the nihilistic logic of efficacy and replaces the violent monotony of *telos* with the generous and plural dimension of dialogue or communication (III, p. 364). The example of men and intellectuals, such as Socrates and Salvador de Madariaga,[1] among many others, helps us not to despair in the contemporary politics of hatred and fear and attests to man's 'honour of living', namely, to a dimension of human existence that is irreducible to power and violence.

Camus is primarily concerned with finding a way to overcome and move past the contemporary 'plague'. Since men have contracted it through the adoption of a particular productive or 'servile' thought, the only way they can overcome it is by changing their way of thinking (III, p. 359); it follows that freedom cannot be renounced. Camus reiterates what he wrote in *Le Mythe de Sisyphe*, identifying freedom with the emancipation from the relationship of domination, which is deeply ingrained in Western teleology. When he makes the affirmation that it is impossible to communicate with an 'enslaved man' (III, p. 361), he is referring to someone who 'measures' his life and actions and those of others according to the logic of efficacy, success and power, thus, to someone who is utterly incapable of recognising the flesh and dignity of other men and women, and is willing to negate his own.

Camus's idea of revolt attests to the existence of a condition of freedom from 'sovereign logic'. Insofar as this type of revolt does not aim at obtaining or gaining power (III, p. 359), there is more to it than a rebellious movement. It is in this differentiation, which is not a difference of degree but a difference of 'economy' or logic of existence, that the 'untimeliness' of Camus's political thinking lies; that is to say, his effort to move beyond the contemporary political theory and practice and speak to the future generations and to those who are and will be able to step out of nihilism was not only before its time but was also considered quite unwelcome, especially, in the French left-wing, Existentialist and Marxist, intellectual milieu. The metaphor of the arrow, reminiscent of Nietzsche, that closes *L'Homme révolté* (*HR*, p. 324) confirms the connection that Camus made between overcoming nihilism through a change in the mode of thinking and the rebirth ('renaissance') of man and

Western civilisation (III, p. 411) out of the ashes of the 'human crisis' that was witnessed by his generation.

The analysis of the concept and act of revolt leads Camus 'au moins au soupçon qu'il y a une nature humaine, comme le pensaient les Grecs, et contrairement aux postulats de la pensée contemporaine (at least to have the suspicion that, contrarily to the postulates of contemporary thought, a human nature does exist, just as the Greeks thought)' (*HR*, p. 73). Born in chains, the movement of revolt is said to reveal the presence of a 'natural community' or a 'metaphysical solidarity' of men and women (*HR*, p. 74). One could not be more mistaken in wanting to detect in Camus's particular form of 'naturalism' an essentialist conception of nature (Isaac 1992, p. 232). The postulates of contemporary political thought that Camus refers to are the organicistic and humanistic concepts of 'nature' and 'natural community', from Rousseau's theory of the natural goodness of men to the twentieth century mystics of Nazi and Fascist communities of blood and soil, which, through Nietzsche and Scheler, Camus traces back to Platonic-Aristotelian teleological thinking. Thus, the Greeks that Camus alludes to are the philosophers and poets of the age of tragedy, who conceive of nature from the a-teleological or 'aesthetic' perspective of *contemplative* intelligence (see Chapter 5) rather than the philosophers of the great tradition of Metaphysics,[2] in which Nietzsche detected the logic and categories of *productive* intelligence.

From Plato to Hegel,[3] and to the French anarchists and Russian nihilists of the second half of the nineteenth century, 'nature' is considered to be the horizon of force, a lawless matter that awaits the domination of and the order bestowed by free Will or Reason. The finalistic or productive logic that is characteristic of this concept of 'nature' is the key to understanding Camus's criticism of anarchic thinking. This criticism, developed in the section of *L'Homme révolté* on 'Trois Possédés' ('Three Possessed') was intended by Camus to bring a 'renewed libertarian thought' into full light, that is, one that is free from the categories and logic of romantic nihilism (III, p. 410).

In his analysis of the three Russian thinkers, Pisarev, Bakunin and Nechayev, who in the second half of the nineteenth century inspired and put into practice the theoretical positions that were immortalised by Dostoyevsky's characters of *The Possessed*, Camus's understanding of nihilism is explicitly identified with the constellation of utility/interest/force/moral fanaticism/radical idealism. Pisarev is seen to provide his political successors with a particular mode of reasoning or intellectual vice ('rationalist obscurantism'), consisting in the negation of everything but (self)interest or utility and that *uses* reason to appro-priate the prejudices of faith (*HR*, p. 194). In doing so, the basis for fanaticism is established. Camus then calls attention to the Hegelian categories and the 'romantic' Manichean struggle between Good (social revolution) and Evil (State/counter-revolution), which, in Bakunin's meditations, are seen to drag nihilism into the very heart of the move-ment of revolt.

In *L'Homme révolté*, Bakunin is the representation of an anarchic thought that conceives of the political foundation of a new world in fabricative terms; the new world is the artwork of a demiurge/master, who condemns this world and by exterminating this evil creation finds final redemption (*HR*, p. 196). According to Camus, Bakunin reduces the movement of revolt to rage, or what he calls the 'naked' or 'bio-logical' principle of revolt (*HR*, p. 195), and identifies the passion for creation with a passion for destruction; thus, he links revolutionary thinking to the festive joy of the oppressed, who, through destruction and cruelty, obtain compensation for the anger that they felt for the wrongs that they have suffered.[4]

Camus warns against the temptation, which lies at the core of con-temporary anarchic or libertarian theories, to 'read' the movement of revolt through the nihilistic lenses of productive or teleocratic logic; in doing so, confusion between revolt and *ressentiment* could be gen-erated.[5] Destruction of all existing law and endless extermination are still attributable to the illusory postulate of free will and attest to the persistence of a logic of domination, which identifies action or creation with the violent prerogative of a master who judges and condemns that which exists according to his inflexible ideal end goals and objectives.

Camus's criticism of nihilism in modern and contemporary polit-ical thought was reinforced by the reading of *Les Sources et le Sens du Communisme Russe* (*The Origin of Russian Communism*) by Russian émigré Nicolai Berdiaev in 1947, as may be attested to by his reading notes in the *Carnets* (Novello 2004). A leading figure of the Russian 'Legal Marxists' and of the *Vekhi* group, who at the turn of the century rejected the 'communal romanticism' of populist social theories in the name of an anti-rationalist 'revolution' of the spirit (Glatzer Rosenthal and Bohachevsky Chomiak 1982), Berdiaev's analyses of the relation-ship between Russian and nihilistic movements and Communism were reminiscent of Nietzsche's 'immoralist' criticism of the Western 'servile' or moral reason.[6]

Berdiaev particularly emphasises the link that exists between the utilitarian logic that he detects in revolutionary thinking and the moral justification of revolutionary action, which persisted in spite of the apparent rejection of traditional moral and civic values – all that which *serves* the revolution, is *moral*.' (Berdiaev 1963, p. 84; II, p. 1101.) By propounding total negation of State, morals, art and science, Russian anarchists and nihilists are seen by Berdiaev to subject their movement of destruction to the finalistic perspective of traditional 'apocalyptism', thus, to a moral interpretation that judges the world to be *evil*. Bakunin, in particular, speaks of the creative or 'constructive' power of the revolutionaries' passion for destruction and, by retrieving Marcion's thesis of the struggle against the creation of the evil God (Berdiaev 1963, pp. 56–7), he incorporates the Gnostic idea of redemption through extermination into the heart of the Russian revolution (Berdiaev 1963, p. 88).

Berdiaev detects a 'romantic' contempt of the world in the Russian 'apocalyptic' nihilism that culminates in the moral ascetic surrender of the individual to the final accomplishment of the 'good of the people' that is identified with the people's material interest.[7] By referring to populism as the ethical drive of the Russian intelligentsia, it is conceived to be the expression of the logic of calculation and efficacy characteristic of teleological reason as it is applied to the concept of revolt. Camus's interest in *Les Sources et le Sens du Communisme Russe*, as may be confirmed by various pages of notes in his *Carnets* (II, pp. 1100–3), can easily be explained by the fact that Berdiaev's theses supported the French author's criticism of the utilitarian 'sovereign' logic of political reason, which he had already begun to expound upon through his analysis of the 'romantic' attitude of the Gnostics in *DES*.

By reducing men and women to 'expendable capital' to be used in succeeding in obtaining the ultimate realisation of the revolutionary objective (*HR*, p. 200), Bakunin and Nechayev express an anarchic theory that identifies total freedom with the wild universe of the *outlaws* (*HR*, p. 198), in other words, with a movement of rebellion that rejects reason's laws and constructs (the traditional moral, social and political order) without, nevertheless, relinquishing the logic of domination upon which they are founded. Thus, the Russian nihilists take Karamazov's phrase 'Everything is permitted' to the letter but fail to comprehend and live the essential consequence of these abysmal words, which lies in the negation of the logic of domination that underlies the hierarchies of teleological reason.

Yet, is a world without law a *free* world? (*HR*, p. 196). According to Camus, the concept of freedom (from law) that is embraced by the Russian anarchists still 'enslaves' men and women to the logic of efficacy and to the 'servile' exercise of force that are implicit in teleological thinking; this results in the disseverment of the vital connection with love and friendship that is constitutive of revolt. His criticism of both liberal and libertarian theories, evident in his letter, 'Révolte et Romantisme', addressed to the journal *Libertaire* (III, p. 410), and in his homage to Salvador De Madariaga (IV, p. 569), concerns that which he refers to as the nihilistic 'prejudices' of modern political philosophy, namely, the 'sovereign logic' that shapes our mode of thinking and our behaviour in all aspects of economic, social and political life.

In his *Actuelles II*, Camus denounces '*romantic* nihilism', which he considers to be an intellectual vice or murderous inconsistency, as the common denominator of bourgeois and alleged revolutionary thinking (III, p. 452). Romantic nihilism conceives of 'nature' as an abstract construct (II, p. 492), a 'stage' without order (*an-archè*) on which the 'drama' of History is played out and it reduces 'human nature' to (free) Will that competes to gain power under the direction of teleological reason. Camus rejects these postulates of contemporary philosophy (*HR*, p. 73) but does not fall back and rely on an essentialist interpretation of 'nature' and 'human nature'; he approaches his understanding of both terms from the Heraclitean perspective of contemplative rather than productive intelligence, in other words, from *an artist's point of view*. From this 'aesthetic' or a-teleological perspective, nature is not devoid of order but, from the lucid or 'divine' point of view of this Heraclitean intelligence, the 'harmony of the contraries' is revealed (II, p. 493).

Beauty is the 'law' of nature and is not only distinct from but finds itself in opposition to the utilitarian laws of teleological reason; it is the unity that a creator or artist discovers after a long *ascesis*, which has nothing to do with the 'romantic' ascesis of *ressentiment* (III, p. 364). The artist's ascesis expresses his attitude of love and admiration, rather than an attitude of pride and hatred. Admiration and love indicate where the *limit* of action lies and, more importantly, of political action as it has been conceptualised in the Western philosophical political tradition; in other words, these attitudes delineate a space that is not subjected to the sovereign master/slave or executioner/victim logic of domination that is characteristic of contemporary political reason.

Like Simone Weil, Camus places beauty and love outside and beyond the nihilistic bounds of efficacy and force. The concept and act of revolt is not reduced to the mere 'biological' or psycho-political dimension of anger; this last coincides with the rebel's '*No*' that is raised against all forms of humiliation of men and women. Nonetheless, a '*Yes*' is necessarily incorporated in the act of revolt, that is to say, revolt takes a stand against and opposes the movement of contempt, which abases and adopts hostile action against human life. Revolt is a movement of love (III, p. 329) for which all lives are equivalent (*HR*, p. 206). Camus describes the source of revolt as 'un principe d'activité surabondante et d'énérgie (a principle of overabundant activity and energy)', which 'fracture l'être et l'aide à déborder (fractures the being and helps it to overflow)' (*HR*, p. 75). The image of the raging torrent, breaking free from the dykes of 'fatalism', in other words, from the fixed constructs of teleological reason that engender *ressentiment*, emphasises the rupture, from the nihilistic straitjacket of hatred of all that exists, that revolt represents.

The rebel does not have any desire to be what s/he is not, a feeling that is typical of self-contempt, and refuses the 'anthropometric virtue' of *romantic* nihilism that enslaves human life to a potentially endless quest for and accumulation of power. The rebel struggles for her/his integrity and for that of others against all violent and violating attempts to touch or alter one's existence. In this struggle, the rebel discovers that s/he belongs to a 'natural community' and this goes beyond the feeling of belonging to a 'community of *interests*' (*HR*, p. 74, my italics). It is this last feeling of belonging that inspired the terroristic political actions of the Russian nihilists, anarchists and revolutionaries between the end of the nineteenth century and the twentieth century.

In approximately 1946, Camus begins to work on the project of a tragedy and an essay on the Russian revolutionaries of 1905, 'les meurtriers délicats' ('the delicate murderers'), to whom he devotes *Les Justes* and a section of his *L'Homme révolté*. The question that he raises in these texts is reminiscent of Camus's earlier *Lettres à un ami allemand* and his articles written for *Combat*. The contradiction that was experienced by the men of the Résistance, who had to come to terms with the use of violence and killing in order to combat for and defend their integrity from *logical* murder, in other words, from the systematic attempts at their lives, which were perpetrated in the name of a logic of efficacy and power, exhibits tragic affinities with the profound contradiction that was experienced by the Russian terrorists in the early years of the twentieth century.

The Russian 'delicate murderers' are the symbol of a revolt that rises up against negation, abasement, humiliation and mutilation of human 'flesh' and life; they testify to their love (of men and women) against the contemporary 'calculating men', who consider human life to be of little or no value at all when *compared* to the act of reaching or obtaining their final goals (*HR*, p. 207). In Camus's view, teleological or productive thinking is what justifies the systematic humiliation and annihilation

of men and women, and it is this way of thinking on which the contemporary age of State terrorism and executioners-philosophers is based.
In a world that justifies oppression, negates freedom and honour and
is populated by men who are not receptive to other points of view and
cannot be persuaded because they refuse to recognise that those whom
they humiliate and kill exist, these 'delicate' rebels are torn by the contradiction between their incapacity to violate life and to make attempts
upon (*'toucher à'*) the life of others and the feeling that there is no other
choice than making use of violence to stop the violence itself and defend
that which they hold dear and love most. For the Russian revolutionaries
of 1905, as well as for the 'terrorists' of the French Résistance, violence
and murder are as inevitable and 'necessary' as they are unjustifiable
(*HR*, p. 206).

It is in this murderous 'fatality' that the contradiction that was
brought to Camus's attention by Scheler's phenomenological analysis of
ressentiment, between the attitudes of hatred and love of the world lies,
in other words, between two opposite and opposed 'economies' of life
wherein revolt is seen to have a participatory role in both (*HR*, p. 205).
Within the movement of revolt against humiliation, a 'community of
love' (*HR*, p. 207) is discovered, the basis of which lies in a constellation of values ('generosity', 'honour', 'honesty') that are considered to
be 'heretical' according to the hegemonic constellation of teleology and
power. The nihilistic logic of efficacy dissolves living men and women,
who are made of flesh and blood, in favour of the abstract construct of
the 'individual', who is condemned to utter solitude by his/her endless
competition against others for higher status and greater power. The
'aesthetic' or 'illogical' movement of revolt, on the other hand, affirms
the plural dimension of human lives and the unavoidable fact that they
touch-*together* or come in contact with each other (*'complicity'*, *'con-
spiration'*), which is made manifest by the new *cogito* of this different
mode of thinking, 'Je me révolte, donc nous sommes (I revolt, therefore
we are)' (*HR*, p. 79).

In 1958, Camus writes the preface to the German edition of the poems
of his friend, René Char, who had fought in the Résistance. Camus considered Char to be a poet of revolt inspired by the tragic optimism or
the 'sagesse aux yeux pleins de larmes (wisdom of eyes filled with tears)'
of pre-Socratic Greece (IV, pp. 618–19), who demonstrated that revolt
cannot be confused with temper or emotion ('l'humeur'). Camus makes
a distinction between two types of revolt, one that aspires to instate
global servitude and the other that desperately attempts to establish a
free order (IV, p. 619). His 'delicate murderers', just as the men of the

Résistance, demand that an order free from humiliation be established, in other words, an order that does not belong to the hierarchy of utility and *telos*.

Although they use terroristic means to fight a system of humiliation and oppression, the 'delicate murderers' chose to pay their crime with their lives, thus, their revolt evokes the value of the ancient Greeks (*HR*, p. 208), who indicate the possibility of a different way of evaluating existence that is irreducible to the utilitarian values of efficacy and force and is the historical testimony of this absurd freedom ('*we* are'). In *Réflexions sur la guillotine*, Camus observes that the Greeks believed that an unpunished crime infected the city (e.g. the plague that decimates Thebes after the murder of the king in Sophocles's *Oedipus Rex*) (IV, p. 155), and that such guilt could only be washed away by the murderer's death. Camus situates the Russian terrorists of 1905, much like Oedipus, between innocence and guilt (*HR*, p. 208); they die so that the future community of men and women will be free from humiliation and may not be infected by their crime. Camus places their example in opposition to the twentieth century revolutionaries, who, on the contrary, accept humiliation and total and unpunished culpability (*HR*, p. 209) by introducing the category of *useful* or profitable murder.

Over the centuries, and especially in contemporary times, the scaffold has been the symbol of the contagion of the plague or the 'disorder of nihilism'(IV, p. 164), the evidence that a man or a woman's life ceases to be sacred the moment one judges that abusing or killing her/him is *useful*. Camus writes that nihilism, which is intimately connected to the movement of a 'disappointed' or despairing religion ('religion déçue'), culminates in terrorism (*HR*, p. 203); he also calls the Russian terrorists of 1905 'fanatics' (*HR*, p. 204), although he admits that they are fanatics of a rare kind, who have scruples when it comes to making attempts on human lives, even if this is *useful* in the fight against an oppressing power and in winning the cause of freedom.

Fanaticism is a movement of 'disappointed religion', which Camus detects at the core of nihilism and which he sees to be embedded in all forms of terrorism or *logical* murder, be the murderous act carried out by an individual or by a State. The Russian terrorists of 1905 choose to take on the profession of *executioner* (*HR*, p. 205), that is to say, their murderous acts are subjected to the same logic, which, in Camus's view, is the basis of the contemporary concept of justice. In particular, the analysis of the practice of the death penalty in France, England and United States, from the eighteenth century to the post-Second World War years, which Camus develops in his *Réflexions sur la guillotine*, sheds light on what Camus understands to be a 'movement of a disappointed religion' (*HR*, p.203).

A movement of hatred and contempt is incorporated in fanaticism; this movement is expressed through the application of a negative *moral* judgement that abases and condemns men and women. Executioners are described as 'humanists' (IV, p. 165), who Camus, just as Max Scheler, considers to be the philosophical expression of *ressentiment* (see Chapter 6).[8] Modern humanists look *down* upon other human beings, they *accuse* them and proclaim the definitive judgement of their absolute guilt and final elimination (IV, p. 156). Capital punishment must be understood to be the extreme consequence of moral reason's nihilistic logic.

Camus detects the intellectual vice that Nietzsche calls 'radical idealism' to be at the core of capital punishment, and it is on this that the fanatic's claim of absolute reason is founded. In concurrence with Nietzsche, Camus identifies the assertion of absolute reason, which places the fanatic's beliefs in a 'safe' or ideal space that transcends facts and is beyond the reach of intelligence and doubt, to be a movement of 'religion without transcendence' (IV, p. 163); this last is intimately connected and intertwined with the utilitarian logic of Western philosophy.

Camus writes that the *death penalty is to death what concentration camps are to prisons* (IV, p. 144). The eliminative punishment acts much like a revenge or a premeditated reaction to a crime, but its logic that drives the principle of compensation or retaliation off its hinges. The death penalty incorporates a form of organisation that is in itself a source of moral sufferings more terrible than death (IV, p. 144) and that uses methods of terror to annihilate the criminal and reduce him/her to inert matter ('patient') or to a mere thing ('parcel') (IV, p. 145). Fear eliminates equity and dignity (IV, p. 147) and reduces men and women to powerlessness and solitude.

In his refutation of capital punishment, Camus denounces the inherent 'sovereign logic' of domination and the extreme consequences of teleological reasoning, which lower human life to a function or 'expendable capital'. The parallel Camus draws between capital punishment and concentrations camps is not a rhetorical image used to stir emotional reactions in the reader; the French writer is convinced that the machine of the death penalty puts into practice the techniques of fear and hatred, which are the distinctive element of all forms of *legal* terrorism in 'free' (Liberal) States as well as in so-called 'totalitarian' States. Capital punishment brings the 'disorder of nihilism', in other words, the murderous consequences of teleological reasoning to the surface: the humiliation

and annihilation of human life that is considered to be capital/utility/
matter; the 'religious' or 'illusory' assertion to have absolute reason,
which incorporates the postulate of free Will, that judges and condemns
(master/demiurge); the application of the postulate of individual responsibility, a construct of moral reason used to justify the extermination of
life; the definition of *legal* murder as an eliminative punishment that is
useful for maintaining and preserving society (IV, p. 151).

It is particularly in the concept of *'useful* murder', which is distinctive
of terrorism, that Camus detects a finalistic argument that is rooted in the
delusory 'romantic' opposition between absolute evil and absolute good
upon which the twentieth century 'political utopias' are founded. 'State
crime' or *legal* murder is the result of the transformation of society or the
political body into an end objective in and of itself; the preservation and
success of society has become the final objective to the service of which
human lives are fetishistically subjected and sacrificed (IV, p. 162).

Teleology is the basis of the religious character of such political claims,
which Camus refers to and denounces with the expression 'romantic
nihilism' (III, p. 452). His criticism of twentieth century Marxism must
be understood in light of his criticism of modern humanitarianism;
in 'L'Artiste et son temps', Marxists are defined as 'humanists', that is
to say, *accusers* of men and women, who negate their existence in the
name of a new man and a 'Paradise on earth' to come (III, p. 452).
The moral interpretation entailed in this teleological argument is what
renders murder *useful*.

In *L'Homme révolté*, Camus's interpretation of Marx's political theory
is a confirmation of an argument, that he first formulated in *DES* after
having read Scheler. Marx is described as an 'eye-opener'; his 'theory
of mystification' is a universally valid demand for honesty and intelligence – it is also applicable to alleged revolutionary mystifications – that
reveals the reality that lies hidden behind formal values and principles,
'fat words' and illusory constructs: 'Si les principes mentent, seule la
réalité de la misère et du travail est vraie. (If principles are deceptive,
only the reality of poverty and work is true.)' (*HR*, p. 233.) Camus makes
a distinction between this part of Marx's theory and his philosophical
interpretation of politics and political action, which, in his opinion,
is embedded in the teleological and productive model of the Western,
Platonic and Christian tradition and, more precisely, in the tradition of
'apocalyptic' or 'romantic' Historicism. This 'romantic' historicist vision
culminates in that which Camus calls the nineteenth century 'bourgeois prophecy' and may be illustrated by Comte's positivistic religion
of progress and divinisation/adoration of society.

By highlighting the link that exists between the Positivistic divinisa-tion of that which is relative (e.g. society) and the Jacobin cult of Reason, Camus denounces the 'intellectual vice' that consists in affirming the transcendence of principles ('ideals') and Reason, in other words, in placing a particular, all too human opinion beyond the reach of doubt, critical reason and constructive discussion; Nietzsche defines this 'radical idealism' (*A*, V, 543) and Camus identifies it as a movement of 'religion without transcendence', that Marx placed at the very core of his concept of politics (*HR*, p. 228). Camus traces 'political reason' in Liberal as well as in revolutionary theories back to Jacobin radicalism or moral fanati-cism, which are rooted in hatred and fear; in his *Réflexions sur la guillo-tine*, he considers this to be a nihilistic disorder ('cancer') of the political body rather than, as it is willingly declared, its logical necessity.

From his earlier writings right up to his last articles and essays, Camus's effort has been directed toward fighting this 'fatalism' or 'sovereign' logic and has aimed at demonstrating that a different mode of thinking not only is possible but exists and to which the ancient Greek tradition is tes-timony. In *L'Homme révolté*, Christianity, especially, Gnostic Christianity, and Marxism are seen to combine the moral concept of punishment with the philosophical concept of history (*telos*), thus, to replace contempla-tion with *transformation*, which is the reverse side of total destruction (*HR*, p. 223);[9] the ancient 'love of the world' that the Greeks understood to be ordered (*cosmos*) was ignored by the early Gnostic Christians, who considered it to be evil and eagerly awaited its demise.[10]

Camus traces the Christian and Marxist justification of the domina-tion, violation and transformation of nature, including human nature ('the new man'), which culminated in the use of atomic bomb, back to this moral interpretation and places this murderous teleology in oppo-sition to the ancient Greek and Plotinian concept of *mediation*. Camus bases 'mediation' in an attitude of love of man and the world and con-siders it to be rooted in *contemplative* intelligence; this last does not aim at subduing nature but rather it 'obeys' the law of beauty, just as an art-ist does when expressing the creative process. Camus declared his belief in ancient values (Camus 1972, p. 1615) and identified his anti-modern political position with the rejection of fanaticism (II, p. 1061).

Simone Weil[11] was among the writers who, in Camus's view, testified to the possibility of (re)thinking the world and political action so that they would rest outside the murderous limits of the logic of productive intelligence and force. Simone Weil understood the 'disease' that affects the contemporary age and denounced the act wherein men and women are reduced to a mere function as a third form of oppression alongside the traditional forms of oppression imposed upon man by money and arms (III, p. 885). She also individuated the remedies to nihilism in '*enracinement*', the 'need for roots' and the 'return to tradition', which consists in 'penser juste, à voir juste (thinking in a just way, seeing in a just way)' (Camus 1972, p. 1700). In his preface to Weil's *L'enracinement*, in June 1949, Camus refers to her book as a 'treatise of civilisation' that provokes the age of efficacy and power by affirming the 'truths of love' (III, p. 864), which, without sentimentalism, mean the refusal of the logic of efficacy and the rejection of humiliation.

Camus detects a concept of justice in Weil that is different from that of political realism; to the '*effective* justice' claimed by Communist State terrorism, as well as by the Algerian terroristic movements,[12] and that is founded on *hate* (IV, p. 570), Camus places in opposition a *generous* justice that recognises and incorporates the '*love* of man and the world' and is characteristic of the 'aesthetic' or tragic perspective of contemplative intelligence. By evading the royal way of teleological reason and breaking free of the logic of utility and power, beauty plays a crucial part in Camus's understanding of a *just* way of thinking and acting. The concept and act of revolt, which are considered to be a crime against the laws of moral or productive reasoning, are inseparable from beauty.

In 1947, Georges Bataille provocatively traced a parallel between Camus and Sade and detected in the two writers the same refusal of *legal* murder and attack against the laws of Reason (Bataille 1947). Bataille maintained, however, that, by refusing suffering and murder (crime) in *La Peste*, Camus reintroduced the 'trivial' morality of utility, which aims at preserving life ('happiness') and rejects the aesthetic dimensions of 'play' and risk, which denote freedom or 'insubordination' to reason (Bataille 1947, p. 15). In a note in his *Carnets*, Camus agrees with Bataille's understanding of Sade on legitimate murder (II, p. 1093); however, in the literary or fictional crimes of Marquis de Sade's works he sees the exemplary illustration of the servile logic of Western thinking, which Bataille had asserted that he had rejected.

Camus had began to work on de Sade in approximately 1941, and, in *L'Homme révolté*, he devotes an entire chapter to this 'man of letters' (*HR*, p. 91), which he considered to be an author that had presented one of the possible paths of absurdity and a temptation to metaphysical revolt. De Sade is the anti-artist, the 'philosopher in chains', who identifies total freedom (from the laws of morality) with the unleashing of sexual instinct; nature is sex, and lawless sexual desire needs crime (*HR*, pp. 92–3). In de Sade's novels, which were written during his imprisonment in the Bastille, the dream of philosophical or moral reason reaches its climax in a creative process in which reality cannot intervene nor refute. The philosophical *hatred* of the world culminates in the literary execution of nature, which replaces the joyful acquiescence of the lovers, whose bodies are made accomplice, with the mathematical equivalence of victims and the mechanical *equality of things* (*HR*, p. 93).

De Sade's fictional writings illustrate the paroxysmal consequences that the logic of power and the rule of force have; contemporary 'romantic' sensibility was bound to appropriate his 'frantic' freedom, along with his detailed descriptions of the techniques and methods used to dehumanise man that were conceived by an all too human (productive) intelligence, only to put them into practice in the extermination and concentration camps (*HR*, p. 100). The paradox, in Camus's view, is that the murderous imagination of this man of letters, theoretician of sexual crime, was used by contemporary executioners to accomplish that which he abhorred most: *legal* murder.

Camus traces this transition from fiction to reality back to a particular mode of thinking that he defines by using Nietzsche's term, 'romanticism'. This last brings the problem of artistic creation to the foreground as the crucial point of contemporary politics, or more precisely, the distinction between two different forms of revolt, that have generally been confused: political action and creation or art (II, p. 493). Camus asserts that the root of this distinction lies in the nostalgia for unity or the thetic drive of human thought, which is situated at the core of the movement of revolt. On one hand, reason satisfies this thetic drive by means of radical idealism (intellectual vice) and interprets political action through the productive lenses of teleology, thus, in terms of domination (master/slave relationship); in Camus's view, the modern conqueror, *by the very logic* of his attitude of hatred of the world, becomes an executioner (II, p. 493). On the other hand, the artist embodies an 'honest' way of thinking that rejects the productive logic, that lies behind the violent effort to *transform* the world, or the absolute realisation of human thetic aspiration, as may be represented by Caligula's desire for the moon. Camus's Heraclitean artist lives and creates out of his passion for that which is relative, that is to say, he refuses radical idealism or moral fanaticism and embodies a type of action that honours others and refuses to humiliate or make attempts upon their living 'flesh' (II, p. 493) – the reduction of life to 'naked' matter is a dishonest or mystifying construct of productive intelligence.

Camus rejects the opposition Bataille makes between law/reason/ utility/servitude, on one hand, and crime/passion/freedom, on the other; as he writes in 1950, servitude may be considered to be the strongest of twentieth-century passions (IV, p. 1097), and, if the refusal of 'servile' or utilitarian reason may be understood to be a crime against the laws of efficacy and power, revolt does not necessarily entail murder. As a matter of fact, Camus understands freedom to be the rejection of the structures of domination, which are embedded in contemporary thought, speech and action; the artist testifies to a freedom from the alternative victim *vs.* executioner, which is an intrinsic part of contemporary politics, as well as at all levels of social intercourse.

Like Scheler, Camus considers the principle of security or preservation of life to be a utilitarian construct of existence, typical of modern humanist thinking; he affirms that freedom and risk are in opposition to the (total) freedom of the contemporary conquerors. His artist embodies the Hellenic a-teleological mode of thinking that, through Nietzsche, he associates with the absurd indifference to all forms of 'safety' or security of the body, life and well-being (IV, p. 1096). The artist creates *dangerously* (*HR*, p. 297) because he thinks and creates outside the laws of utility, of which the modern concern for safety or 'petty happiness' is the expression, and because his freedom is considered to be a threat to the laws of power and efficacy (IV, pp. 264–5).

The artist's indifference to 'security', however, is opposite and opposed to the acceptance of humiliation, which his typical of the aesthetic pose of the dandy. In *L'Homme révolté*, nineteenth century dandyism is an illustration of the movement of 'romantic nihilism',[13] which characterises the modern concept of action that is identified with pure dynamism and force under the Nazi system of State terrorism (*HR*, p. 214)[14] and inaugurates the political 'aesthetics' of the twentieth-century revolutionaries, which culminates in mass production of corpses of concentrations camps (*HR*, p. 272).[15]

Frenzy or power (*HR*, p. 255), from the French Revolution to contemporary terrorisms, is the final word of contemporary 'romantic' nihilism against which Camus proposes a change of perspective that actively replaces the murderous 'sovereign logic' with the artist's honest or *just* way of thinking, which would *transfigure* society and politics.[16] Revolt is the preliminary condition for the 'renaissance' to be made possible in an entire civilisation affected by nihilism; in Nietzsche's own words, revolt consists in replacing the judge with the *creator* (*HR*, p. 296). In Camus's view, this 'transfiguration' must begin from the workers' condition, by restoring their dignity as creators.

In the concluding pages of *L'Homme révolté*, Camus refers to revolutionary syndicalism to support his conviction that such a 'transfiguration' of society and work is possible.[17] Judged to be 'ineffective' by

Communist thinkers, syndicalism intervenes to improve the workers' condition, that is to say, it starts from the concrete basis of professional employment, 'qui est qui est à l'ordre économique ce que la commune est à l'ordre politique, la cellule vivante sur laquelle l'organisme s'édifie, tandis que la révolution césarienne part de la doctrine et y fait entrer de force le réel. (that which is to the economic order as the Commune is to the political order, the living cell upon which the organism builds itself, while the Caesarian revolution starts from the doctrine and forcibly introduces reality into it.)' (*HR*, p. 316.) Revolutionary trade unionism, just like the Commune,[18] is evidence of a revolt that refuses 'romanticism', or 'bourgeois nihilism' (*HR*, p. 318), and is the basis on which a 'realistic' politics may be found, a form of politics that is exercised without the use of terror and defends those 'truths of the flesh' against bureaucratic and abstract centralism (*HR*, p. 317).[19]

In the 1946 text 'The Human Crisis', Camus outlined a political agenda for the world governments, in which he invited them to eliminate terror beginning with the abolition of the death penalty; for legislators and the makers of constitutions, whom he exhorted to affirm freedom by eliminating the fetishistic primacy of politics over life that was experienced in twentieth century State terrorisms; for philosophers, to whom he asks a creation or re-evaluation of positive values that would reconcile pessimistic thinking with optimistic action (II, p. 744). Camus considered this change of attitude, which consists in replacing hatred and fear with love and honour, to be the work of each and everyone.

The artist, through his work, brings the example of a 'creative revolution' against the new adventurers of nihilistic revolutions into the light; in other words, the 'harmonious revolt' of beauty, in its *useless* creativity, over the centuries and in the midst of crime, attests to human greatness (*HR*, p. 299). It is for this reason that Camus, in November 1951, concluded:

Il n'y a pas un bon et un mauvais nihilisme, il n'y a qu'une longue et féroce aventure dont nous sommes tous solidaires. Le courage consiste à le dire clairement et à réfléchir dans cette impasse pour lui trouver une issue. (There is neither a good nor a bad nihilism; there is only a long and fierce adventure in which we are all involved. Courage consists in saying it clearly and in thinking through this impasse in order to find a way out of it). (III, p. 395)

Notes

Introduction: An 'Untimely' Political Thought for Serious Times

1. Deleuze 2005, p. 3.
2. *HTH*, II, Preface, 1.

1. The Twentieth-Century Politics of Contempt

1. 'Le Pari de notre génération', Interview in *Demain* (24–30 October 1957), English translation 'The Wager of Our Generation' (Camus 1961, pp. 169–75).
2. Dismissed 'as an early modern polemical weapon for symbolically annihilating cultural opponents' (Woolfolk 1990, p. 105), sociologists have recently attempted to sketch a viable theory of 'nihilism', distinguishing two theoretical approaches to this much contested notion: the first defines nihilism as the denial of ultimate transcendent foundations; the second approach, originating from Nietzsche's work, traces nihilism in the Platonic–Christian dichotomy of sensory and supra-sensory Being (God, Truth), of immanence and transcendence, and in the devaluation of the immanent sphere of the phenomena as appearance and illusion.
3. Arendt refers to the three Marxian sentences 'The philosophers have only interpreted the world differently; the point is, however, to change it'; 'Labor created man'; 'Violence is the midwife of every old society pregnant with a new one' (Arendt 1993, p. 21).
4. See I, p. xix; Garfitt 2007, p. 27; Garfitt 1983, pp. 103–11.
5. Grenier published the essay 'Le Nihilisme Européen et les Appels de l'Orient' in two parts under the pseudonym of Jean Caves in *Philosophies* between March and May 1924 (Garfitt 2007, p. 34).

2. 'Undisguised influences'

1. 'Rencontres avec André Gide', in *Hommage à André Gide* (November 1951) in III, 881–5.
2. See Viggiani 1968; Arnold 1984, p. 123.
3. 'La Philosophie du siècle', *Sud*, n. 7 (June 1932), p. 144, in I, 543–5.
4. 'Sur la musique', *Sud*, n. 7 (June 1932), pp. 125–30, in I, 522–40.
5. Between 1931 and 1932, the *NRF* devotes a series of articles to Nietzsche, Kierkegaard, Dostoyevsky and Bergson; to Andler's *Nietzsche sa vie et sa pensée*. VI. *La Dernière philosophie de Nietzsche* and Podach E.F. (1931) *L'effondrement de Nietzsche* (Paris: Gallimard) – both texts are listed in Camus's private library (see Favre 2004, pp. 204–5) – and to Stefan Zweig's *Nietzsche*.
6. According to Roger Grenier, in 1932 Camus paraphrases *La Naissance de la tragédie*, in particular the opposition of the Apollonian and the Dionysian'

(in Le Ridier 1999, p. 143), but textual analysis confirms that the source of Camus's commentary of the 1872 work is Nietzsche's 1886 preface, which roots the desire for beauty in pain and the creation of the 'God-artist' in a liberation from pain through illusion, namely, in a 'symbolised ecstasy' that is opposed to reason's *moral* interpretation of existence ('Essay of self-criticism', 4–5). The fact that Camus bases the Apollonian in the Dionysian is not due to an error on the part of the young student (Arnold 1984, pp. 126–7), but to the reading of the 'Essay of Self-Criticism', and, more precisely, to the inspiration he gets from the pages Nietzsche writes on the opposition between the pessimism of the 'Dionysian Greek', creator of symbolic forms, and the optimism of (Socratic) withering logic; see Vattimo 2000, p. 158.

7. See Vattimo 2000, pp. 143–83.
8. Preface to the re-edition of Grenier's *Les Îles* (1959).
9. As Deleuze notes, 'Nietzsche was first introduced in France not by the 'right' but by Charles Andler and Henri Albert, who represented a whole socialist tradition with anarchical colourings' (Deleuze 2004, p. 129.) The language and style of Albert's translations especially contributed to Nietzsche's success in French literary circles, confirming the image, dear to Gide and Valéry, of a writer and thinker that was opposed to the 'professional philosopher' (Le Ridier 1999, p. 61). In 1932, Gide is one of the 'undisguised influences' of Camus's early writings and his favourite literary example (see Camus and Grenier 1981, p. 11).
10. A copy of the 1930 edition of *Aurore*, translated by Henri Albert (Paris: Mercure de France), that was underlined and annotated by Camus, is part of his private library collection (Favre 2004, p. 203). According to his friend and poet, Blanche Balaine, in the mid-1930s, *Aurore* was Camus's favourite book by Nietzsche (Balaine 1999, p. 104).
11. A copy of the 1932 French edition of Lou Andréas-Salomé's *Nietzsche* (Paris: Grasset) was listed in the catalogues of Camus's private library until 1971 (Favre 2004, p. 204).
12. I respect the order proposed in the first volume of the new Pléiade edition of the complete works (Camus 2006), which differs from that proposed by Viallaneix (CAC2; Camus 1980).
13. According to the biographer, Nietzsche's philosophical experience rejects all abstract systems and culminates in the 'mystical apotheosis' of the thinker (Andréas-Salomé 2002, p. 287). Camus's emphasis on his mystical soul's 'fervour' and 'desire for superhuman communions' (I, p. 941) suggests that he understands mysticism from the perspective of the Nietzschean theory of knowledge, in other words, as a liberation from rationalism.
14. The figure of the absurd comedian in *Le Mythe de Sisyphe* evokes the Nietzschean thinker portrayed by Andréas-Salomé (see Andréas-Salomé 2002, pp. 35, 39).
15. The striking affinity between the two figures in 'Incertitudes', the one who commands and the one who obeys, and the philosophical experience evoked in Andréas-Salomé's biography of Nietzsche suggests that Camus uses this text to reflect his personal investigation ('reveries') in the thinker's 'tragic split' that 'transfigures' the individual and allows him to conquer health through illness (Andréas-Salomé 2002, pp. 44–5).
16. The vigorous discipline of his 'anarchy of instincts' is the thinker's way to 'greatness' (*'grandeur'*) (in Andréas-Salomé 2002, p. 38). Exhortation to

(self-)control was also spoken of by Jean Grenier to Camus (see Garfitt 2007, pp. 29–30).

17. In *Ecce Homo*, Nietzsche insists on the crucial role that illness plays in the genesis of his thought, which allows for 'liberation' and a 'return to himself' (*EH*, 'Pourquoi j'écris de si bond livres', 'Humain, trop humain', 4). In similar terms, Camus evokes tuberculosis as a 'fortunate illness', which marked the transition from the 'happy barbarity' (IV, p. 621) of his youth, which was absorbed by the sensual pleasures of the Algerian beaches, to the artist's creative period, which was rooted in suffering and the tragic confrontation with a precocious death.

18. The image of the labyrinth recurs in Nietzsche's *Aurore* (III, p. 169), also quoted in Andréas-Salomé 2002, p. 40.

19. Anticipating *Le Mythe de Sisyphe*, Camus renounces the accessibility of Truth without relinquishing his unquenchable desire for the ideal and the infinite (I, pp. 950–1).

20. Andler employs the notion of 'intuitions sentimentales (sentimental intuitions)' to address the different phases of Nietzsche's philosophy, whose criticism of rationalism is said to stem from a primitive 'éclairage émotionnel' ('emotional light') (Andler 1958b, pp. 14–15). Although it is not cited in the bibliography of 'Sur la musique', we cannot exclude that, in 1932, Camus read this book that devotes an extensive analysis to Nietzsche's philosophy of tragedy. A copy of the 1921 edition of *Le pessimisme esthétique de Nietzsche* figures in the inventories of Camus's private library, along with the other five volumes of Charles Andler's *Nietzsche, sa vie et sa pensée* (Paris: Gallimard) (see Favre 2004, p. 204).

21. Camus's pages on the anthropomorphic character of thinking in *Le Mythe de Sisyphe* are reminiscent of Andler's emphasis on the schemes or value judgements by means of which men impress their seal of order and reason upon reality.

22. It is not possible to say whether Camus read Nietzsche's *Zarathustra* in 1932 or not; the book does not figure in Arnold's inventory (1979), while Favre (2004) refers to a copy of the 1942 French edition of *Ainsi parlait Zarathoustra* translated by M. Betz (Paris: Gallimard). Nonetheless, there are reasons to believe that even in the early 1930s Camus was acquainted with the text of *Zarathustra* through his teacher, Jean Grenier. The island is also a recurring theme in the writings of Grenier, whose 'Îles Kerguélen' ('The Kerguelen Islands') was published in *NRF* in May 1931. At the time Camus was completing his 'reveries', Grenier was working on 'Les Îles Fortunées' ('The Fortunate Isles'), then on 'L'Île de Pâques' ('The Easter Island'). In 1933, Grenier published *Les Îles* (*Islands*), which was to have a great influence on Camus (IV, pp. 621–24). As Garfitt observes, 'for Grenier, the island is a place of inevitable confrontation with the self, in the absence of all other distractions, and is therefore in its essence metaphysical. One is confronted with the truest image of oneself, and it is that experience that can then release one's inner song [...]. There is a genuine desire to understand (on the part of Camus), a sense of almost surprised recognition, and at the same time a fair amount of resistance to Grenier's line of thought, which is strongly influenced by Indian philosophy and is constantly pulling away from the human, relegating it to the periphery. Camus is struggling with Grenier's essentially metaphysical and potentially antisocial approach, and wanting

to assert the possibility of a definitive commitment to the values of the here-and-now' (Garfitt 2007, pp. 31–2). I suggest that Nietzsche provided the arguments for the assertion of such commitment in Camus's early writings.

23. *EH*, 'Pourquoi j'écris de si bons livres' – 'La Naissance de la tragédie', 2. In Camus's copy of *Ecce Homo*, this passage is underlined (Arnold 1979, p. 96).

24. Cited in Ansell-Pearson 1994, p. 85. I argue that Camus develops his criticism of Bergson's philosophy from the Dionysian or tragic perspective of Nietzsche's 1880s writings, which is essentially a theory that rejects *ratio* without evading its logic (*'dédoublement'*) and, therefore, is a fine expression of the modern *'faiblesse'* (weakness) and *'lâcheté'* (cowardice) (I, p. 944). Both in his articles and in *Intuitions*, Camus rejects the Bergsonian theory, which he believes to be an attempt to fight *with* reason *against* reason (I, p. 544), cf. Nietzsche's letter to Mathilde Maier (5 July 1878), in Nietzsche F. (1986) *Sämtliche Briefe. Kritische Studienausgabe*, 8 Bde, (eds) Von G. Colli und M. Montinari (München–Berlin–New York), Bd. V, pp. 337–8.

25. In the second part of *The Origins of Totalitarianism*, Arendt uses the term 'nihilism' to denote this utilitarian logic, which she finds at the core of political modernity (Arendt 1951b, p. 144).

26. Andreas-Salomé insists on the question of mysticism in Nietzsche's philosophy, which she associates with the destruction (by excess) of the human, of which the (sub)human and the *over*human are the opposite consequences (Andréas-Salomé 2002, p. 251).

27. See Camus's letter to Claude de Fréminville (Todd 1996, p. 59).

28. *A*, V, 546 ('Esclave et idéaliste'). According to Viggiani, Camus reads Epictetus during his first convalescence in the hospital aged seventeen (cited in Todd 1996, p. 47).

3. Tragic Beginnings

1. Camus defines Dream as a 'disorder of reality' (I, p. 953). Nietzsche's criticism of so-called 'idealism' is constantly evoked throughout his writings of 1933–34 (see I, p. 96).

2. See also the fragment ('Tu vas mieux...') of the unfinished project (1934–36) of an autobiographical novel, *Louis Raingeard* (I, p. 95).

3. See Camus's letter to Fréminville (in Todd 1996, p. 62).

4. See Andler 1958c, pp. 19 ff. In 1932, Camus reads the third book of Schopenhauer's *Le Monde comme Représentation et comme Volonté*, which tackles the liberating force of art from the categories of space, time, causality and finality, as well as from the suffering related to them. According to the German philosopher, art is beyond common knowledge, which is submitted to the principle of reason, and fixes into eternal formulas that which flows in the uncertainty of appearances (I, p. 965).

5. In his 1933 writings, Camus insists on the emancipatory force of art, which breaks the chains of modern enslavement with its 'miraculous' newness, and frees the subject from the suffering that is related to harsh everyday experience. The 1933 aesthetic theory echoes Nietzsche's pages on the 'aesthetic pessimism' of the ancient Greeks. Charles Andler's emphasis on Nietzsche's 'psychology of Art' is more than likely to have influenced young

Camus, whose early writings recall Andler's books, *Le pessimisme esthétique de Nietzsche* (1921), *Nietzsche et le transformisme intellectualiste* (1922), and *La dernière philosophie de Nietzsche* (cf. I, pp. 961, 964 with Andler 1958a, pp. 29, 141; Andler 1958c, p. 472).

6. See Camus's preface to the 1959 edition of *Les Îles* (IV, pp. 621–4) and Camus and Grenier 1981, pp. 13–14.

7. J.S.T. Garfitt detects in Jean Grenier's spiritualist philosophy a strand of Bergsonism, thus confirming a Bergsonian influence in Camus's early reflection via his teacher (see Garfitt 1983, p. 4).

8. Reflecting Nietzsche's considerations on art in *Human, All too Human* (I, 147), Camus writes that 'l'Art lutte contre la mort. À la conquête de l'immortalité l'artiste cède à un orgueil vain, mais à un juste espoir (Art struggles against death. In seeking to conquer immortality, the artist yields to a vain pride, but a legitimate hope)' (I, p. 960; Camus 1980, p. 172). The verb 'to immortalize' is employed by Andler with reference to the aesthetic process (Andler 1958c, pp. 476, 485); seemingly inspired by Schopenhauer, the emphasis on creative 'fixation' recurs in Bergson's *Essai sur les données immédiates de la conscience*.

9. In 1932, Camus reads Plotinus' *Enneads* I, 6 in Émile Bréhier's French translation (I, p. 1363). He then studies Bréhier's commentaries of the Hellenic philosopher for his *DES* on Neo-Platonism. On the Bergsonian influence on Bréhier's interpretation of the *Enneads*, see Mossé-Bastide 1954, p. 2.

10. Camus uses the Bergsonian term 'synthèse' ('synthesis') to denote the peculiar internal unity of the artistic process that reaches beyond ordinary life and is rooted in the artist's particular perspective and sensibility (I, p. 962). Art recreates a special world, different from the three-dimensional one that is submitted to *ratio*. In *L'Art dans la Communion*, which reflects the argument of Bergson's *Essai sur les données immédiates de la conscience*, Camus resorts to the Plotinian notion of beauty to confirm the Bergsonian thesis that architecture 'evades' ordinary existence (I, p. 961).

11. See Garfitt 2007, p. 29. 'Beyond Christianity, [Grenier] was interested in the mystics of all traditions, and in Eastern metaphysical systems which are as much religious as philosophical' (in Garfitt 1983, p. 73).

12. According to Eric Werner, the lyrical essays of *Noces* define a 'descending' dialectics that does not transcend but brings back to the world and is, therefore, opposed to the Plotinian mystical 'ascent' outside this world (Werner 1972, p. 66). I argue that Camus's 1933 texts betray the influence of Bréhier's reading of Plotinus, which insists on an 'immanent' interpretation of Plotinus' *logos*.

13. By identifying history with political action *tout court*, commentators find it difficult to explain why, for Camus, 'the temptation to quit history and identify with nature is futile' in the end (Isaac 1992, pp. 232–3). I suggest that 'history' represents a specific model of action submitted to *ratio*, that the experience of freedom in ecstatic 'Communion' with nature exposes and allows to dispel, paving the way to the primacy of action outside the straitjacket of teleology.

14. According to R. Gay-Crosier, Camus refers to the pétainist literature (II, p. 1391, n. 10). The expression 'mentalité primitive' echoes L. Lévy-Bruhl's *Le Surnaturel et la Nature dans la mentalité primitive*, reviewed in the *NRF* in June 1932 (n. 225) and cited by Camus in *DES* (I, p. 1046).

15. Camus was familiar with the theses of Rosenberg's *Myth of the 20th century*, as well as with Nazi racial mysticism through the articles of B. Parain and E. Vermeil in the *NRF* (No. 263, pp. 280–2). He was critical of the French fascist neo-nationalist doctrines propounded by Charles Maurras (I, p. 565) and Thierry Maulnier, that conceived of the human community in 'biological' terms, and appealed to the myths of blood and soil (see Carroll 1995).

16. Philippe Lacoue-Labarthe draws attention to this Aristotelian interpretation of *mimèsis* and to the reduction of politics to art (*technè*) that is revelatory of *physis* itself (Lacoue-Labarthe 1998, pp.102–3).

17. As Philippe Lacoue-Labarthe notes, the notion of *ergon* ('work') lies at the core of the totalitarian 'organic' model of politics as Total Art (Lacoue-Labarthe 1998, pp. 108–9).

18. Cf. Noys 2000, pp. 46–8.

19. See Corbic 2003, pp. 128 ff.; Corbic 2007. Corbic's reading draws on François Noudelmann's interpretation of Camus's lyrical essays (Noudelmann 1997, pp. 133–55).

20. According to Pierre Nguyen Van-Huy, the lyrical essays of *Noces* illustrate a paradisial 'State of Union', an original 'Garden of Eden' that Camus's man experiences on earth (Nguyen Van-Huy 1968, pp. 27–8). From this perspective, *Le Mythe de Sisyphe* marks the 'Fall' from the original Unity/Paradise to a condition of separation, associated with knowledge and conscience. This thesis recurs in various commentators, who oppose the pre-rational primordial union with nature to the Cartesian method of Camus's absurdist philosophy (see Corbic 2003, pp. 135–6; Sherman 2009, pp. 23 ff.).

21. In the 1937 conference on 'La culture indigène. La nouvelle culture méditerranéenne' at the Maison de la culture of Algiers, Camus explicitly speaks of the abstractions of rationalisation that justify the violent and murderous actions of fascist and imperialist power politics (I, p. 571).

22. In his letter to Blaise Romeyer, dated 1933, Bergson states having turned mystics into a philosophical method (Bergson 1972, p. 1506). The texts of Camus's *La Maison Mauresque* attest to the influence of Bergson's considerations on the mystics (cf. Mossé-Bastide 1954, pp. 7 ff.). Like the Plotinian architect, the author recreates his own 'house of emotions' in a procession that evades the despotic *ratio* of ordinary life and moves towards the simplicity and unity of Communion (*ascent*). This experience 'transfigures' existence, and is the commencement of a different form of life that is then recollected in memory and art (*descent*).

23. Echoing Bergson's interpretation of *Enneads*, Camus understands love and ecstasy in mystic terms. Bergson identifies ecstasy as a form of super-conscience with participation in creative Love (cf. Mossé-Bastide 1954, pp. 21 ff.).

24. As J. Lévi-Valensi observes, the author is a witness to the union of the elements, and his body is their 'couche nuptiale' (I, p. xxvi).

25. In the unfinished novel, *La Mort Heureuse* (*The Happy Death*), written around 1936 and published posthumously in 1971, wherein the lyrical essays of *L'Envers et l'Endroit* and *Noces* are recalled, Mersault's self-discipline consists in attuning the pounding of his blood to the violent pulsation of the sun. For the analysis of this text, see Susan Tarrow 1985, pp. 34–49, and Grenier 1987, pp. 65–78.

26. The plenitude of 'Communion' is expressed through a series of dynamic sensual images – 'torrent de lumière (torrent of light)', 'confuse symphonie de la lumière (intricate symphony of light)', 'l'attirance infinie de l'horizon marin (the infinite attraction of the sea and the maritime horizon)' – which emphasise the mobility and tension that characterise this union as 'un arrêt vertigineux et tourmenté (dizzying and tormented pause)' (I, p. 972; Camus 1980, p. 149).

27. According to Sharad Chandra, the celebration of the nuptials between man and nature signals a mystical experience that dissolves the false ego or subjectivity (Chandra 1995, pp. 55, 130).

28. Influenced by Bergson and Emile Bréhier's commentaries (I, pp.1077–8), Camus seems to distinguish two 'layers' in Plotinus' thought and to reject his essentialist (Aristotelian) solutions in favour of an 'immanent' reading of the *logos* (see Mossé-Bastide 1954, pp. 1–2).

29. The Bergsonian influence is apparent in the verses of Scipio, the young poet of *Caligula* in the 1941 version of the tragedy (Act II, scene XIV) (I, pp. 356–7).

30. Jean-François Mattéi seems to place Camus's lyrical pages in what Lévinas calls the twentieth-century philosophies of the 'elemental' (Mattéi 1997, pp. 277–8).

31. On the assimilation of love and knowledge in mystic literature, see Cuozzo 2000, pp. 58 ff.

32. *Enneads* VI, 9, 11, 23; see also Schürmann 1996, pp. 202, 206.

33. The author refers neither to a dispersion of the unitary subject of knowledge in sheer sensory perception, nor to an intellectual abstraction of the physical being. The Plotinian notion of consciousness (*synaisthesis*), understood as the extreme degree of 'concentration' in contemplation, is, in my view, more appropriate in expressing the meaning of Camus's notion of 'chair *consciente*' (I, p. 133) than the modern concept of 'conscience'. Bréhier's commentaries of Plotinus may have inspired Camus's understanding of contemplation as a movement of expansion of spiritual life, which identifies thinking with a deepening of sensation beyond abstraction (Bréhier 1982, p. xvi). See also Grenier 1987, p. 61.

34. In 'L'Inde imaginaire', Grenier detects the attempt to go beyond the limits of life and *create a new man* in the contemporary forms of political romanticism (in Grenier 1959, p. 140).

35. Associated with the principle of non-activity and indifference, passivity is a recurrent element in the work of Jean Grenier, who was an attentive reader of Dionysius the Areopagite, Sextus Empiricus, Nicholas of Cusa and the quietists, as well as of Indian and Chinese thought (see Baishanski 2002, p. 86).

36. Camus takes his distance from Bergson's 'experimental philosophy', understood to be the active liberation from the pettiness of the 'human'. According to Hannah Arendt, Bergson merges two contradictory models, the model of contemplation (intuition) and that of fabrication which is identified with violent *activity* (Gk. *energeia*) exerted upon oneself. Bergson speaks of the 'essentially active, I might almost say violent, character of metaphysical intuition' (in Arendt 1978a, p. 123).

37. See Camus's 1934 letter to Fréminville (cited in Todd 1996, p. 71). It is more than likely that Camus's reading of Pascal was influenced by Jean Grenier. In his doctoral thesis devoted to the philosophy of Jules Lequier, Grenier dwells

on the Pascalian criticism of rationalism and of the Cartesian method of the 'Cogito', as well as on the primacy of freedom over the so-called scientific method (Grenier 1936, pp. 43-ff.); see Garfitt 1983.

38. '[...] the philosopher-king applies the ideas as the craftsman applies his rules and standards; he "makes" his City as the sculptor makes a statue; and in the final Platonic work these same ideas have even become laws which need only be executed.' (Arendt 1998, p. 227.)

39. Cf. Schürmann 1982.

40. Camus understands Plato's dialectics in Nietzschean terms, namely, as the construction of a 'romantic' or philosophical reason that separates man from the Good (*DES*, p. 1012).

41. See also Severino 1989.

42. The metaphoric constellation of 'touch' and 'contact' recurs in Jean Grenier's 'L'attrait du vide' in *Les Îles* (Grenier 1959, p. 24) to distinguish contemplation from philosophical thought. In 'L'Inde imaginaire', Grenier suggests that there is a connection between the Greek teleological understanding of becoming and nihilism, or attraction of nothingness (*nihil*), and he explicitly distinguishes the Greek notion of contemplation, identified with the intellectual *vision* of the Absolute, from the Hindu communion, which abolishes the distance between the philosopher and his object of contemplation (Grenier 1959, pp. 138–9). Grenier resorts to the metaphor of touch to refer to the pre-ontological constellation of Hindu thought, which, in his view, negates the teleological primacy of the end (the artwork) and inspired the thought of such authors as Diogenes and Plotinus (Grenier 1959, p. 130).

43. Jean Grenier identifies contemplation with the effort to become *close* (cf. Grenier 1959, p. 149). Jean-Luc Nancy has recently linked the notion of 'presence' (*près-ence*, or being-close) to the dimension of contact (Nancy 2001, p. 196).

44. Camus dwells on these issues in the first chapter of *DES*, pp. 1009–12.

45. From Camus's early written fragments intended for his autobiographical novel, *Louis Raingeard*, through to *L'Envers et l'Endroit* (I, p. 63), the hopes, which are engraved on the tombs of a small cemetery overlooking the bay of Algiers, justify the absurdity of suffering and death by resorting to an otherworldly eternity. Camus rejects them as the creations of an 'idealistic' mind.

46. On the relation between Aeschylus's tragedy, *Prometheus bound*, and the emergence of Greek ontological thinking, see Severino 1989.

47. A reference to the vulture may also be found in Andler's *Le pessimisme esthétique de Nietzsche* and in Victor Hugo's poem, 'Quand Eschyle au vautour dispute Prométhée', in *Les Quatre Vents de l'esprit*. According to Olivier Todd, Hugo's complete works figured in the private library of Camus's uncle, Gustave Acault, with whom the young man lived for a few months after his first bout of tuberculosis (Todd 1996, p. 48).

48. As Susan Tarrow notes, 'the experience of chronic illness deepened [Camus's] perception of the body as the vital source of all human activity [...] for Camus, recurrent bouts of tuberculosis served as constant reminders of his mortality [...]. A sick body is yet another form of oppression. This sense of the role of the body in one's life is reflected in Camus's horror at the inflicting of pain on individuals, his intransigent opposition to violence, torture, and the death penalty.' (Tarrow 1985, pp. 4–5.)

49. In a note in *Carnets* (1939), Camus identifies Prometheus as a revolutionary model (II, p. 889).
50. See the fragment, 'Sans lendemains' (March 1938) (I, p. 1200). The image disappears in O'Brien's English translation (Camus 1960, p. 51).
51. Cited in Todd 1996, p. 68.
52. Camus and Grenier 1981, p. 22.
53. The contemplation of beauty is described as 'cette initiation [qui] prépare à des illuminations plus hautes. (this initiation [which] prepares one for higher illuminations.)' (*N*, p. 131.)
54. In the 1930s, Camus shares with Georges Bataille a special concern for the question of the 'futility' or 'uselessness' of action, namely, of the liberation of the spiritual energies from the finalities and justifications of teleological reason (I, p. 1198); see also Chapter 5.
55. In 'La Mort dans l'âme', Camus notes the inscription on the fronton of an Italian villa: '*In magnificentia naturae, resurgit spiritus*' (*EE*, p. 61). In this essay he reworks and incorporates the earlier fragment 'Tu vas mieux...' (I, p. 96 and *EE*, pp. 62–3).
56. In 'Amour de vivre', the beauty of the Mediterranean landscape brings the futility of reason's questions to the foreground; it does not provide a Platonic 'redemptive vision', but it provokes the 'Nada' (Nothing) and 'désespoir de vivre (despair of living)' (*EE*, p. 67) – beyond *telos*, life designates the time of a desire *without object* (*EE*, p. 68).
57. See I, pp. 1278, 1463.
58. Letter to Jean Paulhan (August 1930). Grenier detects in Bergson's intuitive philosophy an illustration of the contemporary 'naturalistic' reduction of thinking to life, and he specifically refers to the philosophies of the Vedas and of Plotinus to emphasise the tragic limit that separates the two (Paulhan and Grenier 1984, p. 32). Insisting on the affinities of Camus's thought with Indian philosophy, in particular, with the *Gîtâ*, Chandra insists on the distance that exists between the absurd thought of *Le Mythe de Sisyphe* and Bergsonism, which, in her view, traces intuition back to the instinctual 'animal' depths of human thought and remains anchored to a naturalistic perspective (Chandra 1995, pp. 47–8).
59. Anticipating Pindar's epigraphy to his essay on the absurd (*MS*, p. 217), Camus writes in October 1933: 'Mais qu'importe vraiment ce qui nous manque quand ce que nous avons n'a pas été *épuisé*. (But what does it truly matter what we lack when what we have is not *exhausted*.)' (I, p. 984, my italics.)

4. An Artist's Point of View

1. Author of an *Introduction à la philosophie allemande depuis Nietzsche* (1926), Groethuysen plays a pivotal role in the circulation of the works of Nietzsche, Max Scheler and Marx, as well as in the diffusion of German sociological and psychoanalytical thought in France (see Le Ridier 1999, p. 134).
2. Interviewed by Carl Viggiani, Camus recalls reading Shestov, Spinoza, Descartes, Max Scheler and the philosophy of Hinduism between 1930 and 1936 (Viggiani 1968, pp. 200–8, cited in Chandra 1995, p. 31).

3. Grenier uses this expression to refer to Camus's activity in the PCF (in Grenier 1968, p. 40). See also Camus and Grenier 1981, p. 22.

4. In *Le Choix* (1941), Jean Grenier draws attention to 'this paradoxical operation of a blind action which bestows principles upon thought by the very fact that this action is exerted' (cited in Garfitt 2004, p. 105).

5. For both Nietzsche and Scheler, this pessimistic logic culminates in the Hegelian theory of the 'creative value of negation', which illustrates the apostate's rationalism of *ressentiment* (Scheler 1958, p. 46).

6. In 'Remarques sur l'idée de progrès' (1936), Grenier refers to the Marxist pejorative use of 'the Middle Ages' to denote an economic, social and cultural backwardness (servitude, irrationalism); he uses the same term 'Middle Ages' with a strong negative acceptation to denote the twentieth-century totalitarian regimes (in Grenier 1967, p. 161).

7. See Scheler 1958, p. 165. Max Scheler confirms the young student's early criticism that teleological reason is at the service of utility and refers to Bergson's attempt at liberating the vital phenomena from the tyranny of *ratio*, in *L'Évolution créatrice*, as an 'honest' way of considering things beyond the mode of thinking of *ressentiment* (Scheler 1958, p. 184).

8. 'De qui et de quoi en effet puis-je dire: "Je connais cela!" Ce cœur en moi, je puis l'éprouver et je juge qu'il existe. Ce monde, je puis le toucher et je juge encore qu'il existe. Là s'arrête toute ma science, le reste est *construction*. (Of whom and of what indeed can I say: "I know that!" I can feel this heart within me, and I judge that it exists. I can touch this world, and, likewise, I judge that it exists. There ends all my knowledge, the rest is *construction*.)'(MS, p. 232, my italics.)

9. Lev Braun seems to understand generosity in the lyrical essays to mean a 'readiness to give up what is most vital' (Braun 1974, p. 23). But generosity comes into existence through ecstatic contemplation; thus, it coincides with a liberation and overabundance of energies, rather than with a renouncement.

10. Camus was aware of Nietzsche's criticism of pity in modern philosophical political thought; he seems to echo Nietzsche's use of the terms 'piety' and 'uprightness' with reference to the immoralist 'artist's conscience' in *Aurore*.

11. Camus and Grenier 1981, p. 22.

12. Scheler rebuts Nietzsche's identification of the Christian notion of love with *ressentiment*, and distinguishes the mystics' love, understood to be an intense concentration of vital energies, from the notion of love that is the basis of modern humanitarianism. The last is described as a refined and rationalised product of the submission of sexual instincts to the utilitarian logic of self-preservation (see Scheler 1958, pp. 101, 115).

13. Camus does not refuse Marxian notions of class struggle and historical materialism but rather the teleological illusions that they take on in later Marxist theories. In his analysis of the relationship between Christian morality and utilitarianism and modern humanitarianism, Scheler separates class *hatred*, which is the expression of *ressentiment*, from the notion of class struggle, which he detects already in early Christian morality and is revived in contemporary Marxist theory (Scheler 1958, p. 136).

14. Cf. Grenier 1968, p. 47 and the letter of 26 July 1936 (Camus and Grenier 1981, p. 26).

15. I, p. 1209; Camus and Grenier 1981, p. 23. After joining the PCF Camus actively supported the Arabisation of the party and the Blum-Viollette project (see Tarrow 1985, pp. 22–4).
16. According to Jean Grenier, Camus's decision to join the Communist Party was not determined by a theoretical preference for the Marxist doctrine. He confirms that Camus's study of the relationships between Hellenism and Christianity in *DES* was an important source of meditation that challenged the meaning of his political engagement (Grenier 1968, p. 42).
17. '[...] rien de moins que la destruction complète d'une création ([...] no less than the complete destruction of a creation)' (*DES*, p. 1029). See Sloterdijk 2007.
18. Instead of directing his attention to the single doctrines and discussing their validity from an historical perspective, the young student of philosophy proves to be essentially concerned with the origins of these theoretical solutions, which he traces back to a distinct and particular attitude towards the world. The terminology used in *DES* confirms the influence Scheler's phenomenological work had on Camus, especially, the distinction Scheler makes between attitude and doctrine in the analysis of the early Christian and Neoplatonic philosophies, which is essential for the later formulation of Camus's method of thought in *Le Mythe de Sisyphe*.
19. As Camus observes, Plotinus' philosophy anticipates Pascal's '*cœur*' (*DES*, p. 1041). It is not surprising to find echoes of the mystic images of the Fathers of the Church, explored in the first chapter of *DES*, in the lyrical pages of *Noces* – e.g, Saint Ignatius' image of the 'eau vive' (*DES*, p. 1015) recurs in 'Le désert' (*N*, p. 137). In the mystic notion of 'flesh' ('la chair'), Camus detects the emblem of a spiritual condition of nobility and greatness that lies beyond philosophical rationalism (*N*, p. 129); he rejects philosophical materialism considering it to be a product of abstraction (*N*, p. 131), in favour of a dimension that is in-between misery and love ('a mi-chemin entre la misère et l'amour', *N*, p. 130). Like Grenier, Camus is 'unable to go on from that point to rejoice in the assurance of either a pantheistic union [...] or a union with the personal God of the Christian or Islamic tradition.' (Garfitt 1983, pp. 70–1).
20. Scheler proffers the example of the notion of *ascesis* in primitive Christian thought, which he understands as a spiritual liberation rather than the eradication of man's vital energies, thus, as a way to 'evade' the utilitarian mechanisms of basic preservation of life. This form of *ascesis* is the opposite of the asceticism of redemption or what Camus defines the 'ascétisme d'orgueil' ('asceticism of pride') of the Gnostics (I, p. 1029). Scheler ascribes the notion of 'pride' to the moral constellation of *ressentiment* (Scheler 1958, p. 28).
21. See Sloterdijk 2007, pp. 133 ff.
22. Bréhier interprets Plotinian intelligible as the 'internal face of things' (in Bréhier 1982, pp. xvi ff). In his essays, Camus uses the terms *envers/endroit* (reverse side/right side) with a connotation that is reminiscent of Bréhier's Bergsonian commentaries of Plotinus. On Camus's reception of Bréhier, see Archambault 1972, pp. 50 ff.
23. Bréhier 1982, pp. xvi, vi–ix, and pp. xvi–xvii; see also chapter 5 on the soul (ibid.), pp. 183 ff.

24. Camus insists on Plotinus' use of the image of light to express a notion of unity that is not a con*fusion* ('indifference') and lies outside the abstract divisions of discursive reason (*DES*, p. 1050). Camus's early Bergsonism is apparent in his interpretation of Plotinus' philosophy (cf. Deleuze 2008, pp. 37ff.) and deserves more extensive exploration and study.
25. Jeanne-Paule Sicard's letter to Francine Camus (20 June 1960), I, pp. 1208–9.
26. Walter Langlois emphasises the historical accuracy of *La Révolte dans les Asturies* and its authors' optimistic belief in the possibility of improving the workers' condition through the realisation of the social and political reforms, for which the Asturian workers had died (see Langlois 1981).
27. The company was denied permission to use the hall, where the play was to be performed, by Augustin Rozis, the mayor of Algiers who was elected by a coalition of the political local right and extreme-right. The text was immediately published by Edmond Charlot and, a year later, extracts of *Révolte dans les Asturies* were read at the Maison de la Culture under the title 'Espagne 1934. Chœur parlé' (I, pp. 1209–10).
28. Without heading or date, this fragment is classified in the 1933 notes for *L'Envers et l'Endroit* (I, p. 1424).
29. Camus calls attention to the Neoplatonic effort to conciliate rationalism and mysticism (*DES*, p. 1005).
30. See the opening lines of his 1935 *Carnets* (II, p. 795).
31. The question of colonialism is a central issue of the Communist International from 1920 and thereafter. The process of arabization of the Algerian section of the PCF, actively promoted by Jean Chaintron (Barthel) in September 1935, inserts itself in the political programme of the 'anti-imperialist revolution'. The Communist position on the 'indigenous question' in favour of the independence of the North-African colony is likely to have persuaded Camus to join in the PCF (Lévi-Valensi 1986, p. 139). Reference to the Internationalist political programme may be found in Camus's conference of February 1937. Camus rejects the contemporary Fascist nationalisms as 'signs of decadence' (I, p. 566) and sees in Internationalism a condition for the creation of a popular Mediterranean culture against the nihilistic abuses of intelligence with the finality of conquest and dominion (I, p. 572). In the early phase of his political engagement, Camus's recruitment of Moslems in the nationalist party Étoile Nord-Africaine (ENA), under the auspices of the Communists, reflects the support given by the PCF in favour of the Arabs' demand for independence. After the Stalin–Laval pact (May 1935) and the change in the party's priorities, for which the 'indigenous question' was strongly downplayed in favour of anti-Fascist activity, Camus openly criticises the party's leadership. His dissent regarding the new political stance of the PCF, in his opinion, responsible for sacrificing the social question of the Algerian people oppressed by colonialism and for paving the way to radical nationalism, culminates in Camus's expulsion from the political party in 1937 (see Tarrow 1985).
32. In the articles published in the *NRF* and his letters written around 1936, Jean Paulhan calls attention to the Manichean attitude common to both fascism and anti-fascism (see Cornick 1995).
33. According to Grenier, the idea of progress replaces the ancient idea of a personal effort of obtaining perfection with the idea of pure chronological

succession that occurs *in spite of* men. Therefore, it is the main cause of contemporary stupidity ('L'intellectuel dans la société' (1935) in Grenier 1967, p. 121).

34. In his 1936 'L'âge des orthodoxies', Grenier detects an economic theory as well as a philosophy, or even a 'theology' in Marxism (Grenier 1967, p. 29).

35. In Camus's opinion, Plotinus' 'aesthetic' thought provides the example of a true materialism that is opposed to the abstract or 'romantic' materialism of the philosophers; these last pass dead ideas off as living realities (I, p. 131).

36. The first two numbers of the review were published in December 1938 and February–March 1939; a number devoted to García Lorca was confiscated by the police of Vichy in 1941 (cf. I, pp. 1402–3).

37. In opposition to the 'romantic' uses of poverty in contemporary revolutionary ideologies, the author employs the term from an a-teleological perspective that evokes the figure of the mother, on one hand, and, on the other, the Plotinian process of 'purification' from the constructs of philosophical reason (*N*, p. 125).

38. Préface à l'édition américaine (1958) (I, p. 215).

39. 'Pour un Collège de Sociologie', *NRF*, n. 298 (July 1938) (Bataille 1988).

40. Sartre, J.P. (1955) 'Camus, *The Outsider*', in *Literary and Philosophical Essays* (New York: Criterion Books).

41. Grenier 1987, p. 66. See note in the *Carnets* (II, p. 895).

42. See Abbou 1972 and the critical introduction to the articles of *Alger républicain* and *Soir républicain* (I, pp. 1368–98) and to *L'Étranger* (I, pp. 1246–55).

43. '[...] les pouvoirs meurtriers de la presse s'expliquent autant par la corruption de ceux qui la dirigent que par le manque de sens critique de ceux qui la lisent. ([...] the murderous powers of the press are explained by the corruption of the directors as much as by the lack of critical sense of the readers)'; 'Notre position' (6 November 1939) in *Soir républicain* (I, p. 1372). Lack of critical sense in the population is also a crucial concern in Jean Grenier's essays of 1936 on political orthodoxy, as well as in his correspondence with Jean Paulhan (Paulhan and Grenier 1984, p. 82). The question of Jacobin radicalism or fanaticism is a recurring theme in the *NRF* throughout the mid-1930s, as well as in Paulhan's *Les Fleurs de Tarbes ou La Terreur dans les Lettres* which investigates the question of terrorism as a specific form of *misology* (Trudel 2007, p. 12). Passionately debated with Grenier, Camus could not ignore these issues. See also the letter to Grenier (5 May 1941), in Camus and Grenier 1981, p. 53.

44. Those who judge Meursault do not behave as his peers and fellow men. Insofar as they do not preserve him from baseness and diminution – and 'radical idealism' elevates Truth by diminishing and abasing that which exists – they do not show *love* toward him (II, p. 895). In agreement with Nietzsche, but also with Grenier and Scheler, Camus detects a perspective of (self-)contempt and nausea of man in radicalism or *moral* fanaticism (see Caves 1924a, p. 56).

45. In 'Sans lendemains', Camus figures the man condemned to death as a leper (I, pp. 1198, 1201).

46. In prison, Meursault is deprived of that profound freedom from *telos*, of which his life in the first part of the novel is the illustration.

47. The fragments of 'Sans lendemains' recall Nietzsche's criticism of the 'priestly errors' present in *Genealogy of Morals* and in *Crépuscule des Idoles*;

Camus's reading notes in *Carnets* attest to the fact that he works on Henri Albert's translation of *Crépuscule* in August 1938 (II, pp. 857, 889–90).

48. See *MS*, p. 259 n. *. Camus demonstrates that the notion of humility is engrained in the moral interpretation of reason; he is of the same mind as Nietzsche, according to whom, humility is a virtue of *ressentiment* and is founded on the false construction of the free Subject, who is supposed to restrain himself from committing evil deeds (*GM*, I, 13).

49. Preface to the 1958 American edition (I, p. 215).

50. A draft of a preface to *L'Envers et l'Endroit* (1937) suggests that there is a continuity between the author's refusal of rational justification in the lyrical essays and the issue that he develops in his novel (see II, pp. 815–16).

51. In *L'Étranger*, the magistrate calls Meursault 'monsieur l'Antéchrist' (I, p. 182).

52. Camus, against moral and political fanaticism, delineates the 'marche difficile vers une sainteté de la négation – un héroïsme sans Dieu – l'homme pur enfin [...] Qu'est-ce qui fait la supériorité d'*exemple* (la seule) du christianisme? Le Christ et ses saints – la recherche d'un *style de vie*. (difficult walk that leads to a holiness of negation – a heroism without God – the pure man at last [...] What determines the (only) superiority of *example* of Christianity? Christ and its Saints – the research of a *life style*' (II, p. 951).

53. See also II, p. 888.

5. Commencement of Freedom

1. This was the opinion in 1941 of Jean Paulhan, who considered *Le Mythe de Sisyphe* a clever chronicle of the metaphysical events of the 1920s–1930s (Camus and Pia 2000, p. 74).

2. Interview for the *New York Post* (5 June 1946) (II, p. 676, my italics).

3. Cf. Arendt 1961, p. 30.

4. A series of notes in the *Carnets* substantiate the belief that Camus read *Crépuscule des Idoles* and *Humain, trop humain* in 1938 (II, p. 857). Two notes confirm that he had already read Bianquis' translation of *La Naissance de la philosophie à l'époque de la tragédie grecque* (cited as 'Origine de la philosophie') by 1943, and that he intended to use his reading notes of the book together with those of Scheler's *Homme du ressentiment* for his essay on revolt (II, pp. 984, 986).

5. Camus was in possession of the following editions: Nietzsche, F. (1934) *Œuvres posthumes*, translation H.J. Bolle (Paris: Mercure de France); Nietzsche, F. (1923) *La Volonté de puissance*, translation by Henri Albert (Paris: Mercure de France); Nietzsche, F. (1935/1937) *La Volonté de puissance*, two volumes, translation Geneviève Bianquis (Paris: Gallimard) (Favre 2004, pp. 203–4).

6. The letter to Pierre Bonnel (19 March 1943) concerning *Le Mythe de Sisyphe* confirms that Camus, in the early 1940s, was already acquainted with Nietzsche's reading of Heraclitus (I, p. 322). Camus particularly dwells on Nietzsche's interpretation in *La Naissance de la philosophie* of Heraclitus' 'divine' thought in his article on 'Nietzsche et le nihilisme' (1950).

7. The Hellenic thinker is said to replace 'aesthetic' reason for the 'logic' or 'ethic' reason of the Platonic-Aristotelian tradition, and to replace images for the syllogism of traditional Logic (II, p. 861).

8. Published in F. Nietzsche (1913) *19. Unveroffentlichtes zur antiken Religion und Philosophie* (Leipzig: Kröner Verlag), pp. 184–6.
9. As Arendt observes, the fabricative process 'falls into two parts: first, perceiving the image or shape (*eidos*) of the product-to-be, and then organizing the means and starting the execution' (Arendt 1998, p. 225).
10. Bianquis makes a distinction between 'contempler' ('to contemplate') and 'observer' ('to observe') in order to respectively convey the contemplative and productive forms of intelligence detected by Nietzsche in his text on the pre-Platonic philosophers (*NP*, p. 75).
11. According to Audin, the reading of Jean Grenier's *Essai sur l'esprit d'orthodoxie* (1938) brought the myth of Sisyphus to Camus's attention (I, p. 1272) and, in particular, the question of the *hubristic* aspiration of men to act like gods that is embedded in the utopian idea of a 'new man' typical of twentieth-century revolutionary ideologies (Grenier 1967, p. 162 n. 2). I maintain that *La Naissance de la philosophie à l'époque de la tragédie grecque*, also published in 1938, allows Camus to connect the mythic figure to the 'useless' or aesthetic perspective of the absurd logic that he develops in the first part of *Le Mythe de Sisyphe*.
12. This title is suggested by Camus in a letter to Gaston Gallimard written in 1942 (I, p. 320).
13. According to A. Comte-Sponville, the wisdom of Sisyphus is moulded on Stoicism (Comte-Sponville 1997, p. 168). I suggest that Camus's understanding of wisdom is influenced by Nietzsche's early pages on Heraclitus and pre-Socratic philosophy. In *La Naissance de la philosophie*, and then again in *Ecce homo*, the Stoics are said to inherit almost all of their fundamental ideas from Heraclitus and to have distorted Heraclitean 'aesthetic' philosophy by submitting it to a logic of prudence (*NP*, p. 71). See Camus's note on Stoicism in Nietzsche's *Volonté de Puissance* ('Stoïciens non révoltés, ils adhèrent'), cited in Favre 2004, p. 199.
14. One of Camus's favourite books by Nietzsche, *Aurore*, is the work that begins the campaign of the 'immoralist' thinker against the causal interpretation and prejudices of reason. It is described by Nietzsche as a book that 'says *yes*' (*EH*, 'Pourquoi j'écris de si bons livres' – 'Aurore', 1).
15. Camus's reading of the Greek myth of Sisyphus as the symbol of the modern human condition evokes the one that was developed in the mid-1920s by Italian philosopher Giuseppe Rensi. Influenced by the thoughts of Leopardi, Nietzsche and Schopenhauer, Rensi develops an 'absurdist' or anti-historicist criticism of political rationalism in the contemporary bourgeois society of progress and labour. In particular, he takes European nihilism into account as a distinct philosophy of authority, rather than as a doctrine of the dissolution of foundations. Jean Grenier devoted special attention to the ideas of this philosopher, who held Sextus Empiricus in high esteem and was also a strenuous opponent of the philosophy of Gentile under the Fascist regime. Editor of the works by Sextus Empiricus (1917), Rensi dwells on the figure of Sisyphus in *Filosofia dell'assurdo* (first edition 1923; second edition 1937). Camus's teacher devotes an essay to Rensi's philosophical position in the mid-1920s (see Grenier, J. (1926) 'Trois penseurs italiens : Aliotta, Rensi, Manacorda', *Revue philosophique de la France et de l'Etranger*, n. 5–6, pp. 361–95). It is more than likely that Camus, through Grenier, took up

the association Rensi had made between the endless and meaningless work of the Danaides, Tantalus, and Sisyphus and the modern labour process. See also Emery 1997, pp. 30–2.

16. In his notebooks of April 1938, Camus meditates on a two-fold liberation, from money and from one's cowardice and vanities, in order to be able to escape from the most miserable of conditions: that of the worker in a civilisation founded on workers (II, p. 849). In his 1942 draft of a preface for *Le Mythe de Sisyphe*, he concludes that the solution to nihilism lies in re-establishing the foundations of all of civilisation (II, p. 948).

17. Bataille's correspondence confirms that in 1937 he was already acquainted with Nietzsche's *Die Philosophie in tragishen Zeitalter de Griechen*, that is to say, before the publication of Bianquis's translation of 1938 (*NP*). His correspondence also confirms that he incorporated the philosopher's theses in his articles of the late 1930s (see Bataille 1997, p. 128). It is more than likely that Camus had read Georges Bataille's article, 'L'Apprenti-Sorcier', which was published in Paulhan's *NRF* in July 1938 (n. 298).

18. See Camus's letter to Ponge, 'Au sujet du *Parti pris*', which discusses the relationship between absurd thought and the question of language (I, pp. 883–8). On Camus's aesthetics of the absurd, see Audin 1997; Morot-Sir 1981, 1985b; Gay-Crosier 1985b.

19. As Audin points out, just as Plotinus' images provided a new mould for a feeling that was rooted in the early Christian experience and exceeded the conceptual definitions of traditional logic, Camus resorted to metaphors and especially to the 'forms' characteristic of the Christian language to bestow an unprecedented 'direction' on the process of thinking (Audin 1991, p. 49) and to incorporate the anti-modern (tragic) perspective of the 'flesh' ('la chair').

20. In 1942, Camus notes in his *Carnets*: 'Le monde absurde ne reçoit qu'une justification esthétique (The absurd world can only be justified aesthetically)' (II, p. 974).

21. A copy of the 1920 edition of *Crépuscule des Idoles*, translated by Henri Albert (Paris: Mercure de France), figures in the inventory of Nietzsche's books filed in Camus's private library (Favre 2004). The page number in his reading notes of 1938 confirms that this text is one of the sources used to aid him in his reflections on freedom and 'conscious' death (II, p. 857) developed in the lyrical essays of *Noces* and in the unfinished novel *La Mort Heureuse* (*A Happy Death*). Susan Tarrow confirms Camus's rejection of the vertical relation of dominion of traditional politics in *La Mort Heureuse* (see Tarrow 1985, pp. 33 ff).

22. In a note on Maurice Blanchot's metaphysical novels written in 1942, Camus observes that death is a knowledge that makes knowledge not only *useless* but also renders it a *sterile* progress (II, p. 975).

23. According to Sherman, the problem of the Absurd 'is not the particular epistemological problem of skepticism but rather the universal existential problem of nihilism, the thoroughgoing belief in nothing [...] Camus commences his philosophical inquiries straightforwardly from Descartes' dualistic perspective: there is consciousness and there is the material world.' (Sherman 2009, p. 30.) The comparative analysis of Camus's sources, in particular, *La Naissance de la philosophie* and *Crépuscule des Idoles*, dispels what I consider

to be a fundamental misunderstanding regarding Camus's notion of absurd consciousness in *Le Mythe de Sisyphe*. In *Noces* and in *Le Mythe*, the notions of 'lucidity' and 'consciousness' incorporate the Nietzschean criticism of modern rationalism, of which the Cartesian subject is the pivot.

24. That same month, two notes attest to his reading of Nietzsche's *Crépuscule des Idoles* and *Humain, trop humain* (I, 'De l'âme des artistes et des écrivains', 149).

25. Camus does not cite the source of this quote, but the Nietzschean paternity is obvious; the formula recurs in *VP*, I, V, 559.

26. Like Georges Bataille, Camus is aware that the so-called 'death of God' radically challenges all categories of philosophy, especially, those of Subject and materialism (Sichère 2006, p. 72). In 1944 Bataille offered Camus a copy of his *Nietzsche* with a dedication (Favre 2004, p. 204). The two authors adopt the legacy of nihilism and attempt to think outside the dominant theoretical approaches; the Nietzschean parentage between Camus's absurd thought and Bataille's 'inner experience' has not been systematically analysed yet and deserves a careful examination.

27. As Jaspers observes, to interpret Nietzsche's 'God is dead' as the affirmation that God *does not exist*, is to turn it into the expression of a trivial atheism, which was not in the author's intention (Jaspers 1996, p. 228). In counterposition to Sherman, who defines Camus as an atheist (Sherman 2009, p. 30), I contend that Camus, like Nietzsche, bases nihilism in the belief in the categories of reason rather than in the negation of the existence of God. The absurd reasoning that permeates *Le Mythe de Sisyphe* refutes an atheist conclusion.

28. The same argument is developed in Nietzsche's *Twilight of the Idols* ('The Four Great Errors', 3).

29. Camus explicitly refers to the 'royal road of reason' as opposed to the 'direct paths of truth' (*MS*, p. 235), when citing Scheler and the phenomenologists among a group of like minds, from Jaspers to Heidegger, from Kierkegaard to Shestov, who rejected it. In April 1938, the *NRF* published Heidegger's 'Qu'est-ce que la métaphysique?', and Jasper's 'Descartes et la philosophie' in September that year. Camus is likely to have had these texts in mind when he referred to these various authors' criticism of rationalism. Camus read Shestov's *La Philosophie de la tragédie*, a copy of the 1926 edition of *Dostoïevski et Nietzsche* is listed in the inventories of his private library.

30. According to Compte-Sponville, the absurd is a third term that may be found at the heart of the duality of man-to-the-world or world-with-man (Compte-Sponville 1997, p. 162). I assert that Camus's notion of the absurd must be understood consistently with the 'aesthetic perspective' that is taken in the essay as the limit or threshold of man and the world's appearing-*together* (*con*tact); Camus's notion of the absurd is closer to Simone Weil's interpretation of the Heraclitean *logos* as a (cor)relation that harmonises contradictions (see Rasoamanana 2005, p. 346). Furthermore, the absurd can neither be reduced to the traditional acceptation of 'absence of meaning' nor designate, properly speaking, a 'contradictory meaning' (Compte-Sponville 1997, p. 161) without falling back on a substantialist approach that absurd reasoning rejects. There is an essential difference between stating, with Compte-Sponville, that the meaning of the absurd is contradictory and

saying, as Camus does in 1945, that the absurd is contradictory *in existence* (*RR*, p. 337).

31. The notion of 'tragic differend' in Reiner Schürmann's seminal study on broken hegemonies (see Schürmann 1996) fully describes, in my view, the particular 'contradiction' of Camus's notion of the Absurd found in *Le Mythe de Sisyphe*.

32. According to Camus, both the rationalist and irrationalist doctrines of the nineteenth and twentieth centuries perpetuate this logical error, to which the chapter on 'Philosophical Suicide' is devoted. In *Le Mythe de Sisyphe*, the criticism of Shestov and Kierkegaard is grounded on the rejection of the logical connection: 'This transcends the human scale; *therefore*, it must be super-human.' (*MS*, p. 246, my italics). According to Camus, there is 'therefore' one too many; the first sentence does *not prove* anything, it justifies nothing.

33. 'Réponse à un orthodoxe' (1936), in Grenier 1938, p. 64.

34. Nietzsche detects the 'agonal' point of view in Greek tragic thought (*NP*, p. 60).

35. Negating all moral judgement, absurd thought is beyond good and evil (I, p. 321). Camus's description of the absurd creators evokes Nietzsche's aphorism on 'nihilism of the *artists*' (*VPII*, III, 472).

36. Between 1939 and 1942, Camus meditates over the Nietzschean writings on the conduct of the artist (*VPI*, III, 441 and *NP*, II) and dwells on sexual chastity and of thought as conditions for a life 'style' or perfection '*without reward*' (II, p. 901). According to Camus, unbridled sexuality leads to a philosophy of the meaninglessness of the world (II, p. 968).

37. Absurd thought does not coincide with thoughtlessness or stupidity. The rejection of the moral or teleological interpretation of reason involves the refusal of the dualisms reason/passion, mind/body that are characteristic of traditional metaphysics. Echoing Nietzsche's *Crépuscule des Idoles*, Camus understands freedom as a higher spiritualisation or discipline of one's instincts. The absurd figures of Don Juan and the conqueror respectively embody a 'spiritualised' love – a mixture of desire, affection and intelligence that binds the lovers (*MS*, p. 270) – and a 'spiritualised' action, that refuses moral and political fanaticism.

38. Karl Jaspers links the notion of 'example' to the rejection of the category of the end or final objective presented in Nietzsche's thought (see Jaspers 1996, p. 229). A review of Jaspers' book on Nietzsche by Pierre Klossowski was published in *Acéphale*, n. 2, 'Nietzsche et les fascistes: une réparation' (21 January 1937), and a letter of Georges Bataille to Brice Parain (22 June 1945) confirms that the interpretation of the author was well known and debated in the circle of the *NRF* (Bataille 1997, p. 238). The French translation of Jaspers' *Nietzsche, une introduction à sa philosophie* was published by Gallimard in 1950; a copy of the book is also listed in Camus's private library (Favre 2004, p. 205).

39. Anticipating Hannah Arendt's lectures on *Kant's Political Philosophy*, the notion of example plays a relevant part in Camus's articles and essays of the 1940s and 1950s, and acquires its full meaning in the author's refusal of the nihilistic teleology of contemporary power politics (see Chapter 6). Camus uses the term 'example' from the 'aesthetic' perspective that is developed in *Le Mythe de Sisyphe* in opposition to the teleological model of action of

the Western political tradition. Rather than a model (*idea*) to be imitated/ executed, 'example' denotes an especially noteworthy illustration (*MS*, p. 266). In his review on '*Sur une philosophie de l'expression* de Brice Parain', published in *Poésie 44* (January–February 1944), Camus also defines Socrates as a thinker who believed more in the virtue of example than in logic (I, p. 904).

40. In the fourth *Lettre à un ami allemand*, dated July 1944, Camus refers to the Nazi opponents and writes: 'vous avez choici l'injustice, *vous vous êtes mis avec les dieux. Votre logique n'était qu'apparente.* (you chose injustice and *sided with the gods. Your logic was merely apparent).*' (*LAA*, p. 26; Camus 1961, p. 21; my italics.)

41. According to Bataille, Parain approaches the political question of the relationship between action and art or language in the twentieth century in terms extremely close to his own (see Bataille 1997, p. 237).

42. Camus is clearly referring to Jean Paulhan's critical interrogation on the relationship between language and thought that culminates in *Les Fleurs de Tarbes ou La Terreur dans les Lettres* and in a series of articles for *Mesures*. A first version of *Les Fleurs* was published in four parts in *NRF* in 1936 (No. 273–7); the final version is dated 1941. Camus received a copy of *Les Fleurs de Tarbe* from Pascal Pia in September 1942 (Camus and Pia 2000, p. 101).

43. Camus devotes a 'Lettre au sujet du *Parti pris*' (27 January 1943) to the work of Francis Ponge, that is published in *NRF* in 1956. He defines Ponge's *Parti pris* an 'absurd work' (I, p. 883) that radically challenges the problem of expression and approaches the question of language primarily as a metaphysical question (I, p. 886). In Camus's view, language is not just a metaphysical problem, but the root of metaphysics itself (I, p. 903).

44. According to Camus, men are not free until they become aware that death alone is fatal, and that, outside this single fatality, 'everything is permitted' (*MS*, p. 300).

45. In 1944, Camus writes: 'Nous ne connaissons que par les mots (We only know through words)' (I, p. 902).

46. Cf. Bataille 1997, pp. 239–40.

47. Bataille directed the Cahiers d'*Actualité* edited by Calmann-Lévy. This report on literature and politics for the second issue of the review was never published (Bataille 1997, p. 235).

48. Camus cites Nietzsche's pages on morality so that he may be able to introduce the extra-moral code of conduct of the absurd man: 'Quand Nietzsche écrit: 'Il apparaît clairement que la chose principale au ciel et sur la terre est d'*obéir* longtemps et dans une même direction : à la longue il en résulte quelque chose pour quoi il vaille la peine de vivre sur cette terre comme par exemple la vertu, l'art, la musique, la danse, la raison, l'esprit, quelque chose qui transfigure, quelque chose de raffiné, de fou ou de divin', il illustre la règle d'une morale de grande allure. Mais il montre aussi le chemin de l'homme absurde. (When Nietzsche writes: 'It clearly seems that the primary thing in heaven and on earth is to *obey* at length and in a single direction: in the long run something results for which it is worth the trouble living on this earth just as, for example, virtue, art, music, the dance, reason, the mind – something that transfigures, something delicate, mad, or divine' he elucidates the rule of a distinguished code of ethics. But he also points the way of the absurd man.) (*MS*, p. 263; Camus 1960, p. 55). The terminological correspondence between

Camus's commentary on *La Volonté de Puissance* and the pages on absurd freedom and the lucid *tabula rasa* of metaphysical 'illusions' in *Le Mythe de Sisyphe*
suggest that the French writer believed that the tragic thought expressed in his
1942 essay inherited the positive legacy of Nietzsche's criticism of reason (*HR*,
p. 116).

49. Agamben dwells on the figure of the bandit or outlaw (*friedlos*), which he
    associates with that of the man-wolf or werewolf (*wargus*), as an illustration
    of the *homo sacer*. From ancient German law to Hobbes, a man who was con-
    demned and banned from the community could be killed without it being
    considered a homicide or could even be considered as already dead. The figure
    of the bandit as a werewolf, who represents an indifferent threshold between
    nature (*physis*) and the law of the city (*nomos*), sheds light on the Hobbesian
    state of nature of the *homo homini lupus* (Agamben 1995, pp. 116 ff.).
50. See *VPII*, III, Introduction, 16. A note in the *Carnets* in 1943 confirms that
    Camus identified the nihilism of the statement 'Everything is permitted'
    ('Tout est permis') with the negation of the vertical relation of judgement,
    thus, with the rejection of the teleological interpretation of the agent and of
    his actions in terms of crime and punishment (II, p. 991).

6. The Absurd and Power

1. Chiaromonte was to read *Le Mythe de Sisyphe* only a few years later in New
   York. The Italian intellectual became a close friend of Camus and introduced
   the French author's work to the American post-war debate, especially, to
   Dwight MacDonald and the *politics* circle (see Sumner 1996), that contributed in shaping the American definition of totalitarianism in the decade
   prior to the publication of Arendt's *Origins of Totalitarianism* (Witfield 1980,
   p. 11). As one of the editors of *Partisan Review*, and the founder of *politics*,
   MacDonald brought the work of Albert Camus to the attention of the
   American public. Two chapters from *Le Mythe de Sisyphe* that were translated
   by William Barrett (vol. 13 n. 2, 1946), 'Between Yes and No' (vol. 16, n. 11,
   1949), the chapter on 'Art and Revolt' from *L'Homme révolté* translated by J.
   Frank (vol. 19, n. 3, 1952), and the text of the conference 'A Writer and His
   Time' (vol. 22, n. 3, 1955) were published in the *Partisan Review*.
2. Quotes refer to the last edition revised by the author in 1958.
3. See Bataille 1988a, 1988b.
4. In 'L'Intelligence et l'Échafaud', published in the special issue of *Confluences*
   that was devoted to the novel as a literary genre in July 1943, Camus writes
   that as much as action constitutes the universe of drama, intelligence constitutes that of the novel (I, p. 897).
5. In 1958, Camus defines the Emperor a rare example of 'intelligent tyrant',
   whose conduct exposes the impossibility of justifying tyranny (I, p. 451).
6. In a letter to Brice Parain (29 June 1945), Bataille uses the term 'morality' to
   indicate both the position of an unconditional value and the subordination
   of this value to 'utility', thus, to fabricative logic (Bataille 1997, p. 239).
7. Organ of the union of movements of the Résistance, founded by Henri
   Frenay in December 1941, the first public issue of *Combat* in the French
   capital liberated from Nazi occupation is dated 21 August 1944. Under the

direction of Bourdet and Pia and the influence of Malraux, the journal was independent from economic and political organisations and was created with the intention of providing 'informations précises puisées aux meilleures sources (detailed information obtained from the best sources)' in order to fight 'l'anesthésie du peuple français (the anaesthesia of the French people)' (CAC8, pp. 23–24). Camus joined *Combat* in 1943 and was chief editor for a year after the Liberation, leaving a profound mark on the high civic and moral example of journalism of the newspaper.

8. Cf. Bataille 1997, pp. 217–24. Camus shared Bataille's analysis of Nietzsche's criticism of utilitarian or 'servile' morality, which based the concept of political freedom on the modern enslavement to interest and utility (Bataille 1988a, p. 11).

9. Caligula places love in opposition to the 'servile' logic of life that is symbolised by the public Treasury (I, p. 339). By entering into this logic, in which contempt is incorporated, he declares that love is nothing.

10. Blanchot uses 'absurd' as a synonym of 'absurdity'; thus, he neglects the distinction between the two terms introduced by Camus in *Le Mythe de Sisyphe*, which, in my view, is essential to the argument of the essay on the Absurd, as well as to the comprehension of *L'Homme révolté*.

11. See Blanchot 1954b, pp. 1060–1.

12. In the editorial of 15 September 1944, Camus speaks of the sacrifice of the happiness of a thousand peoples, which was treated as though it were nothing *in comparison* with the power of a great individual (CAC8, p. 189).

13. Scheler uses 'conscience' in the acceptation of Pascal's 'order or *logic* of the heart' (Scheler 1958, p. 54).

14. Although Camus insisted on the primary importance of the material and historical conditions of the emancipation of men, he did not reduce the 'liberation' of man to the material sphere (see Abbou 1986, p. 119). Spiritual liberation plays an essential part in his political reflections from the mid-1930s on (see Chapter 4).

15. A very similar thesis had already been formulated by Emmanuel Lévinas in *Quelques réflexions sur la philosophie de l'Hitlérisme* (1934). Although he never uses the term 'nihilism', Lévinas bases Hitlerism on an extreme form of scepticism that may be identified with a complacent absence of belief and commitment to any truth. In this sense, Nazi 'philosophy', by celebrating the awakening of elemental feelings and the annihilation of the spiritual values of the Judeo-Christian tradition, is seen as the point marking the collapse of Western civilisation. According to Lévinas, Hitlerism embodies the dissolution of the Platonic–Christian duality Body/Mind, which corresponds to the duality Senses/Ideas, for which the Self is identified with physical existence, and therefore the latter is chained to the fatality of biological laws. This thesis will find an echo in the notion of 'biological Caesarism' in Camus's *L'Homme révolté*.

16. On the relation between logic and suicide in *Le Mythe de Sisyphe* see Chapter 5.

17. In the fourth *Lettre à un ami allemand* (July 1944), Camus explicitly differentiates his own position from the philosophy of Hitlerism, which interprets the Nietzschean phrase 'Nothing is true' in terms of will, power and end objectives and, thus, from the nihilistic or 'moral' perspective of reason.

Hitlerism negates the foundation or principle of traditional metaphysics without rejecting the logic that supports it and arrives at the conclusion that 'Everything is possible'. This conclusion is the rejection, rather than the extreme consequence, of the 'illogical' or absurd thought expressed in *Le Mythe de Sisyphe*. In the first *Lettre à un ami allemand* (July 1943), by having identified the absurd thought with 'intelligence' and 'lucidity' (*LAA*, p. 26), he roots Hitlerism in the 'mépris de l'intelligence (contempt of intelligence)' (*LAA*, p. 10)

18. In the 1945 preface to 'L'Espagne libre', Camus mentions the many 'fathers Ubu' (an allusion to the protagonist of Alfred Jarry's play *Ubu Roi*), who, on the European stage from 1933 on, have put irresistible mechanics at the service of their mediocre frenzy (II, p. 668). 'L'Espagne libre' is the first issue of *Actualité* (n. 1, 4ᵗʰ quarter 1945), the series directed by Georges Bataille.
19. Camus reworks his reading notes of *La Naissance de la philosophie à l'époque de la tragédie grecque* in 1943–44 (II, pp. 984, 986).
20. In the manuscript of the Introduction to *L'Homme révolté*, Camus clearly identifies and differentiates between two models of action, the absurd or a-teleological model of action/play and the traditional model of action intended as realisation and achievement of predefined final objectives. This last subjugates action to the utilitarian logic of efficacy and might and interprets all relations in terms of the vertical relation of domination, which Nietzsche ascribed to the teleological model of productive reasoning (III, p. 1240).
21. In 'Remarque sur la révolte', Camus refers to Nietzsche and Ivan Karamazov to exemplify a 'passion of man for man' that is opposed to Rousseau and the Utilitarian theorists' humanitarian theses, which Scheler propounds as being rooted in the hatred of the world and in *ressentiment* (*RR*, p. 328). This confirms that Camus makes a connection between the phrase of modern nihilism, 'Everything is permitted', and a love of the world and of men that makes this form of nihilism irreducible to the servile logic of contemporary political ideologies ('absolute' nihilism), which he considered to be an expression of contempt.
22. From the a-teleological perspective of the Heraclitean 'play', all actions are equivalent. Thus, one can conduct millions of innocents to the crematorium or devote oneself to caring for the sick; one can tear a man's ears with one hand only to soothe them with the other (II, p. 740).
23. 'Les Exilés dans la peste' ('The Exiled in the plague') published in *Domaine français (Messages)* in Brussels in 1943, later reworked and incorporated in the novel *La Peste* (II, pp. 275 ff).
24. Caligula takes over and exerts the function of the plague (act IV, scene ix).
25. Contact, touch ('le toucher'), exposure or the appearing to and with an other ('comparution') are brought to the foreground in Jean-Luc Nancy's recent philosophical attempts to reassess the understanding of community and political action in relation to the question of nihilism (see Nancy 1988, 1990a, 1990b, 1993).
26. Camus notes in 1943 that the Eternal Return involves the indulgence in pain (II, p. 1001).
27. In 'Nietzsche est-il fasciste?', Bataille calls attention to a 'solitary' Nietzsche, whose reflection is situated in the fringes of the common and necessary concerns of the public sphere (Bataille 1988a, p. 11).

28. See also Arendt 1982, pp. 74 ff.
29. This formula recalls Camus's criticism of 'universal' or moral reason in *Le Mythe de Sisyphe* (*MS*, p. 233).
30. According to Scheler, Rousseau derives the positive value of political action or rebellion – in opposition to everything (institutions, traditions, moralities) that may constitute an obstacle to the realisation of man's material happiness ('bonheur sensible') – from efficacy (Scheler 1958, p. 115).
31. The parallel to Camus's analysis of the 'romantic' universe of the Gnosis in *DES* is apparent (see Chapter 4).
32. Both Nietzsche and Scheler insist on Rousseau's influence on the Kantian critique of moral reason; while Nietzsche traces this influence in radical idealism, Scheler seems to detect it in the concept of love of man. He ranges the moral reflection of Kant, who identifies love with a pathological emotional condition and, therefore, excludes it from morality, into the spectrum of modern humanitarian theories (Scheler 1958, p. 135 n. 1).
33. According to Corbic, by refusing to consider human lives as a means toward the achievement of any kind of political end, Camus suggests that men are considered *ends* in and of themselves, therefore, he is still influenced by Kant (Corbic 2003, pp. 127–8). I maintain that the perspective of a means-without-an-end is more appropriate when describing Camus's moral and political reflections, which reject the nihilistic teleology of modern rationalism.
34. Sloterdijk calls attention to an 'economy of generosity' in the work of Georges Bataille, who develops Nietzsche's criticism of morality and brings two distinct 'economies' of life to the foreground: one founded on *eros* (desire for possession, erotic impulse) and another on generosity, desire for recognition and respect (Sloterdijk 2007, p. 46). I have documented the influence Nietzsche has had regarding the concern for the utilitarian ('servile') logic that supports the modern thought and action, which Camus and Bataille shared in the early 1940s. Both authors criticise traditional morality and attempt to reformulate the problem of action outside and beyond the limits posed by the nihilistic teleology of *ratio*. In Camus's writings, this effort does not begin with the Liberation and the end of the Second World War, but dates back to the mid-1930s (see Chapter 3) and continues to be present in his 'Remarque sur la révolte', for which Bataille expressed his enthusiastic approval. The mystics are the example of an alternative mode of conceiving of existence beyond the confines of 'reason'; it is not surprising that, in 1944, Camus refers to Meister Eckhart to illustrate the 'love of the world' and the movement of generosity that characterises his notion of revolt (*RR*, pp. 328–9).
35. In the editorial of 9 March 1945 the power of the police and economic power are defined as two ways of infringing upon freedom. Camus observes that the latter can be exercised either directly or indirectly by orienting the way people think and using the press to bias them to favour private interests (CAC8, p. 453).
36. See *GM*, II, 5 and *HTH*, 'Le voyageur et son ombre', 32–33, 50.
37. 'La Crise de l'Homme' is the title of the conference presented at Columbia University in New York (28 March 1946). The text was translated by Lionel Abel and published as 'The Human Crisis' in *Twice a Year* (XIV–XV, 1946–47, pp. 19–33).

38. Moral and political fanaticism is described as a 'blindness' or impossibility to be confronted with and recognise the face of the opponent, which consequently reduces him to a 'silhouette' (II, p. 491).
39. See the project of a preface to *Actuelles* (II, p. 498).
40. Article 'Le pessimisme et le courage' (3 November 1944) (CAC8, p. 310). Camus associates political philosophies with 'universal' or moral reason in 'La Crise de l'homme' (1946) (II, p. 746). See Abbou 1986, p. 120.
41. In a note for the first chapter of *L'Homme révolté* in his *Carnets* (1943), Camus points out that 'la morale existe. Ce qui est immoral, c'est le Christianisme. Définition d'une morale contre le rationalisme intellectuel et l'irrationalisme divin. (morality exists. That which is immoral is Christianity. The definition of a morality against intellectual rationalism and divine irrationalism.)' (II, p. 1016).
42. In his letter to Francis Ponge in 1943, Camus confirms the political relevance of an 'immense, total and lucid revision of values' that he explicitly links to the absurd figure of Sisyphus (I, p. 888).
43. In the editorial of 19 September 1944, the beginning of a revolt is said to lie in a feeling of almost blind refusal to accept an order that sought to put men on their knees (CAC8, p. 198); when the initial (affective) '*No*' moves to the mind, it gives way to a judgement ('*Yes*') that culminates in concerted action – 'that is the moment of revolution' (ibid.).
44. CAC8, p. 149. Camus identifies the initial movement of revolt with the heart (CAC8, p. 198).
45. CAC8, p. 153. The reference to fraternity and friendship recalls the words of the absurd conqueror (*MS*, p. 280).
46. Revolt calls the notion of the individual into question, which is ascribed to the logic of nihilism; it replaces the 'servile' subjugation to the end that is the foundation of the idea of self-sacrifice and martyrdom with a different idea of sacrifice, which affirms the irreducibility of the human being to an abstract function (*RR*, p. 326).
47. See letter to Parain (I, p. 909).
48. Roger Dadoun interprets this convergence of revolt and 'bonheur' ('happiness') as the two-fold suppression of anteriority and authority (*archè*), which embody the order of domination where nobody is recognised (abstraction); see Dadoun 1986, p. 263.
49. 'Ni victimes ni bourreaux' ('Neither Victims Nor Executioners') is the title of a series of eight articles published in *Combat* between 19 and 30 November 1946. These were republished in Dwight Macdonald's independent journal, *politics*, in July–August 1947.

7. Between Sade and the Dandy. Conclusion

1. See 'Le parti de la liberté. Hommage à Salvador de Madariaga' (IV, pp. 567–74) presented on 30 October 1956, on the occasion of the seventieth anniversary of the Spanish writer and exile from Franquist Spain.
2. 'Je me sens à l'aise chez les Grecs, et pas ceux de Platon: les présocratiques, Héraclite, Empédocle, Parménide...J'ai foi en des valeurs antiques... (I feel at ease with the Greeks, and not with those of Plato: the pre-Socratics,

Heraclitus, Empedocles, Parmenides...I believe in ancient values...)' (Camus 1972, p. 1615).

3. In 1947, Camus notes that, for Hegel, 'nature' is an abstract concept, which indicates the existence of a great 'adventure' of intelligence that ends up killing everything (II, p. 1084).

4. See *GM* II, 4.

5. Peter Sloterdijk detects in Camus's concept of revolt the psycho-political sign of a bygone age (Sloterdijk 2007, p.166) and interprets his famous phrase, 'I revolt, therefore we are' to be the expression of an 'economy' of anger (*thymós*) that exceeds the hegemonic 'economy' of Western political theory. However, Camus's notion of revolt has little to do with the anger and indignation of the 'inverted romantics', or professional revolutionaries, who founded a collective militant subject on a mixture of sentimentality and inexorability (Sloterdijk 2007, p. 63) I have extensively demonstrated how Camus understands both these terms to be the expression of *ressentiment*, and how the community that he bases on revolt, as well as the political considerations that he develops around it, cannot be identified with the nineteenth-century 'operational thymotic collectives' or 'choleric bodies' (Sloterdijk 2007, p. 168), nor be reduced to traditional revolutionary militancy.

6. On Nietzsche's profound, widespread, and enduring influence in Russia, and, especially, in Berdiaev's philosophy of freedom and human creativity, see Galtzer Rosenthal 1986 and Grillaert 2008.

7. The *Vekhi* group denounced the Russian *utilitarian* nihilism or nihilistic *utilitarianism* (Berdiaev 1986), which coincided with a moralistic divinisation of the material 'happiness' of the majority of the people. The populist and socialist intelligentsia was conceived to be 'revolutionary' in a moral rather than political sense, their love for future mankind being rooted in a *hatred* for the men and women of the present and in a religious desire for final emancipation or redemption of humanity through the realisation of an earthly paradise.

8. Camus calls attention to the pleasure of torture and murder that executioners feel (IV, p. 142), as well as to the pleasure at the spectacle of cruelty that is enjoyed by some people during public executions.

9. In a note written in 1956, Camus observes that industrial civilisation provokes artificial needs by suppressing natural beauty, thus, it makes it impossible to live and endure poverty (IV, p. 1253).

10. Camus conceives 'the admirable efflorescence of the Albigensian heresy' and Saint Francis to be the expression of a particular combination of the Hellenic *love* of the world with Christianity (*HR*, p. 223). In his view, with the Inquisition and the eradication of the Catharist doctrine, the Christian Church adopted the early Gnostic historicist interpretation and separated itself from beauty and the world (ibid.).

11. Camus's interest in the work of Simone Weil dates back to 1947; he edited *L'Enracinement* (1949), *La Connaissance surnaturelle* (1950), *Lettre à un religieux* (1951), *La Condition ouvrière* (1951) and *La Source grecque* (1953) in the series 'Espoir', which he directed for Gallimard (Basset 2006).

12. Camus's name is often associated with Stockholm's polemic concerning his condemnation of terrorist action in Algeria in the late 1950s. I will not dwell on the details, my intention being to shed light on the internal logic and profound consistency of Camus's political thinking, particularly, in rejecting

the concepts of justice and violent political action of the philosophical political tradition that are subjected to the categories of utility and efficacy. I refer to Carroll 2007 and Tarrow 1985 and to André Abbou's articles for the analysis of Camus's position on the social and political situation in Algeria.

13. Dandies are solitary creators who combine frenzy with desire for total destruction ('apocalypse'), thus, they still feel a nostalgia for morality (*HR*, p. 106). Just like Caligula, they live and die in front of a mirror (*HR*, p. 104) and replace the living 'communion' and complicity with men and women with the pleasure of the beautiful spectacle of cruelty, which is sign of *ressentiment*.

14. Camus calls attention to the theatrical dimension of the Nazi exercise of power – he recalls the anecdote of Goering who received dressed and made-up as the Roman Emperor Nero (*HR*, p. 214 n. *), which calls to mind Caligula-Venus in his homonymous tragedy – and detects in the Nazi and Communist *logic* of terror the oppositional logic ('objective enemy'), which is typical of 'romantic nihilism' or dandyism.

15. In *L'Homme révolté*, Camus rejects Rauschning's thesis and refuses to consider the so-called 'fascist revolutions' of the twentieth century as 'totalitarian revolutions' compared with Russian Communism (*HR*, p. 213). In concurrence with Berdiaev, Camus uses the adjective 'totalitarian' to denote a political system that aims toward achieving the ultimate realisation of the philosophical dream of 'totality' or completion, i.e. the Communist 'end of history' through the ultimate realisation of a classless society. By denouncing the moral or 'romantic' reason, upon which contemporary revolution is based (*HR*, p. 251), Camus defines this last as the extreme contradictory result of traditional teleology and detects in the fetishistic servitude to industrial production (utilitarian logic) the common root of both capitalist and revolutionary societies (*HR*, p. 295).

16. Camus's creator-artist is alien to the logic of power–force–oppression; in his chapter on 'Revolt and Art', he rejects the 'ridiculous illusion' of a city ruled by artists (*HR*, p. 296), which reproduces the logic of domination of the Platonic Republic.

17. Camus refers to the organisation of the Comités Syndicalistes Révolutionnaires. For the writer's support and collaboration to periodicals associated to French Revolutionary Syndicalism, such as Samson and Proix's *Témoins*, Pierre Monatte's *La révolution prolétarienne*, and Maurice Joyeux's *Le Monde libertarie*, see Marin 2008.

18. In *L'Homme révolté*, the revolutionary council systems of the Paris Commune in 1871 and of the Russian Soviets in the early stages of the 1917 Revolution are the examples of a Communard 'revolted' politics or a new form of political action that rejects and is in opposition to the party system and the abstract model of the modern sovereign state, of which 'State terrorism' is the extreme expression. Anticipating Arendt's *Thoughts on Politics and Revolution*, Camus rejects the fabricative model of political action, implicit in the top-down movement of foundation of the body politic, and affirms a 'naturalistic', non-essentialist or tragic model of political action, evoked by the image of the living cell, that rejects the vertical relation of violence.

19. In Camus's view, Scandinavian society, which brought together the political form of constitutional monarchy with syndicalism, offered an example of a *just* society (*HR*, p. 317, note *).

Bibliography

Primary works by Camus

Camus, A. (2006) Œuvres Complètes, I. 1931–1944; II. 1944–48 (Paris: Gallimard).
Camus, A. (2008) Œuvres Complètes, III. 1949–56; IV. 1957–59 (Paris: Gallimard).
Camus, A. (1972) Pléiade Essais (Paris: Gallimard).
Camus, A. (1985) Pléiade Théâtre, récits nouvelles (Paris: Gallimard).
Camus, A. (1960) The Myth of Sisyphus, English translation by Justin O'Brien (London: Hamish Hamilton).
Camus, A. (1961) Resistance, Rebellion and Death (London: Hamish Hamilton).
Camus, A. (1971) The Rebel, translated by A. Bower (Harmondsworth: Penguin Books).
Camus, A. (1980) Youthful Writings (London: Penguin).
Camus, A. (1946) 'The Human Crisis' in B.T. Fitch (ed.) (1972) Albert Camus 5. Journalisme et politique : l'entrée dans l'histoire (1938–1940), La Revue des Lettres Modernes (Paris: Minard), pp. 157–76.
Camus, A. (1973) Cahiers Albert Camus 2. Le premier Camus suivi des écrits de jeunesse, Paul Viallaneix (ed.) (Paris: Gallimard).
Camus, A. (1978) Cahiers Albert Camus 3. Fragments d'un combat 1938–1940 (Paris: Gallimard).
Camus, A. (1984) Cahiers Albert Camus 4. Caligula. Version de 1941, A. James Arnold (ed.) (Paris: Gallimard).
Camus, A. (1987) Cahiers Albert Camus 6. Albert Camus éditorialiste à l'Express, Paul F. Smets (ed.) (Paris: Gallimard).
Camus. A. and Grenier, J. (1981) Correspondance 1932–1960 (Paris: Gallimard).
Camus, A. and Pia, P. (2000) Correspondance 1939–1947 (Paris: Fayard/Gallimard).

Primary works by other authors

Arendt, H. (1951a) The Burden of Our Time (London: Secker & Warburg).
Arendt, H. (1951b) The Origins of Totalitarianism (New York: Harcourt Brace Jovanovich).
Arendt, H. (1968) Men in Dark Times (New York: Harcourt, Brace & World).
Arendt, H. (1972) Crises of the Republic (New York and London: Harcourt Brace Jovanovic).
Arendt, H. (1978a) The Life of the Mind. 1. Thinking (London: Secker and Warburg).
Arendt, H. (1978b) The Life of the Mind. 2. Willing (London: Secker and Warburg).
Arendt, H. (1982) On Revolution (Westport: Greenwood Press).
Arendt, H. (1982) Lectures on Kant's Political Philosophy (Brighton: Harvester Press).
Arendt, H. (1983) Eichmann in Jerusalem: A report on the banality of evil (Harmondsworth: Penguin).
Arendt, H. (1993) Between Past and Future (New York: Penguin Books).

Arendt, H. (1994) *Essays in Understanding 1930–1954* (New York: Harcourt Brace and Co.).

Arendt, H. (1998) *The Human Condition* (Chicago: University of Chicago Press).

Arendt, H. (2000) *Within Four Walls: The correspondence between Hannah Arendt and Heinrich Blücher, 1936–68* (New York: Harcourt).

Arendt, H. (2003) *Responsibility and Judgment*, Kohn, J. (ed.) (NewYork: Schocken Books).

Arendt, H. and Jaspers, K. (1992) *Correspondence, 1926–1969* (New York: Harcourt Brace Jovanovich).

Bataille, G. (1937a) 'Propositions. I. Propositions sur le Fascisme', *Acéphale. Réparation à Nietzsche* (January), pp. 17–20.

Bataille, G. (1937b) 'Propositions. II. Propositions sur la mort de Dieu', pp. 20–1.

Bataille, G. (1947) 'La morale du malheur : *La Peste*', *Critique*, No. 13–14, pp. 3–15.

Bataille, G. (1949) 'Le bonheur, le malheur et la morale d'Albert Camus', *Critique*, No. 33, pp. 184–9.

Bataille, G. (1949) 'Notes. Vue d'ensemble. Nietzsche', *Critique*, No. 34, pp. 271–4.

Bataille, G. (1973a) *Œuvres complètes. 5. La Somme athéologique. 1. L'Expérience intérieure. Méthode de méditation. Post-scriptum 1953. Le Coupable. L'Alleluiah* (Paris: Gallimard).

Bataille, G. (1973b) *Œuvres complètes. 6. La Somme athéologique. 2. Sur Nietzsche. Mémorandum. Annexes* (Paris: Gallimard). English translation (1992) *On Nietzsche* (London: Athlone Press).

Bataille, G. (1988) 'The Sorcerer's Apprentice' in *The College of Sociology (1937–39)*, Denis Hollier (ed.) (Minneapolis: University of Minnesota Press), pp. 12–23.

Bataille, G. (1988a) 'Nietzsche est-il fasciste?' in *Œuvres complètes. 11. Articles I (1944–1949)* (Paris: Gallimard), pp. 9–11.

Bataille, G. (1988b) 'La littérature est-elle utile ?' in *Œuvres complètes. 11. Articles I (1944–1949)* (Paris: Gallimard), pp. 12–13.

Bataille, G. (1997) *Choix de lettres, 1917–1962* (Paris: Gallimard).

Berdiaev, N. (1963) *Les sources et le sens du communisme russe* (Paris: Gallimard).

Berdiaev, N. (1986) *Signposts: A collection of articles on the Russian intelligentsia*, translated and edited by Marshall S. Shatz and Judith E Zimmerman (Irvine, CA: Charles Schlacks).

Bespaloff, R. (2004) *Cheminements et Carrefours* (Paris: Vrin).

Caves, J. (1924a) 'Le Nihilisme Européen et les Appels de l'Orient' in *Philosophies*, No. 1, pp. 51–65.

Caves, J. (1924b) 'Nihilisme Européen et les Appels de l'Orient' in *Philosophies*, No. 2, pp. 185–96.

Grenier, J. (1936) *La philosophie de Jules Lequier* (Paris: Les belles lettres).

Grenier, J. (1959) *Les Îles* (Paris: Gallimard).

Grenier, J. (1967) *Essai sur l'esprit d'orthodoxie* (1938) (Gallimard: Paris).

Grenier, J. (1968) *Albert Camus: Souvenirs* (Paris: Gallimard).

Heidegger, M. (1977) 'The word of Nietzsche: "God is dead"' in *The Question Concerning Technology* (New York: Harper).

Jaspers, K. (1996) *Nietzsche. Introduzione alla comprensione del suo filosofare* (Milano: Mursia).

Nietzsche, F. (1901) *L'Origine de la Tragédie ou Hellénisme et pessimisme*, translation J. Marnold, J. Morland (Paris: Mercure de France).

Nietzsche, F. (1921) *Ecce homo* (Paris: Mercure de France). English translation (1992) *Ecce homo: How one becomes what one is* translated by R.J. Hollingdale (London, England–New York: Penguin Books).

Nietzsche, F. (1934) *Œuvres posthumes*. Translation Henri Jean Bolle (Paris: Mercure de France).

Nietzsche, F. (1941) *Crépuscule des Idoles*, suivi de *Le cas Wagner, Nietzsche contre Wagner, L'Anthéchrist*, translation by Henri Albert (Paris: Mercure de France).

Nietzsche, F. (1951) *La Naissance de la philosophie à l'époque de la tragédie grecque* translated by G. Bianquis (Paris: Gallimard) (1938).

Nietzsche, F. (1964–) *Opere*, G. Colli and M. Montinari (eds) (Milano: Adelphi).

Nietzsche, F. (1987) *Aurore*, translated by Henri Albert (Paris: Hachette). English translation (1982) *Daybreak: Thoughts on the prejudices of morality* (Cambridge–New York: Cambridge University Press).

Nietzsche, F. (1988) *Humain, trop humain*, translated by A.M. Destrouneaux and H. Albert (Paris: Hachette). English translation (1986) *Human, All too Human*, vol. I (Cambridge: Cambridge University Press).

Nietzsche, F. (1994) *On the Genealogy of Morality* (Cambridge: Cambridge University Press).

Nietzsche, F. (1995) *La Volonté de Puissance*, vols. I, II, F. Würzbach ((ed.)), translation G. Bianquis (Paris: Gallimard).

Nietzsche, F. (1999) *The Birth of Tragedy* (Cambridge: Cambridge University Press).

Nietzsche, F. (2005) *The Twilight of the Idols*, in A. Ridley and J. Norman (eds) *The Anti-Christ, Ecce homo, Twilight of the Idols, and Other Writings* (New York: Cambridge University Press).

Nietzsche, F. (2006) *The Pre-Platonic Philosophers* (Urbana&Chicago: University of Illinois Press).

Paulhan, J. and J. Grenier (1984) *Correspondance 1925–1968* (Paris: Quadrigrammes).

Rauschning, H. (1939) *The Revolution of Nihilism: Warning to the West* (New York: Alliance book corporation Longmans, Green & Co.).

Scheler, M. (1958) *L'homme du ressentiment* (Paris: Gallimard).

Critical works

Abbou, A. (1972) 'Combat pour la justice' and 'Variations du discours polémique' in *Albert Camus 5. Journalisme et politique*, pp. 35–81; pp. 107–26.

Abbou, A. (1986) 'Nature et place d'une théorie de la libération de l'homme dans la pensée d'Albert Camus' in *Camus et la politique*, J.-Y. Guérin (ed.) (Paris: L'Harmattan), pp. 117–27.

Agamben, G. (1995) *Homo sacer: il potere sovrano e la nuda vita* (Torino: Einaudi). English translation (1998) *Homo Sacer: Sovereign Power and Bare Life* (Meridian: Stanford University Press).

Agamben, G. (1996) *Mezzi senza fine: note sulla politica* (Torino: Bollati Boringhieri). English translation (2000) *Means without Ends: Notes on Politics* (Minneapolis: University of Minnesota Press).

Agamben, G. (2002) *L'aperto: l'uomo e l'animale* (Torino: Bollati Boringhieri).

Albert Camus: parcours méditerranéens, Actes du Colloque de Jérusalem (10–13 November 1997), in *Perspectives* (1998/5), revue de l'Université de Jérusalem (Jérusalem: Éditions Magnes).

Amiot, A.-M. (1997) 'Nature et fonction du lyrisme de *Caligula* dans la redéfinition de la tragédie moderne', *Camus et le lyrisme* (Paris: SEDES), pp. 133–46.

Amiot A.-M. and J.-F. Mattéi (eds) (1997) *Albert Camus et la philosophie* (Paris: Presses Universitaires Françaises).

Andler, C. (1958a) *Nietzsche. Sa vie et sa pensée. I. Les Précurseurs de Nietzsche. La jeunesse de Nietzsche*, Bibliothèque des idées (Paris: Gallimard).

Andler, C. (1958b) *Nietzsche. Sa vie et sa pensée. II. Le pessimisme esthétique de Nietzsche. La maturité de Nietzsche*, Bibliothèque des idées (Paris: Gallimard).

Andler, C. (1958c) *Nietzsche. Sa vie et sa pensée. III. Nietzsche et le transformisme intellectualiste. La dernière philosophie de Nietzsche*, Bibliothèque des idées (Paris: Gallimard).

Andréas-Salomé, Lou (2002) *Nietzsche* (Paris: Editions Archives Contemporains).

Ansell-Pearson, K. (1994) *An Introduction to Nietzsche as Political Thinker*, (Cambridge: Cambridge University Press).

Ansell Pearson, K. and D. Morgan (eds) (2000) *Nihilism Now! Monsters of Energy* (London: Macmillan Press).

Arnold, A.J. (1979) 'Camus lecteur de Nietzsche, in Brian T. Fitch *Albert Camus 9. La pensée de Camus*, La Revue des Lettres Modernes (Paris: Minard), pp. 95–9.

Arnold, A.J. (1984) 'La poétique du premier Caligula', in *Cahiers Albert Camus 4. Caligula* (Paris: Gallimard), pp. 123–89.

Archambault, P. (1972) *Camus' Hellenic Sources* (Chapel Hill: University of North California Press).

Archambault, P. (1979) 'Camus: le problème du mal et ses "solutions" gnostiques', in *Albert Camus 9. La pensée de Camus, La Revue des Lettres Modernes* (Paris: Minard), pp. 27–40.

Audin, M.-L. (1985) *Pour une sémiotique du Mythe de Sisyphe de Camus: thèmes et métaphores au service de l'absurde*. Thèse de doctorat d'état en Lettres et Sciences Humaines, Université de Nancy II.

Audin, M.-L. (1991) 'Le Mythe de Sisyphe ou "L'autre scène"' in *Albert Camus 14. Le texte et ses langages, La Revue des Lettres Modernes* (Paris: Minard), pp. 11–49.

Audin, M.-L. (1992) 'Le paradigme du théâtre dans *Le Mythe de Sispyhe*' in *Albert Camus et le théâtre*, J. Lévi-Valensi (ed.) (Paris: Imec), pp. 105–22.

Audin, M.-L. (1997) 'La "condensation furieuse de l'image" ou le double lyrisme camusien' in J. Lévi-Valensi and A. Spiquel (eds) (1997) *Camus et le lyrisme*, pp. 21–34.

Baishanski, J. (2002) *L'Orient dans la pensée du jeune Camus. L'Etranger un nouvel évangile ?* (Paris–Caen: Lettres Modernes Minard).

Balaine, B. (1999) *La Récitante. Récit autobiographique. Alger – Théâtre de l'Equipe – Albert Camus*. Tome I (1937–39) (Antibes: La Tour des Vents).

Balaine, B. (2006) *La récitante, Tome 2 – les années de paille* (1940–44) (Nice: Maison d'édition Baie des Anges).

Bartfeld, F. (1988) *L'effet tragique. Essai sur le tragique dans l'œuvre de Camus* (Paris-Genève: Champion-Slatkine).

Bartfeld, F. (ed.) (1995) *Albert Camus voyageur et conférencier, Archives Albert Camus 7* (Paris: Lettres Modernes).

Bartlett, E. (2004) *Rebellious Feminism: Camus's Ethic of Rebellion and Feminist Thought* (New York: Palgrave Macmillan).

Basset, G. (2006) 'Camus éditeur de Simone Weil', *Cahiers Simone Weil. 'Albert Camus et Simone Weil'*, n. 29 (Paris: Association pour l'étude de la pensée de Simone Weil), pp. 249–63.

Bergson, H. (1972) *Mélanges* (Paris: PUF).

Berry, D. (2002) *A History of the French Anarchist Movement, 1917–1945* (Westport–London: Greenwood Press).

Birchall, I. (1994) 'Camus contre Sartre: quarante ans plus tard' in *Albert Camus. Les Extrêmes et l'équilibre* (Amsterdam: Rodopi).

Blanchot, M. (1943) 'Le Mythe de Sisyphe' in *Faux pas* (Paris: Gallimard).

Blanchot, M. (1954a) 'Recherches. Réflexions sur le nihilisme (II)' in *La Nouvelle N.R.F.*, n. 17 (May), pp. 850–9.

Blanchot, M. (1954b) 'Recherches. Tu peux tuer cet homme (III) in *La Nouvelle N.R.F.*, n. 18 (June), pp. 1059–69.

Braun, L. (1974) *Witness of Decline. Albert Camus: Moralist of the Absurd* (Cranbury: Fairleigh Dickinson University Press).

Brée, G. (1972) *Camus and Sartre, Crisis and Commitment* (London: Calder & Boyars).

Bréhier, E. (1982) *La philosophie de Plotin* (1923) (Paris: Vrin).

Carroll, D. (1995) *French Literary Fascism. Nationalism, Anti-Semitism, and the Ideology of Culture* (Princeton: Princeton University Press).

Carroll, D. (2007) *Albert Camus, the Algerian. Colonialism, Terrorism, Justice* (New York: Columbia University Press).

Caussat, P. (1997) 'Le prélude d'une pensée: *Métaphysique chrétienne et néoplatonisme*', in A.-M. Amiot and F. Mattéi (eds) (1997) *Albert Camus et la philosophie* (Paris, PUF), pp. 223–39.

Cavarero, A. (2002) 'Politicizing Theory' in *Political Theory*, vol. 3 No. 4, pp. 506–32.

Chabot, J. (2002) *Albert Camus, ' la pensée de midi'* (Aix-en-Provence: Édisud).

Champigny, R. (1981) 'Compositions philosophiques et concepts' in *Albert Camus 1980* (Gainesville: University Presses of Florida), pp. 49–54.

Chandra, S. (1995) *Albert Camus et l'Inde*, English translation by S. Crossman (Paris: Editions Balland).

Chiaromonte, N. (1952) 'Paris Letter: Sartre versus Camus', *Partisan review*, Vol. XIX, No. 6, pp. 680–6; republished in E. Kurzweil (ed.) (1996) *A Partisan Century. Political Writings from 'Partisan Review'* (New York: Columbia University Press), pp. 146–51.

Chiaromonte, N. (1977) 'Albert Camus', *The Worm of Consciousness and Other Essays*, edited by Miriam Chiaromonte; preface by Mary McCarthy (New York, London: Harcourt Brace Jovanovich), pp. 50–7.

Clayton, A. (1971) *Étapes d'un itinéraire spirituel: Albert Camus de 1935 à 1944* (Paris: Les Lettres Modernes).

Clemens, J. and C. Feik (2000) 'Nihilism, Tonight...', in K. Ansell Pearson and D. Morgan (eds) *Nihilism Now! Monsters of Energy* (London: Macmillan).

Comte-Sponville, A. (1997) 'L'absurde dans *Le Mythe de Sisyphe*' in *Albert Camus et la philosophie* (Paris: PUF), pp. 159–71.

Conway, D.W. (1996) *Nietzsche and the Political* (London–New York: Routledge).

Corbic, A. (2002) *Camus et Bonhoeffer: Rencontre de deux humanismes* (Genève: Labor et Fides).

Corbic, A. (2003) *Camus. L'absurde, la révolte, l'amour* (Paris: Editions de l'Atelier).

Corbic, A. (2007) *Camus et l'homme sans Dieu* (Paris: Editions du Cerf).

Cornick, M. (1995) *Intellectuals in History. The Nouvelle Revue Française under Jean Paulhan, 1925–1940* (Amsterdam–Atlanta: Rodopi).

Crépon, M. (2005) 'Le nihilisme dans la culture', in *Nietzsche et le temps des nihilismes* (Paris: PUF), pp. 85–95.

Crosby, D.A. (1988) *The Specter of the Absurd: Sources and Criticisms of Modern Nihilism* (Albany: State University of New York Press).

Cruickshank, J. (1959) *Albert Camus and the Literature of Revolt* (London: Oxford University Press).

Cuozzo, G. (2000) *Mystice videre* (Torino: Trauben).

Dadoun, R. (1986) 'Albert Camus: Fondations d'anarchie' in J. Guérin (ed.) *Camus et la politique*, pp. 257–67.

Deleuze, G. (1983) *Nietzsche et la philosophie* (Paris: PUF).

Deleuze, G. (2004) *The Desert Islands and Other Texts*, Semiotext(e) Foreign Agents Series (Cambridge, MA–London: MIT Press).

Deleuze, G. (2005) *Différence et répétition* (Paris: PUF).

Deleuze, G. (2008) *Le bergsonisme* (Paris: PUF).

Del Vecchio, M. (1979) *La fenomenologia dell'assurdo in Albert Camus* (Firenze: La Nuova Italia).

Dunwoodie, P. (1971) 'Chestov et *Le Mythe de Sisyphe*' in *La Revue des Lettres Modernes: Albert Camus 4. Sources et influences* (Paris: Minard), n. 264–70, 43–50.

East, B. (1984) *Albert Camus ou l'homme à la recherche d'une morale* (Montréal-Paris: Bellarmin & Cerf).

Emery, N. (1997) *Lo sguardo di Sisifo. Giuseppe Rensi e la via italiana alla filosofia della crisi* (Settimo Milanese: Marzorati).

Engel, V. (1992) 'Ni Dieu ni néant: pour une éthique camusienne de la solidarité' in *Ethica*, vol. 4, no. 1, pp. 83–99.

Esposito, R. (1996) *L'origine della politica. Hannah Arendt o Simone Weil?* (Roma: Donzelli Editore).

Esposito, R. (1998) *Communitas : origine e destino della comunità* (Torino: Einaudi).

Esposito, R., C. Galli and V. Vitiello (eds) (2000) *Nichilismo e politica* (Roma-Bari: Laterza).

Favre, F. (2004) 'Quand Camus lisait Nietzsche' in *Albert Camus 20, 'Le premier homme' en perspective* in 'La Revue des lettres modernes' (Paris: Minard), pp. 197–206.

Fitch, B.T. (ed.) (1972) *Albert Camus 5. Journalisme et politique : l'entrée dans l'histoire (1938–1940) / textes par André Abbou et Jacqueline Lévi-Valensi, La Revue des Lettres Modernes* (Paris: Minard).

Flores d'Arcais, P. (1996) 'L'assurdo e la rivolta: Albert Camus filosofo del finito', in *Micro-Mega – Almanacco di Filosofia*, pp. 201–23.

Forti, S. (2001) *Il totalitarismo* (Roma-Bari: Laterza).

Forti, S. (2003) 'Biopolitica delle anime', *Filosofia Politica*, anno XVII, n. 3, pp. 397–417.

Fülop-Miller, R. (1927) *The Mind and Face of Bolshevism. An Examination of Cultural Life in Soviet Russia* (London–New York: Putnam's Sons).

Garfitt, J.S.T (1983) *The Work and Thought of Jean Grenier (1898–1971)* (London: Modern Humanities Research Association).

Garfitt, J.S.T (2004) 'L'exigence de la vérité et le problème des croyances : De Jean Grenier à Albert Camus' in *Albert Camus et le mensonge* (Paris: Bibliothèque Centre Pompidou), pp. 99–114.

Garfitt, J.S.T. (2007) 'Situating Camus: the formative influences', in E.J. Hughes (ed.) *The Cambridge Companion to Camus* (Cambridge: Cambridge University Press).

Gay-Crosier, R. (1967) *Les Envers d'un échec. Étude sur le théâtre d'Albert Camus* (Paris: Les Lettres Modernes Minard).

Gay-Crosier, R. (ed.) (1979) *Albert Camus 9. La pensée de Camus* (Paris: Minard).

Gay-Crosier, R. (ed.) (1981) *Albert Camus 1980. Second International Conference, February 21–23, 1980* (Gainesville: University Presses of Florida).

Gay-Crosier, R. (1985a) 'La révolte génératrice et régénératrice', in *Albert Camus : œuvre fermée, œuvre ouverte ?* (Paris: Gallimard), pp. 113–34.

Gay-Crosier, R. (ed.) (1985b) *Albert Camus 12. La révolte en question, La Revue des Lettres Modernes* (Paris: Minard).

Gay-Crosier, R., (ed.) (1991) *Albert Camus 14. Le texte et ses langages* (Paris: Minard).

Gay-Crosier, R. (1992) 'Caligula ou le paradoxe du comédien absurde', in *Albert Camus et le théâtre* (Paris: Imec), pp. 19–28.

Gay-Crosier, R. (1998) 'Les enjeux de la pensée de Midi' in *Albert Camus: parcours Méditerranéens. Actes du Colloque de Jérusalem, 10–13 Novembre 1997, Perspectives*, n. 5, pp. 93–108.

Gay-Crosier, R. (2000) *Albert Camus : Paradigmes de l'ironie – révolte et négation affirmative* (Toronto: Paratexte).

Girard, R. (1964) 'Camus's *Stranger* Retried' in *PMLA*, LXXIX, pp. 519–33.

Girard, R. (1968) 'Pour un nouveau procès de l'étranger' in *Revue des Lettres Modernes* (Paris: Minard), pp. 15–52.

Gjørven, C. (1997) 'L'absence du lyrisme dans *L'Étranger*', in *Camus et le lyrisme* (Paris: SEDES), pp. 147–59.

Glatzer Rosenthal, B. (1986) *Nietzsche in Russia* (Princeton, NJ: Princeton University Press).

Glatzer Rosenthal, B. and M. Bohachevsky Chomiak (1982) *A Revolution of the Spirit: Crisis of Value in Russia, 1890–1918* (Newtonville, MA: Oriental Research Partners).

Gleason, A. (1995) *Totalitarianism. The Inner History of Cold War* (New York–Oxford: Oxford University Press).

Grenier, R. (1987) *Albert Camus. Soleil et ombre. Une biographie intellectuelle* (Paris: Gallimard).

Grillaert, N. (2008) *What the God-seekers Found in Nietzsche: The reception of Nietzsche's Übermensch by the philosophers of the Russian religious renaissance* (Amsterdam–New York: Rodopi).

Groethuysen, B. (1935) '"L'homme du ressentiment" par Max Scheler', in *N.R.F.*, n. 257, pp. 308–10.

Guérin, J. (ed.) (1986) *Camus et la politique. Actes du Colloque de Nanterre, 5–7 Juin 1985* (Paris: L'Harmattan).

Guérin, J.-Y. (1992) 'Le tragique, la tragédie et l'histoire', in *Albert Camus et le théâtre* (Paris: Imec), pp. 159–70.

Guérin, J. (1993) *Camus. Portrait de l'artiste en citoyen* (Paris: F. Bourin).

Guérin, J. (1994) 'Actualité de la politique camusienne' in D.H. Walker (ed.) (1994) *Albert Camus. Les Extrêmes et l'équilibre* (Amsterdam: Rodopi), 103–14.

Guérin, J. (1995) 'Camus, Albert' and 'Combat' in *Dictionnaire de la vie politique française au XXe siècle*, J.F. Sirinelli (ed.) (Paris: PUF), pp. 128–30, 206–7.

Guérin, J. (2007) 'Camus the Journalist' in E.J. Hughes (ed.) (2007) *The Cambridge Companion to Camus* (Cambridge: Cambridge University Press), pp. 79–92.

Haar, M. (1998) *Par-delà le nihilisme* (Paris: PUF).

Halberstam, M. (1999) *Totalitarianism and the Modern Conception of Politics* (New Haven–London: Yale University Press).

Havas, R. (1995) *Nietzsche's Genealogy: Nihilism and the Will to Knowledge* (Ithaca–London: Cornell University Press).

Honig, B. (1993) *Political Theory and the Displacement of Politics* (Ithaca: Cornell University Press).

Hughes, E.J. (ed.) (2007) *The Cambridge Companion to Camus* (Cambridge: Cambridge University Press).

Isaac, J.C. (1989/90) 'Arendt, Camus, and Postmodern Politics', in *Praxis International*, No. 9, pp. 48–71.

Isaac, J.C. (1992) *Arendt, Camus, and Modern Rebellion* (New Haven–London: Yale University Press).

Judt, T. (1992) *Past Imperfect. French Intellectuals, 1944–1956* (Berkeley–Los Angeles–Oxford: University of California Press).

Judt, T. (1998) 'The Reluctant Moralist. Albert Camus and the Discomfort of Ambivalence', in *The Burden of Responsibility. Blum, Camus, Aron, and the French Twentieth Century* (Chicago, Chicago University Press), 87–135.

Judt, T. (2008) *Reappraisals. Reflections on the Forgotten Twentieth Century* (New York: Penguin Press).

Kessler, M. (1999) *Nietzsche et le dépassement esthétique de la métaphysique* (Paris: PUF).

Kurzweil, E. (ed.) (1996) *A Partisan Century: Political Writings from Partisan Review* (New York: Columbia University Press).

Lacoue-Labarthe, P. (1998) *La fiction du politique. Heidegger, l'art et la politique* (Paris: Ch. Bourgeois Éditeur).

Lacoue-Labarthe, P. and J.L. Nancy (eds) (1983) *Le retrait du politique: travaux du centre de recherches philosophiques sur le politique* (Paris: Galilée). English translation (1997) *Retreating the Political*, S. Sparks (ed.) (London: Routledge).

Lacoue-Labarthe, P. and J.L. Nancy (1991) *Le mythe nazi* (La Tour d'Aigues: Ed. de l'Aube).

Langlois, W.G. (1981) 'Camus et le sens de la révolte asturienne', *Albert Camus 1980* (Gainesville: University Presses of Florida), pp. 163–77.

Le Ridier, J. (1999) *Nietzsche en France : de la fin du XIXe siècle au temps présent* (Paris: PUF).

Lévi-Valensi, J. (2006) *Albert Camus ou la naissance d'un romancier* (Paris: Gallimard).

Lévi-Valensi, J. (1970) *Les critiques de notre temps et Camus* (Paris: Garnier).

Lévi-Valensi, J. (1972) 'L'engagement culturel' in *Albert Camus 5. Journalisme et politique. L'entrée dans l'Histoire*, La Revue des Lettres Modernes, n. 315–22 (Paris: Minard), pp. 83–106.

Lévi-Valensi, J. (1986) 'L'entrée d'Albert Camus en politique' in *Camus et la politique* (Paris: L'Harmattan), pp. 137–51.

Lévi-Valensi, J. (1992) *Albert Camus et le théâtre* (Paris: Imec).

Lévi-Valensi, J. (1997a) 'Entre La Palisse et Don Quichotte' in *Camus et le Lyrisme*, pp. 35–42.

Lévi-Valensi, J. (1997b) 'Si tu veux être philosophe...' in *Albert Camus et la philosophie* (Paris: PUF), pp. 21–33.

Lévi-Valensi, J. (ed.) (2002) *Camus à Combat, Cahiers Albert Camus. 8* (Paris: Gallimard). English translation: (2006) *Camus at Combat: writings. 1944–1947* (Princeton: Princeton University Press).

Lévi-Valensi, J. (2002a) 'Un journal dans l'histoire' in *Camus à 'Combat'*. *Cahiers Albert Camus 8* (Paris: Gallimard), pp. 17–65.

Lévi-Valensi, J. (2002b) 'Un écrivain face à l'histoire' in *Camus à 'Combat'*. *Cahiers Albert Camus 8* (Paris: Gallimard), pp. 66–103.

Lévi-Valensi, J. (2004) 'Albert Camus, une écriture de la vérité' in *Albert Camus et le mensonge : actes du colloque organisé par le BPI les 29 et 30 decembre 2002* (Paris: Bibliothèque publique d'information. Centre Pompidou), pp. 13–19.

Lévi-Valensi, J. and A. Spiquel (eds) (1997) *Camus et le lyrisme* (Paris: SEDES).

Lévi-Valensi, J., A. Garapon and D. Salas (eds) (2002) *Albert Camus. Réflexions sur le terrorisme* (Paris: Nicolas Philippe).

Lévinas, E. (1997) *Quelques réflexions sur la philosophie de l'hitlérisme* (Paris: Rivages).

Lottman, H.R. (1979) *Albert Camus: A Biography* (London: Weidenfeld and Nicolson).

Magnus, B. and K. Higgins (eds) (1996) *Cambridge Companion to Nietzsche* (Cambridge: Cambridge University Press).

Margerrison, C., M. Orme and L. Lincoln (2008) *Albert Camus in the 21st Century. A Reassessment of His Thinking at the Dawn of the New Millenium* (Amsterdam–New York: Rodopi).

Marin, L. (2008) *Albert Camus et les libertaires* (Marseilles: Égrégores Éditions).

Marmande, F. (1985) *Georges Bataille politique* (Lyon: Presses Universitaires de Lyon).

Mattéi, J.-F. (1997) 'Terre et ciel d'Albert Camus', in *Albert Camus et la philosophie* (Paris: PUF), pp. 277–94.

Mattéi, J.-F. (2005) *Nietzsche et le temps des nihilismes* (Paris: PUF).

McBride, J. (1992) *Albert Camus, Philosopher and 'Littérateur'* (New York: St. Martin's Press).

Michel, H. and B. Mirkine-Guetzévitch (1954) *Les idée politiques et sociales de la Résistance (Documents clandestins – 1940–1944)* (Paris: PUF).

Modler, K.W. (2000) *Soleil et mesure dans l'œuvre d'Albert Camus* (Paris: L'Harmattan).

Montano, A. (2003) *Camus : mistico senza Dio* (Padova: Messaggero).

Montinari, M. (1996) *'La Volonté de Puissance' n'existe pas* (Paris: Editions d'Eclat).

Morani, R. (2007) *Soggetto e modernità. Hegel, Nietzsche, Heidegger interpreti di Cartesio* (Milano: Franco Angeli) .

Morot-Sir, E. (1981) 'Logique de la limite, esthétique de la pauvreté: théorie et pratique de l'essai', in Gay-Crosier, R. (ed.), *Albert Camus 1980*, pp. 189–209.

Morot-Sir, E. (1982) 'Georges Bataille : critique d'Albert Camus', *Stanford French Review*, VI, n. 1, pp. 101–12.

Morot-Sir, E. (1985a) *'L'Homme Révolté*: entre non et oui', in *Albert Camus 12 – la révolte en question*, 'La Revue de Lettres Modernes' (Paris: Minard), pp. 35–64.

Morot-Sir, E. (1985b) 'L'esthétique d'Albert Camus : logique de la limite, mesure de la mystique' in *Albert Camus : œuvre fermée, œuvre ouverte ?* (Paris: Gallimard), pp. 93–112.

Mosse-Bastide, R.-M. (1954) *Bergson et Plotin* (Aix-en-Provence, Bouches-du-Rhône : Office universitaire de polycopie).

Münster, A. (1995) *Nietzsche et le nazisme* (Paris: Editions Kimé).

Nancy, J.-L. (1988) *L'Expérience de la liberté* (Paris: Galilée).

Nancy, J.-L. (1990a) *La Communauté désœuvrée* (Paris: Bourgois). English translation (1991) *The Inoperative Community* (Minneapolis–London: University Minnesota Press).

Nancy, J.-L. (1990b) *La pensée finie* (Paris: Galilée).

Nancy, J.-L. (1993) *Le sens du monde* (Paris: Galilée).

Nancy, J.-L. (1993/94) 'Entre la destruction et l'extinction' in *Traversées du nihilisme* (Paris: Editions Osiris), pp. 105–11.

Nancy, J.-L. (1996) *Etre singulier pluriel* (Paris: Galilée).

Nancy, J.-L. (2001) *Le sens du monde* (Paris: Galilée).

Nguyen-Van-Huy, P. (1968) *La métaphysique du bonheur chez Albert Camus* (Neuchâtel: Editions de la Baconnière).

Nicolas, A. (1964) *Une philosophie de l'existence : Albert Camus* (Paris: PUF).

Noudelmann, F. (1997) 'Camus et Sartre ; le corps et la loi' in *Albert Camus et la philosophie* (Paris: Presses Universitaires Françaises), pp. 133–55.

Novello, S. (2004) 'Du nihilisme aux théocraties totalitaires : *Les sources et le sens du communisme russe* de Berdiaev dans les *Carnets* d'Albert Camus', in *Albert Camus 20. ' Le Premier homme' en perspective, La revue des lettres modernes* (Paris: Minard), pp. 175–95.

Novello, S. (2007) 'La liberté de ne pas être moderne : le paradigme tragique de l'action politique dans l'œuvre d'Albert Camus', in *Albert Camus et la Grèce* (Arles: Écritures du Sud), pp. 125–41.

Novello, S. (2008) 'Tragedy and Aesthetic Politics. Re-thinking the Political beyond Nihilism in the work of Albert Camus', in C. Margerrison, M. Orme and L. Lincoln (eds) *Albert Camus in the 21st century*, pp. 259–76.

Noys, B. (2000) *Georges Bataille: A Critical Introduction* (London–Sterling: Pluto Press).

Nussbaum, M. (1986) *The Fragility of Goodness. Luck and Ethics in Greek Tragedy and Philosophy* (Cambridge: Cambridge University Press).

O'Brien, J. (ed.) (1958) *From the N.R.F. An Image of the Twentieth Century from the pages of the Nouvelle Revue Française* (New York: Farrar, Straus and Cudahy).

Parain, B. and G. Blumberg (1933) 'Documents sur le National-Socialisme' in *N.R.F.*, n. 239, pp. 234–62.

Parker, E. (1965) *The Artist in the Arena* (Madison-Milwaukee: University of Wisconsin Press).

Passeri Pignoni, V. (1965) *Albert Camus, uomo in rivolta* (Imola: Cappelli).

Pisier, E. and P. Bouretz (1986) 'Camus et le marxisme' in *Camus et la politique* (Paris: L'Harmattan), pp. 269–80.

Ponton, O. (2005) 'Le "caractère equivoque" du nihilisme', in *Nietzsche et le temps des nihilismes*, sous la direction de Jean-François Mattéi (Paris: PUF), pp. 9–28.

Ramirez Medina, A. (2001) *La filosofia tragica de Albert Camus. El transito del absurdo a la rebelion* (Analecta Malacitana: Universidad de Malaga).

Rasoamanana, L. (2005) 'Simone Weil et Camus lecteurs d'Héraclite', in *Cahiers Simone Weil*, Vol. 28, No. 4, pp. 341–64.

Rey, P.-L. (2000) *Camus une morale de la beauté* (Paris: SEDES).

Risset, J. (ed.) (1987) *Georges Bataille: Il Politico e il Sacro* (Napoli: Liguori Editore).

Rosenthal, B. (1977) *Die Idee des Absurden. Friedrich Nietzsche und Albert Camus*, (Bonn: Bouvier).

Rosset, C. (1988) *Le principe de cruauté* (Paris: Minuit).

184   *Bibliography*

Rosset, C. (1993) *Logique du pire. Éléments pour une philosophie tragique* (Paris: Quadrige PUF).
Rustichelli, L. (1992) *La profondità della superficie: senso del tragico e giustificazione estetica dell'esistenza in Friedrich Nietzsche* (Milano: Mursia).
Schürmann, R. (1996) *Des hégémonies brisées* (Mauvezin: Trans-Europ-Repress).
Schürmann, R. (1982) *Le principe d'anarchie: Heidegger et la question de l'agir* (Paris: Seuil). English translation (1987) *Heidegger on being and acting: From principles to anarchy* (Bloomington: Indiana University Press).
Severino, E. (1982) *L'essenza del nichilismo* (Milano: Adelphi).
Severino, E. (1989) *Il giogo. Alle origini della ragione : Eschilo* (Milano: Adelphi).
Sherman, D. (2009) *Camus* (Oxford: Wiley-Blackwell).
Sichère, B. (2006) *Pour Bataille. Être, chance, souveraineté* (Paris: Gallimard).
Sloterdijk, P. (2000) *Le penseur sur scène. Le Matérialisme de Nietzsche* (Paris: Christian Bourgeois Editeur).
Sloterdijk, P. (2007) *Colère et temps* (Paris: Libella-Maren Sell Editions).
Smith, D. (1996) *Transvaluations: Nietzsche in France. 1872–1972* (Oxford: Clarendon Press).
Soulez, P. (1989) *Bergson politique* (Paris: PUF).
Sprintzen, D. (1988) *Camus. A Critical Examination* (Philadelphia: Temple University Press).
Strong, T.B. (1988) 'Nietzsche's Political Aesthetics', in M.A. Gillespie, and T.B. Strong (eds) *Nietzsche's New Seas. Explorations in Philosophy. Aesthetics and Politics* (Chicago: University of Chicago Press), pp. 153–74.
Strong, T.B. (2000) *Nietzsche and the Politics of Transfiguration* (Urbana: University of Illinois Press).
Sumner, G.D. (1996) *Dwight MacDonald and the* politics *Circle. The Challenge of Cosmopolitan Democracy* (Ithaca and London: Cornell University Press).
Tarrow, S. (1985) *Exile from the Kingdom: A Political Rereading of Albert Camus* (Alabama: University of Alabama Press).
Thody, P. (1957) *Albert Camus: A Study of His Work* (London: Hamish Hamilton).
Todd, O. (1996) *Camus une vie* (Paris: Gallimard).
Traverso, E. (2001) *Le Totalitarisme. Le XXe siècle en débat* (Paris: Seuil).
Trundle, R.C. Jr. (1986) *Beyond Absurdity. The Philosophy of Albert Camus* (Lanham, MD: University Press of America).
Trudel, E. (2007) *La Terreur à l'œuvre. Théorie, poétique et éthique chez Jean Paulhan* (Saint-Denis: Presses Universitaires de Vincennes).
Various authors (1984) *Albert Camus et les libertaires* (Antony: Groupe Fresnes-Antony de la Fédération anarchiste).
Vasil, D. (1986) *The Ethical Pragmatism of Albert Camus. Two Studies in the History of Ideas* (New York: Peter Lang).
Vattimo, G. (1974) *Il soggetto e la maschera. Nietzsche e il problema della liberazione* (Milano: Bompiani).
Vattimo, G. (1985) *La fine della modernità. Nichilismo ed ermeneutica nella cultura postmoderna* (Milano: Garzanti); translated as Vattimo, G. (1988) *The End of Modernity: Nihilism and Hermeneutics in Post-Modern Culture* (Cambridge: Polity Press in association with Blackwell).
Vattimo, G. (1988) *Le avventure della differenza. Che cosa significa pensare dopo Nietzsche e Heidegger* (Milano: Garzanti); translated as Vattimo, G. (1993) *The*

Adventure of Difference: Philosophy after Nietzsche and Heidegger (Baltimore: Johns Hopkins University Press).

Vattimo, G. (2000) *Dialogo con Nietzsche. Saggi 1961–2000* (Milano: Garzanti); translated as Vattimo, G. (2006) *Dialogue with Nietzsche* (New York: Columbia University Press).

Vattimo, G. (2003) *Nichilismo ed emancipazione. Etica, politica, diritto* (Milano: Garzanti).

Vertone, T. (1989) *L'oeuvre et l'action d'Albert Camus dans la mouvance de la tradition libertaire* (Lyon: Atelier de la création libertaire).

Viggiani, C. (1968) 'Note pour le futur biographe d'Albert Camus', *Revue des Lettres Modernes*, No. 170–4 (Paris: Minard), pp. 200–18.

Villa, D. (1992) 'Beyond Good and Evil. Arendt, Nietzsche, and the Aestheticization of Political Action', in *Political Theory*, Vol. 20, No. 2, pp. 274–308.

Villa, D. (1996) *Arendt and Heidegger. The Fate of the Political* (Princeton University Press).

Vintiadis, E. (2001) *Nietzsche's 'Secular' Christians: 'Modern Ideas' and the Slave Revolt in Morality* (MPhil Dissertation; Cambridge University).

Voegelin, E. (1968) *Science, Politics and Gnosticism* (Chicago: Regnery Company).

Volpi, F. (1999) *Il Nichilismo* (Bari: Laterza).

Walker, D.H. (1997) 'In an out of history: Albert Camus', in *French Cultural Studies*, pp. 103–16.

Warren, M. (1985) 'Nietzsche and Political Philosophy', in *Political Theory*, vol. 13, No. 2, pp. 183–212.

Warren, M. (1988) *Nietzsche and Political Thought* (Cambridge – London: MIT Press).

Werner, E. (1972) *De la violence au totalitarisme, essai sur la pensée de Camus et Sartre* (Paris: Calmann-Lévy).

Weyemberg, M. (1985) 'Révolte et ressentiment' in *Albert Camus 12. La révolte en question, La Revue de Lettres Modernes* (Paris: Minard), pp. 65–82.

Weyemberg, M. (1998) *Albert Camus ou la mémoire des origines* (Paris–Bruxelles: De Boeck Université).

Whitfield, S.J. (1980) *Into the Dark: Hannah Arendt and Totalitarianism* (Philadelphia: Temple University Press).

Willhoite, F.H. Jr. (1968) *Beyond Nihilism: Albert Camus' Contribution to Political Thought* (Baton Rouge: Louisiana State University Press).

Woolfolk, A. (1990) 'Toward a Theory of Nihilism', in *Sociological Analysis*, Vol. 51, No. 1, pp. 105–7.

Index

Abbou, André, 2, 77, 160n. 42, 168n. 14, 171n. 40, 173n. 12
absurd, 2, 4, 8, 9, 49, 50, 53, 56, 60, 78, 81, 82, 86–94, 96–116, 119–22, 127, 129–30, 140, 146, 149n. 14, 156nn. 58 and 59, 162n. 11, 163nn. 18 and 20 and 23, 164nn. 26 and 27 and 30, 165nn. 30 and 31 and 35 and 37, 166nn. 43 and 48, 167n. 48, 168n. 10, 169nn. 17 and 20, 171nn. 42 and 45
absurdity, 34, 48, 49, 51, 52, 57, 70, 76, 87–90, 94, 97, 99, 102, 107, 115, 120, 144, 155n. 45, 168n. 10; wall of (*murus absurditatis*), 48
Aeschylus, 49–50, 155n. 46
aestheticisation of politics, 7, 40, 122
Agamben, Giorgio, 38, 107, 167n. 49
Alger républicain (journal), 77, 160n. 42
Algeria, 172n. 12; Algerian nature, 19, 41–3, 56, 61, 73, 150n. 17; Algerian people, 74; terrorist movements, 144; Algerian section of the French Communist Party, 159n. 31
Amsterdam-Pleyel, Comité, 71
anarchy, 65, 104, 149n. 16
Anaxagoras, 83–5
Anaximander, 126
Andler, Charles, 27, 148n. 5, 149n. 9, 150nn. 20 and 21, 151nn. 3 and 5, 152nn. 5 and 8, 155n. 47
Andréas-Salomé, Lou, 23–5, 27, 149nn. 11 and 13 to 16, 150n. 18, 151n. 26
Ansell Pearson, Keith, 11, 28, 151n. 24
Antichrist, 79, 161n. 51
apocalyptism, 65, 136, 142

Apollonian, 21, 148n. 6, 149n. 6
Arendt, Hannah, 11, 12, 16, 37, 45, 46, 72, 84, 132, 148n. 3, 151n. 25, 154n. 36, 155n. 38, 161n. 3, 162n. 9, 165n. 39, 167n. 1, 170n. 28, 173n. 18
Aristotle, 83; Aristotelian tradition of philosophy, 7, 68, 84, 89, 97, 123, 134, 154n. 28, 161n. 7; on perfection, 16, 40; on nature, 41, 132; on action, 17, 54; on art and beauty, 36, 153n. 16; on prudence, 85
Arnold, A. James, 20, 22, 148n. 2, 149n. 6, 150n. 22, 151n. 23
Aron, Raymond, 105
ascesis, 4, 44, 54, 62, 91, 99, 104, 122, 137, 158n. 20
atheism, 164n. 27
Augustine, 64, 66, 123

Balaine, Blanche, 55, 149n. 10
Bakunin, M.A., 134–6
barbarian, 73–4, 79
Bataille, Georges, 7, 40, 75, 88–9, 101, 103, 109–12, 114, 122, 126, 144–5, 156n. 54, 160n. 39, 163n. 17, 164n. 26, 165n. 38, 166nn. 41 and 46 and 47, 167nn. 3 and 6, 168n. 8, 169nn. 19 and 27, 170n. 34
beauty, 21–2, 36–7, 43, 46, 55–6, 64–5, 67, 73–4, 91, 121–2, 126, 137, 143–4, 147, 149n. 6, 152n. 10, 156nn. 53 and 56, 172nn. 9 and 10
Berdiaev, Nikolai, 135–6, 172nn. 6 and 7, 173n. 15
Bergson, Henri-Louis, 6, 19–21, 33–7, 39, 41–3, 68, 148n. 5, 151n. 24, 152nn. 8 to 10, 153nn. 22 and 23, 154nn. 28 and 36, 156n. 38, 157n. 7

Bergsonism, 152n. 7, 156n. 58, 159n. 24
Blanchot, Maurice, 4, 81–2, 87–8, 90, 104, 106–7, 111, 115, 119–20, 163n. 22, 168nn. 10 and 11
Blumberg, George, 39
Bolshevism, 17
Bonnel, Pierre, 130, 161n. 6
Bourdet, Pierre, 168n. 7
Bréhier, Émile, 36, 68, 152nn. 9 and 12, 154nn. 28 and 33, 158nn. 22 and 23
Brisville, Jean-Claude, 19

Cahiers d'Actualité, 103, 166n. 47, 169n. 18
Caligula, 8, 81, 106, 108–19, 121, 125, 145, 154n. 29, 168n. 9, 169n. 24, 173nn. 13 and 14
capital execution, 14, 76, 78, 141 *see also* death penalty
capitalism, 69, 87, 125, 132, 173n. 15
Cartesianism, 92 *see also* Descartes, René
Caves, Jean, 148n. 5, 160n. 44 *see* Grenier, Jean
Chaintron, Jean (Barthel), 159n. 31
Char, René, 131, 139
Charlot, Edmond, 159n. 27
Chiaromonte, Nicola, 109–10, 167n. 1
Christ, 65–7, 90–1, 161n. 52
Christianity, 49, 64, 123, 143, 158n. 16, 161n. 52, 171n. 41, 172n. 10; Christian metaphysics, 7, 14, 26, 63, 65–7, 90, 142, 148n. 2, 157n. 12, 158nn. 18 to 20, 168n. 15; mystic literature, 47, 152n. 11, 163n. 19; morality, 28, 61, 123, 157n. 13
Church, 172n. 10; Fathers of the, 66, 158n. 19
Commune, 69, 147, 173n. 18
Communion, 34–8, 40–1, 43–9, 52, 54–5, 57, 62, 66, 149n. 13, 152n. 13, 153n. 22, 154n. 26, 155n. 42, 173n. 13
Communism, 54, 62–3, 73, 135–6, 173n. 15

community, 7, 11, 13, 40, 107, 113, 127, 134, 138–40, 153n. 15, 167n. 49, 169n. 25, 172n. 5
Combat (journal), 8, 14, 98, 114, 116–17, 122, 125–9, 138, 167–8n. 7, 171n. 49
Comte, Auguste, 142
Comte-Sponville, 162n. 13, 164n. 30
contempt, 5–12, 14–15, 22, 61, 64–5, 67, 70, 78, 103, 107, 113, 115–17, 119, 123, 126, 130, 136–8, 141, 160n. 44, 168n. 9, 169nn. 17 and 21
Corbic, Arnaud, 153nn. 19 and 20, 170n. 33
creation, 2, 5, 7–9, 12, 18–19, 21–2, 25, 34–7, 39–40, 43–4, 52–3, 55–7, 59, 64, 69–70, 72, 74, 78, 88, 91, 93–4, 98, 101, 108, 110, 112, 114, 130–1, 135–6, 145, 147, 149, 155n. 45, 158n. 17, 159n. 31
crime, 10, 16, 83–5, 89, 91, 107, 112, 140–2, 144–7, 167n. 50; criminal, 16, 77, 141

death, 6, 8–9, 11, 24, 30, 32, 49–53, 56–7, 61, 70, 73, 76–7, 78–9, 83, 86, 90, 92, 95–6, 106, 110, 112–13, 118, 124, 130, 140, 150n. 17, 152n. 8, 153n. 25, 155, 160n. 45, 163nn. 21 and 22, 166n. 44; of God, 8, 100, 104, 164n. 26; penalty, 130, 140–1, 147, 155n. 48
Deleuze, Gilles, 148n. 1, 149n. 9, 159n. 24
Della Francesca, Piero, 54
De Madariaga, Salvador, 133, 137, 171n. 1
democracy, 11
De Ochoa, López, 69
Descartes, René, 51, 82, 156n. 2, 163n. 23, 164n. 29
dialectics, 8, 25, 27, 53, 66, 72, 152n. 12, 155n. 40
Dike, 85
Dionysian, 21, 28, 148–9 n. 6, 151n. 24
Dionysius the Areopagite, 154n. 35

Rosenberg, Alfred, 39, 153n. 15
Rousseau, Jean-Jacques, 22, 55, 123–4,
134, 169n. 21, 170nn. 30 and
32
Rozis, Augustin, 159n. 27
Russia, 16, 124, 172n. 6; Soviet, 117

Sartre, Jean-Paul, 75, 160n. 40
Schopenhauer, Arthur, 19, 151n. 4,
152n. 8, 162n. 15
Scheler, Max, 6–7, 12–13, 58–67,
71–2, 75, 81, 83, 115–16,
123–5, 134, 139, 141–2, 146,
156nn. 1 and 2, 157nn. 5 and 7
and 12 and 13, 158nn. 18 and
20, 160n. 44, 161n. 4, 164n.
29, 168n. 13, 169n. 21, 170nn.
30 and 32
Schürmann, Reiner, 33, 154 n. 32,
155n. 39, 165n. 31
Sade, Donatien, Marquis de, 131,
144–5, 147
Severino, Emanuele, 155nn. 41 and
46
Sextus Empiricus, 154n. 35, 162n. 15
Shestov, V., 156n. 2, 164n. 29,
165n. 32,
Sisyphus, 81–2, 86–8, 91–2, 106–7,
119–20, 122–3, 128–9, 162nn.
11 and 13, 162–3n. 15,
171n. 42
slavery, 29, 31
Sloterdijk, Peter, 123, 158nn. 17 and
21, 170n. 34, 172n. 5
Socialism, 55, 61; Socialist theory, 29,
40, 149n. 9, 172n. 7
Socrates, 133, 166n. 39
Soir républicain (journal), 32, 77, 80,
160nn. 42 and 43
Sophocles, 90, 121, 140
Spengler, Oswald, 15
Spinoza, Baruch, 156n. 2
State, 105, 135–6, 139–42, 144, 146–7,
173n. 18; Greek, 127; modern,
11
Stoicism, 17, 162n. 13
Sud (periodical), 19, 148nn. 3 and 4
Suetonius, 111

suicide, 7, 8, 80, 94–5, 97, 108,
113–14, 116, 118–19, 165 n. 32,
168 n. 16
Surrealist movement, 104

Temps Modernes, Les (periodical), 104
terror, 12, 104, 112, 118, 125, 130–1,
141, 147, 173n. 14; terrorism,
7–8, 10, 11, 103, 105, 118–19,
131, 138–42, 144, 146–7,
160n. 43, 172n. 12,
173n. 18
Tertullian, 13–4, 113
Théâtre de l'équipe, 71
Théâtre du Travail, 50, 69, 71
Todd, Olivier, 151nn. 27 and 28 and
3, 154n. 37, 155n. 47, 156n. 51
totalitarianism, 11, 12, 105, 132,
151n. 25, 167n. 1; totalitarian
ideology, 7–8, 12, 98, 105, 108,
153n. 17; regimes, 44, 122, 141,
157n. 6; revolution, 173n. 15
tragedy, 8, 20, 45, 49–50, 102, 106,
108–14, 134, 138, 150n. 20,
154n. 29, 155n. 45, 173n. 14;
tragic thought, 8, 21, 23–5, 33,
56–7, 61, 70, 83, 88, 90–1, 93,
95, 97, 100, 103, 107, 114,
118–19, 121, 139, 144, 149n.
15, 151n. 24, 156n. 58, 163n.
19, 165nn. 31 and 34, 166n.
48; hero, 49, 86–7, 106–8,
110–11, 121; tragic
philosophers, 132
Turgenev, Ivan, 11
tyranny, 34, 109–10, 157n. 7, 167n. 5

Ulysses, 68
United States, 109, 140
uselessness, 55, 73, 87, 110, 114,
156n. 54
utility, 2, 7, 9, 40, 58, 61, 71–3, 78,
86–7, 93, 106, 112, 114, 123,
131, 134–5, 140, 142, 144–6,
156n. 54, 157n. 7, 167n. 6,
168n. 8, 173n. 12
utilitarianism, 20, 157n. 13, 172n. 7
Valéry, Paul, 149n. 9
Vattimo, Gianni, 28, 149nn. 6 and 7